Enquiries of Local Authorities and Water Companies: A Practical Guide

CALLOW PUBLISHING

Enquiries of Local Authorities and Water Companies: A Practical Guide

by

Keith Pugsley, LL.B, LL.M, Ph.D., Solicitor,
Former Director of Law and Administration,
Dacorum Borough Council, Hemel Hempstead

Fifth Edition

London
Callow Publishing
2007

ISBN 978 1 898899 95 2

All reasonable care is taken in the preparation of this publication, but the authors and the publisher cannot accept responsibility for the consequences of any error, however caused.

Published by Callow Publishing Limited,
4 Shillingford Street, London N1 2DP
www.callowpublishing.com
Printed and bound in Great Britain by MPG Books Ltd, Bodmin, Cornwall.

Acknowledgements

Grateful thanks are due to Pauline Callow, for encouraging the production of this fifth edition. Thanks also to my wife, Gilly, for her valuable assistance and forbearance. Particular thanks are due to Beryl Evans and the staff of the Legal Services Unit at North Devon District Council, for the generous provision of research facilities with a friendly face to this now retired solicitor, and to Martin Smith, Senior Technical Officer in the Environmental Health Unit for his invaluable assistance with Radon Gas. Finally, thanks are due to Jan Boothroyd, Deputy Chief Executive of the Council for the National Land and Property Information Service for keeping me in touch with the progress of the new forms Con 29.

KMP
June 2007

*For my patron and my inspiration,
the Lady Mallens of Bedfordshire*

Contents

PART II: Optional Enquiries

PART III: Drainage and Water Enquiries

Table of Legislation

Introduction

An integral part of the modern conveyancing process is the conduct of a search of the register of local land charges maintained by the district council, and the raising of enquiries of local authorities. The register of local land charges contains details of all local land charges registered against property situated in the district administered by the council. The register contains details of such matters as outstanding liability for road and other financial charges, home improvement grants, tree preservation orders and notices served consequent upon the making of a compulsory purchase order. There is a multitude of local land charges made registrable under Act of Parliament or regulation; they are outside the scope of this book.

A prospective buyer of property, whether freehold or leasehold, is interested in, and concerned to have, as full a picture as possible of the property in question. The buyer will want to know, for instance, details of any highways proposals, the position regarding planning permission, and whether the council has any proposals which will directly or indirectly affect the property.

Searches of the register of local land charges are conducted either in person, by attendance at the offices of the district, unitary or London borough council, or, much more commonly, by despatch to the appropriate council of form LLC 1, *Application for an Official Search of the Register*. Further information is also elicited by the use of form Con 29. This was for many years a single form, submitted to the local authority by a buyer or prospective buyer. From 1 August 2007, the form has been divided into two: Con 29R: *Enquiries of Local Authority* and Con 29O: *Optional Enquiries of Local Authority*. The former contains the enquiries, the replies to which must now, in a residential conveyancing transaction, be included in a home information pack, pursuant to the Home Information Pack (No. 2) Regulations 2007. The latter contains optional enquiries which, in a residential conveyancing transaction, may be raised either by the seller and included in a home information pack, or by the buyer. Both forms are reproduced in the appendix to this book.

The forms, despatched to the council in duplicate, or often electronically, contain comprehensive enquiries designed to reveal to an intending buyer information about the property to be purchased and the effect on it of the exercise, or proposed exercise, of a wide variety of powers and duties vested in district councils. These powers and duties are exercised by the council's officers on behalf of the council or one of its committees.

The enquiries fall broadly into three categories:

(a) *Planning:* enquiries relating to the control of development under the Town and Country Planning Act 1990.

(b) *Engineering:* enquiries relating to highways, sewers, traffic schemes, railways and pipe-lines etc.

(c) *Environmental health:* enquiries relating to control of the physical environment, for example, overcrowding, noise abatement and contaminated land.

The council will reply to the required enquiries for one inclusive fee.

The optional enquiries are charged for individually; they will elicit a reply from the council only if the person requesting the search places a tick in the appropriate box on the form.

Drainage and water enquiries relating to the property are now usually answered by the water companies direct, and are the subject of a separate form (Con 29DW) and fee. Some councils still maintain an agency arrangement with the water companies and are prepared to reply to the water and drainage enquiries.

It is the purpose of this book to give a commentary on the enquiries of local authority, and the drainage and water enquiries, and on the responses to them. The book is intended for the guidance of those new to the forms and those wanting a ready reference to the meaning of the enquiries and the implications of the replies given. It is not intended as a comprehensive or definitive interpretation of the law, but rather as a guide and a training tool.

The General Notes to form Con 29

There are twelve general notes on form Con 29R, *Enquiries of Local Authority*. They are of an explanatory nature and are designed for the guidance of users. Notes A to F at the end of the form and are instructive. Notes (1) to (6) appear within the body of the form and are interpretative. Similar notes are to be found in Con 29O, *Optional Enquiries of Local Authority*, amended as applicable to the content of that form.

Notes on the Front of the Form

Note A instructs the searcher to enter the name and address of the council for the area in which the property lies. It also advises the searcher to consider raising enquiries of adjoining councils if the property is near to a local authority boundary. This is important in the case of a proposed road scheme which includes cross-boundary roads. Some planning applications also affect properties lying within the boundaries of more than one local authority, and the prudent buyer might check the neighbouring council's views or intentions with respect to planning policy.

Note B instructs searchers to enter the address and description of the property, and to quote any Unique Property Reference Number ("UPRN") relevant to it. Particular care should be taken to ensure this description is accurate, as the replies will relate only to the property as described. Some local authorities have adopted a system of UPRNs for search and other purposes. Enquiry of the council concerned normally reveals whether a UPRN should be quoted, but, again, the searcher should be concerned to ensure that any

UPRN fully, clearly and accurately refers to the boundaries of the property searched. This note also reminds the enquirer that a duplicate plan is required for all searches submitted directly to a local authority. The plan submitted should show the boundaries of the property clearly marked (say, in red). The search may be returned if the land or property cannot be easily identified.

Note C to the required enquiries (Con 29R) relates to roads, footpaths and footways abutting the property, which do not appear in its address, but in respect of which the searcher requires a reply to enquiry 2. Searchers should be careful to elicit sufficient information from their clients to enable a full search to be made, and if there is any doubt at all about responsibility for the maintenance of roads, footpaths or footways abutting on the property (but not being part of the property's description in box B of the form), those roads, footpaths etc. should be named or described in box C. Note C to the optional enquiries (Con29O) is a reminder to the searcher that questions 1 to 3, relating to planning and buildings regulations, roads and other matters, appear on Con29R as "required enquiries". The buyer's legal advisor should become at least sufficiently acquainted with the location and nature of the property, and his client's intentions for it, to enable him to select the relevant optional enquiries.

Note D informs the searcher that details of search fees can be obtained from the council (to which the search is to be sent), or the National Land Information Service ("NLIS") channel or search provider. Generally, an approach to the relevant council is most productive, as the level of fees varies between councils, which have discretion, within reasonable parameters, to set fees as they think fit. The information at the NLIS may at any one time be out of date or incomplete, and a simple telephone call to the local land charges department of the relevant council will save the frustration of a returned search or a request for further fees.

Note E to the required enquiries refers to box E, in which are to be inserted, if relevant, the name of the seller(s) and their estate agents, solicitors or conveyancers and the person providing the home information pack. This is to ensure compliance with the Home Information Pack (No. 2) Regulations 2007, which require search reports to declare whether the searcher or the person who prepared the search report has any personal or business relationship with any person involved in the sale of the property. This does not apply to the optional enquiries.

Note F to the required enquiries (note E to the optional enquiries) simply instructs the searcher to enter the name and address, or document exchange number, of the person or firm to which the replies are to be sent.

Notes at the Foot of the Forms
Note (1) makes clear that any references to Acts of Parliament or regulations (and there are many of these in the enquiries) include references to both earlier legislation replaced by current legislation, and subsequent modifications or re-enactments of current legislation. This obviates the necessity for frequent revision of the enquiries. For example, references in the enquiries to the Town and Country Planning Act 1990 include references to the Town and Country Planning Act 1971.

Note (2) is a little like a disclaimer and a warning that the council or its officers would be legally liable for the replies given to the enquiries only in the event of negligence. It is essential that a council's registers and records are kept up to date on a daily basis since negligent replies may result in claims for substantial damages against the council giving them. Although these claims are normally met by the council's insurers, a proliferation of such claims may result in a substantial increase in the council's insurance premium, or even a refusal by the insurance company to renew the policy. It may not be a defence to a claim to show that the officer replying to a particular enquiry had not been advised by another officer of the necessity to amend or update the records. Liability extends to any buyer of the property, or lender on its security, who had knowledge of the replies to enquiries before entering into a contract for the purchase, or a commitment to lend, whether or not the enquiries were raised on that buyer's or lender's behalf.

Note (3) advises that the forms should be read in conjunction with the guidance notes published separately. A short commentary on the current Guidance Notes follows.

Note (4) makes clear to users that any reference to "the area" (see, for example, enquiries 1.2 and 3.10, and optional enquiries 6.3, 11.1, 12.1, 13, 14, 15 and 17) means an area in which the property enquired about is situated.

Note (5) makes clear that references in the enquiries to "the Council" are intended to include references to any officer or committee or sub-committee exercising powers on its behalf, and to any council which has exercised powers in the past but been superseded by the present council as a result of local government reorganisation; and that "approval" by the council should be taken as denoting a decision to proceed. The note also recognises the fact that there are frequently agency and other arrangements in existence between county and district councils in the shire (that is, non-metropolitan) districts, whereby enquiries addressed to the district council elicit information from both councils. If in doubt, the prudent buyer should enquire of the district council whether the replies given are comprehensive, or whether a further approach should be made to the relevant county council.

Note (6) is a reminder to the search staff that, where relevant, the location of the department from which copy documents may be obtained should be provided. This may be relevant, for example, in any response to enquiries 1.1, 3.3, 3.7, 3.9, 3.12, 6, 11, 16, 18, 19, 20, 21 or 22.

The Guidance Notes

Guidance Notes (the full title is *Guidance Notes Con 29 Part I Standard Enquiries of Local Authority (2002) and Con 29 Part II Optional Enquiries of Local Authority (2002)*) were produced by The Law Society for the guidance of the legal profession and local authorities to coincide with the publication of the 2002 edition of Con 29. They apply to both "hard copy" searches and those submitted electronically via a NLIS channel. At the time of going to press, no new edition of the Guidance Notes has been prepared. However, the advice given in the notes remains relevant to the new, and now partly statutory, forms, and will no doubt be replicated in any revision.

The Guidance Notes explain that two new forms came into force on 1 July 2002, replacing the 1994 edition and 2000 revision, and taking into account changes in legislation and practice.

Since the drainage function is now controlled by local sewerage undertakers in most local authority areas, the separate drainage and water search (Con 29DW) was designed and agreed with Water UK for submission direct to those undertakers. However, as the Guidance Notes 2002 point out, questions on combined drainage and consents for building over sewers have been retained in Con 29 (required enquiries 3.3 (a) and (b)), since agreements and consents relating to these matters may still be recorded in local authority records. The Guidance Notes recommend that the searcher submit the separate Con 29DW to the local sewerage undertaker in addition to submitting the required enquiries to the local authority.

The Guidance Notes 2002 advise both local authorities and enquirers to use the document exchange or first class mail, when not submitting searches electronically, in the interests of speeding up land transactions.

Further explanation is given in the Guidance Notes 2002 as to the format of the forms, the style of replies, the fees to be charged and the footnotes to the forms, which have been commented on above. There is a note on liability for negligent replies which reinforces footnote (2) printed on the new forms and outlined above.

In the rest of the Guidance Notes 2002 it is sought to clarify the origin of each of the enquiries (both required and optional) and to prescribe some "informative" statements that should be included by local authorities in their replies. Where helpful, these clarifications and any advisory informative statements are alluded to or reproduced in the text of the commentary which follows.

Any prospective enquirer and all local authorities should be sure to have at least one copy of the Guidance Notes.

All the above should now be read in the light of the Home Information Pack (No. 2) Regulations 2007, which require home information packs to include a search report containing, as a minimum, the replies to the required enquiries.

Status of the Enquiries

The required enquiries (Con 29R), that were for many years affectionately known as Con 29 Part I, now have, for the first time, a statutory basis. The content of these enquiries is now enshrined in and prescribed by schedule 7 to the Home Information Pack (No. 2) Regulations 2007, which came into force on 1 August 2007 for some properties, and will gradually be rolled out to apply to all residential sales. The replies to the optional enquiries (Con 29O), appearing on a separate form, remain based upon a contractual relationship between the enquirer and authority.

The forms are approved by The Law Society (the professional body representing the interests of solicitors who, in practice, raise the enquiries on behalf of their clients) and the various associations representing the interests of the councils replying to the enquiries. They are also approved by the Local

Government Association, the Council of Mortgage Lenders, Water UK, the Association of Council Secretaries and Solicitors, the Council for the National Land and Property Information Service, the Council of Licensed Conveyancers and the Local Land Charges Institute. It can be assumed that the enquiries have been carefully designed to elicit information relevant to the property and which buyers are generally concerned to have, and that the councils have agreed to reply to the enquiries on receipt of their reasonable charges. Additional specific enquiries may of course also be raised, and will be separately charged for.

Part I: The Required Enquiries

All the enquiries in Con 29R, *Enquiries of Local Authority*, will be replied to by the council, unless there is insufficient information in the search application or the council's records to enable a reply to be made. The composite standard fee remitted by the person requesting the search covers all these enquiries.

Replies to these enquiries are "required" to be included in a search report included in a home information pack in accordance with the Home Information Pack (No. 2) Regulations 2007.

Enquiry 1: Planning and Building Regulations

"1.1. Planning and building decisions and pending applications
Which of the following relating to the property have been granted, issued or refused or (where applicable) are the subject of pending applications?
- (a) a planning permission
- (b) a listed building consent
- (c) a conservation area consent
- (d) a certificate of lawfulness of existing use or development
- (e) a certificate of lawfulness of proposed use or development
- (f) building regulations approval
- (g) a building regulation completion certificate and
- (h) any building regulations certificate or notice issued in respect of work carried out under a competent person self-certification scheme

1.2. Planning designations and proposals
What designations of land use for the property or the area, and what specific proposals for the property, are contained in any existing or proposed development plan?"

The purpose of the first enquiry is to ascertain the general planning and building regulation status of the property.

The first part of the enquiry relates to the register of planning applications which the council is required to keep pursuant to section 69 of the Town and Country Planning Act 1990. It also relates to applications for listed building consent and conservation area consent in respect of the property. Certificates of lawfulness of existing or proposed use or development under sections 191 and 192 of the Town and Country Planning Act and relevant approvals and completion certificates under the Building Regulations are also sought in reply to this part.

Enquiry 1.1.(a): Planning Permissions
The council, as local planning authority, must keep a register containing information relating to applications for planning permission, including information as to the manner in which the applications have been dealt with.

The register provides a public record of planning applications and decisions, and gives the public notification of all applications that have been made.

The register is kept in two parts. Part I contains a copy of every application for planning permission, together with copies of the plans and drawings submitted with them. The council must make an entry in the register within fourteen days of receiving an application. Applications for planning permission must remain in part I until finally disposed of, that is, granted or refused.

Part II is a permanent record of all applications for planning permission and the decisions taken by the council on them. The following matters must be entered in part II of the register:

(i) a copy of the application and any plans and drawings submitted with it;

(ii) any directions given under the Town and Country Planning Act in respect of the application;

(iii) the decision of the council and the date of that decision;

(iv) the date and effect of any decision of the Secretary of State following any appeal in respect of the application;

(v) the date of any subsequent approval (such as approval of reserved matters, that is, matters of detail such as materials to be used in construction).

The council must also keep, in this part of the register, details of any development it has decided to carry out itself and for which planning permission has been granted. The register must include an index for reference purposes.

Summary

Enquiry 1.1.(a) asks for details of any entries relating to planning applications that have been made, or any decisions of the council or the Secretary of State recorded in either part I or part II of the register. A buyer needs to know what applications have been made and whether they have been granted or refused. This gives the buyer an idea of the use(s) to which the property may be put, and whether planning permission for any contemplated development is likely to be forthcoming. Clearly, if the register shows a previous refusal, for example, of commercial development on housing land, this is likely to indicate that a further similar application would also be unsuccessful.

Enquiry 1.1.(b): Listed Building Consents

A listed building is a building of special architectural or historic interest which has been identified as such by the Secretary of State (sometimes on the advice of the Historic Buildings and Monuments Commission), and placed on a list of such buildings in accordance with powers and duties of the Secretary of State now comprised in the Planning (Listed Buildings and Conservation Areas) Act 1990. The number of listed buildings in England and Wales is approaching half a million.

Buildings may be listed either on account of their particular architectural or historic merit, or because of their relationship to other such buildings, and there may be particular features or characteristics which make a building worth listing either for itself or as part of a group of buildings. Once listed, any object or structure fixed to the building or within its curtilage should be treated as part of the building, so that, for instance, a garden wall (if it was in existence before 1 July 1948) surrounding a listed building is also protected by the listing.

Once the lists are compiled by the Secretary of State, they must be deposited with the councils for the areas covering the buildings concerned and the details must be entered in the registers of local land charges by the councils, and appear in an official certificate of search. Copies of the lists must also be kept available for public inspection at the council's offices, insofar as they relate to properties in its area.

There are two main categories of listed building:
- Grade I: Buildings of exceptional interest. Only approximately two per cent of all listed buildings fall into this category.
- Grade II: Buildings of special interest, covering the majority of listed buildings. Some particularly important buildings (about four per cent) in this category are classified Grade II*.

To be listed, a building must normally fall into one of the following classifications:
(i)   built before 1700 and surviving in more or less original condition;
(ii) built between 1700 and 1840 (selection is necessary);
(iii) built between 1840 and 1914 and of definite quality; the principal works of principal architects are included;
(iv) built between 1914 and 1939 and selected for its high quality;
(v)   built after 1939 and of outstanding quality.

The main consequences of listing are that the building attracts all the protection of the Planning (Listed Buildings and Conservation Areas) Act 1990, that is to say:
(i)   any person causing damage to a listed building may be prosecuted for the offence and ordered to pay a fine;
(ii) listed building consent is required for the demolition or alteration of the building;
(iii) special listed building enforcement notices may be served by the council (see the commentary on enquiry 3.9: Notices, etc. under Planning Acts);
(iv) there are limitations on the permitted development rights under the Town and Country Planning (General Permitted Development) Order (again, see the commentary on enquiry 3.9).

It is (ii) above (listed building consent) with which enquiry 1.1.(b) is concerned.

Under section 7 of the Planning (Listed Buildings and Conservation Areas) Act 1990, if a person carries out any works for the demolition of a listed building, or for its alteration or extension in any manner which would affect its character as a building of special architectural or historic interest, and those works have not been authorised, the person carrying out the works is guilty of an offence and may be prosecuted; on conviction, such a person is liable to a fine or may be imprisoned.

Works are authorised only if:

(i) the council or the Secretary of State has granted listed building consent, and any conditions attached to the consent are complied with; and

(ii) in the case of demolition, notice of the proposal to demolish has been given to English Heritage (in relation to Wales, the Royal Commission on Ancient and Historical Monuments in Wales), allowing the opportunity to make a record of the building before it is demolished.

Application for listed building consent must be made to the council as local planning authority. The application must contain sufficient details to identify the building, and plans and drawings sufficient to describe the proposed works. The council then advertises the application in the local newspaper and displays a site notice on the building. The council must also notify the Secretary of State (or English Heritage if the building is in London), and other interested archaeological institutions.

The council may grant listed building consent for the proposed works, and in so doing must have regard to the importance of the building; its architectural merit; its historical interest; its condition; the cost of repairing and maintaining it; and other factors. If listed building consent is refused, the person wishing to carry out the works has a right of appeal to the Secretary of State, who may hold a public local inquiry into the matter and, having heard the evidence, either confirm the council's refusal or himself grant listed building consent, with or without conditions.

Summary

The purpose of enquiry 1.1.(b) is to obtain details of any applications and decisions in respect of listed building consent, including grants of such consent by the Secretary of State on appeal from the council's refusal. If listed building consent has been granted, the buyer will want to know full details, including any conditions which have been imposed on the consent, since carrying out work in breach of any of those conditions will render the buyer liable to prosecution.

Enquiry 1.1.(c): Conservation Area Consents

An outline of the provisions relating to conservation areas is to be found in the commentary on enquiry 3.10: Conservation area. The protection accorded to individual listed buildings by the provisions of the Planning (Listed Buildings and Conservation Areas) Act 1990 is extended, in modified form, to all buildings situated in a conservation area designated by the council as local planning authority, or by the Secretary of State.

In particular, by virtue of section 74 of the Act, a building in a conservation area may not be demolished without the consent of the council as local planning authority, and such consent, if granted, is known as "conservation area consent". Application for consent must be made to the council as local planning authority and must be accompanied by details similar to those required in respect of a listed building consent application. Consent may be granted with or without conditions. An appeal against refusal of consent by the council may be made to the Secretary of State. Contravention of the conditions attached to a conservation area consent renders the owner of the building liable to prosecution, and, on conviction, imprisonment or a fine.

Summary
Enquiry 1.1.(c) is designed to elicit details of any applications and decisions in respect of conservation area consents. If the property enquired about does not lie within a designated conservation area, this part of the enquiry is irrelevant. If conservation area consent has been granted, the buyer will want to know full details, including any conditions which have been imposed on the consent, since carrying out demolition in breach of any of those conditions will give rise to the risk of prosecution.

Enquiry 1.1.(d): Certificates of Lawfulness of Existing Use or Development

These certificates (known as CLEUDs) effectively replace the old regime of "established use certificates". Under that regime, and under the current provisions of section 191 of the Town and Country Planning Act, a person wishing to ascertain the legality of:

- an existing use of buildings or land;
- operations that have been carried out in, on, over or under land; or
- other matters which might constitute failure to comply with any planning condition or limitation,

may make a formal application to the local planning authority, specifying the land and describing the use or operations concerned. If, on considering the application, the local planning authority is satisfied as to the lawfulness of the use, operations or other matters as described at the time of the application, it must issue a certificate to that effect. Such a certificate is now called a "certificate of lawfulness of existing use or development". The certificate specifies the land to which it relates, describes the use, operations or other matters (for example, breach of a planning condition) and give the reasons for determining the use etc. to be lawful. The lawfulness of the development described, on the land defined, is to be conclusively presumed by virtue of the issue of such a certificate. The certificate also specifies the date from which it applies.

The application for a CLEUD allows the landowner to seek a ruling to the effect that current development is immune from enforcement action, and the issue of the certificate is therefore broadly equivalent, in many ways, to the grant of planning permission. If a certificate is refused, there is a right of appeal to the Secretary of State, although the appeal is confined to the narrow question of reviewing the local planning authority's decision. An appeal must be dismissed if the Secretary of State finds that the authority's refusal to issue a certificate was well-founded.

As with CLOPUDs (see enquiry 1.1.(e) below) there is no requirement to advertise, or to notify adjoining owners, when applying for a CLEUD, because the matters to be determined are solely matters of evidence and law. They often fall within the purview of the local planning authority's lawyers, rather than their planning officers, for consideration.

Summary
The purpose of enquiry 1.1.(d) is to obtain details and copies of any certificates (CLEUDs) that have been granted; and details of any applications that have been made but refused, or are still pending. The status of a certificate that has been granted is practically identical to that of a planning permission, and the buyer will be interested in the extent of any use or development that is declared lawful by it. Similarly, any application which has been refused is of interest to a buyer, indicating at least that formal planning permission will need to be sought to pursue change of use or development. Furthermore, any evidence that a use or development is being pursued despite a refused CLEUD, might be an indication that enforcement action on the part of the local planning authority is being considered.

Enquiry 1.1.(e): Certificates of Lawfulness of Proposed Use or Development

Application may be made under section 192 of the Town and Country Planning Act for a certificate of lawfulness of proposed use or development of land, as a device to secure the lawful status of a proposed development (or use) where it is considered by the applicant that formal planning permission is not required.

Application for a CLOPUD (as these certificates are affectionately termed) is made to the council as local planning authority. It must specify:

(i)   whether the application is in respect of a proposed use or in respect of building or other operations;
(ii)   the use of the land at the date of application;
(iii)   which of the prescribed "use classes" the applicant considers is appropriate to the proposed use;
(iv)   the reasons why the proposed use or operations should be deemed lawful; and
(v)   any other supporting information.

An application must be accompanied by a plan identifying the land to which it relates; evidence in verification of the applicant's claim and the applicant's interest in the land; and the name(s) and address(es) of any other parties with an interest in the land.

As in the case of CLEUDs (above), there are no requirements as to advertising, or notifying adjoining owners, because the matters here to be determined by the council are solely matters of evidence and law. It is for this reason that applications are commonly handled by the council's legal, rather than its planning, advisors.

If a certificate is granted by the council, it specifies the land to which it relates, the use or operations in question which are deemed lawful and the reasons for that lawfulness. The date of application is also specified. The lawfulness of the use or operations described in the certificate is conclusively presumed, unless there has been a material change, before the use is instituted or the operations begun, in any of the matters relevant to the determination of lawfulness.

Summary

The purpose of enquiry 1.1.(e) is to obtain copies of any certificates (CLOPUDs) that have been granted; and details of any applications that have been made but refused, or are still pending. The status of any certificate granted is practically identical to that of planning permission, and the buyer will be interested in the extent of any lawful proposed use or development. Similarly, any application which has been refused is of interest to a buyer, indicating at least that formal planning permission will need to be sought to pursue change of use or development.

As the Guidance Notes 2002 pointed out, references in this enquiry to specific types of planning document should be taken by the council to include the equivalent documents under previous planning legislation. The enquirer may thus expect to receive, in reply to this part of the enquiry, details of any "established use certificates" issued under the Town and Country Planning Act 1971 recognising established and lawful planning uses in respect of the property. In a sense, established use certificates could be said to be the forerunners of CLOPUDs as well as CLEUDs (see enquiry 1.1.(d), above).

Enquiry 1.1.(f): Building Regulation Approvals

Part 1.1.(f) of this enquiry relates to breaches of the Building Regulations. The Building Regulations 2000 are designed to control the carrying out of building work in the erection, extension or alteration of buildings. All building work must be carried out in compliance with the detailed requirements contained in schedules to the regulations, and with proper materials and in a workmanlike manner.

Builders or others intending to carry out building works are required to give certain notices to, and deposit certain building plans with, the council and obtain approval before work commences. Further notices must be given to the council at specified stages in the progress of work, to enable the council's officers to inspect.

The particular requirements of the regulations are extremely detailed and cover matters under the following headings:

(A) Structure
  - loading (requirements of dead, imposed and wind loads);
  - ground movement (movements of the subsoil caused by swelling, shrinkage or freezing, landslip and subsidence);
  - disproportionate collapse in the event of accident.

(B) Fire
  - means of warning and escape;
  - internal fire spread (resistance to the spread of flames);
  - external fire spread (roof and external walls);

- access and facilities for the fire service.
(C) Site preparation and resistance to moisture
  - preparation of site (freedom from vegetable matter);
  - dangerous and offensive substances;
  - subsoil drainage (i.e., to avoid the passage of ground moisture into the building);
  - resistance to weather and ground moisture.
(D) Toxic substances
  - cavity insulation (prevention of permeation of toxic fumes).
(E) Resistance to the passage of sound
  - airborne sound (walls, floors and stairs);
  - impact sound.
(F) Ventilation
  - means of ventilation;
  - condensation.
(G) Hygiene
  - bathrooms;
  - hot water storage (to prevent water exceeding 100° C);
  - sanitary conveniences and washing facilities.
(H) Drainage and waste disposal
  - foul water drainage;
  - cesspools, septic tanks and settlement tanks (access for emptying);
  - rainwater drainage;
  - solid waste storage (access for removal).
(I) Heat-producing appliances
  - air supply (i.e. to heat-producing appliances);
  - discharge of products of combustion (i.e. to the outside air);
  - protection of building (from risk of fire).
(J) Stairways, ramps and guards
  - stairways and ramps (safe passage for users);
  - protection from falling (by barriers, guards etc.);
  - vehicle barriers and loading bays;
  - protection from collision, impact or trapping by doors.
(K) Conservation of fuel and power
(L) Access and facilities for disabled people
  - access and use of building;
  - sanitary conveniences;
  - audience or spectator seating.
(M) Glazing
  - safety in relation to impact, opening and cleaning.
(N) Electrical safety
  - design and installation;
  - provision of information.

Under section 35 of the Building Act 1984 (under which Act the regulations are made), it is a criminal offence, punishable by a magistrates' court, to contravene provisions of the Building Regulations.

Developers seeking to carry out building works or, in certain cases, to make a material change of use to an existing building, must either serve on the council a building notice under regulation 13, or deposit full plans under regulation 14. A building notice must describe the proposed works or change of use, and must be accompanied by plans, a statement and other particulars relating to drainage requirements. Alternatively, a developer may deposit full plans with the council, describing the proposed works or change of use. If the building notice route is chosen, the developer may commence works two clear days after service of the notice, but risks inspection by the council, which may reveal breaches of the regulations and require remedial action. If full plans are deposited under regulation 14, the council must approve or reject them within five weeks (two months by agreement with the developer). Proceeding on the basis of approved plans is clearly slower, but more certain of being in compliance with the relevant regulations to the satisfaction of the council's building inspectors. "Building regulation approvals" for the purposes of this part of this enquiry mean plans passed under section 16 of the Building Act 1984 or regularisation certificates given under regulation 21(6) of the Building Regulations 2000. Section 16 of the Act provides that plans deposited with the local authority must normally be passed unless they are defective, or show that proposed work would in fact contravene the Building Regulations. In certain cases defective plans may be passed subject to conditions that modifications will be made, but in any event the authority must, within "the relevant period" (five weeks or two months, as mentioned above) give notice that the plans are passed or rejected. If rejected, the notice must specify the defects in the plans. If passed, the notice operates as an approval of the plans for the purposes of the Building Regulations. If there is a dispute between the local authority and the person proposing to carry out the work, as to whether the plans are in conformity with the appropriate regulations, the matter may be referred to the Secretary of State for his determination.

Regulation 21 of the Building Regulations 2000 deals with the question of unauthorised building work, that is, building work carried out without a building notice having been served on the local authority or full plans having been deposited or a notice of commencement of work having been duly given under regulation 15. In a case of unauthorised building work, the owner of the building may apply to the authority for a regularisation certificate, issued under regulation 21(6). The owner must give a description of the unauthorised work, together with a plan if practicable, and a plan showing any additional work required to secure compliance with the building regulations. On receipt of such an application the local authority may require the applicant to lay open the works for inspection or for the taking of samples and the making of tests. Where the local authority has been able to satisfy itself that the relevant requirements have been satisfied, or can be dispensed with, or that no further work is required to secure compliance with them, it may issue the regularisation certificate, which is evidence (but not conclusive evidence) that the requirements of the certificate have been complied with.

Summary
The purpose of enquiry 1.1.(f) is to elicit details of building regulation approvals and regularisation certificates that the council has granted or refused in respect of the property. A buyer will be concerned to know that any recent

building works have been duly approved, but is not normally concerned with refused applications. Further investigation may be made into the building regulation status of the property if any works are in any sense doubtful. Even though a buyer would not be prosecuted for a breach of the regulations which pre-dates the buyer's ownership, evidence of prosecution for breach or of any regularisation certificates indicates that all may not be well with the property.

Enquiry 1.1.(g): Building Regulation Completion Certificates

Councils are duty bound, by virtue of regulation 17, to give completion certificates on completion of building works. On completion of any relevant works covered by the regulations, the person carrying out the works must give the council notice to this effect within five days. Any buildings proposed to be occupied before completion of building work must similarly be the subject of a notice five days before occupation. The council is then, in accordance with regulation 17, obliged to issue a completion certificate. Completion certificates given in accordance with this regulation are evidence (but, as the regulation states, not conclusive evidence) that the requirements specified have been complied with.

Summary

Enquiry 1.1.(g) concerns building regulation completion certificates. Since such a certificate normally indicates successful completion of authorised building works, a buyer normally prefers to be supplied with copies of any such certificate(s) which relate to the property being purchased. But the buyer should be aware that they are not conclusive evidence of completion. If there is any doubt about the completion of authorised works, physical inspection of the premises by a qualified surveyor or independent building inspector is advisable.

Enquiry 1.1.(h): Competent Person Self-Certification Schemes

Building Regulation 16A relates to minor building works, consisting only of the installation of, for example, replacement windows, rooflights, roof windows, or a replacement glazed door; or the installation of a heat-producing gas appliance, oil storage tank, central heating system, sanitary convenience, washing facilities or a bathroom. The work may be carried out, without formal building regulation approval, by an installer who is registered with the appropriate professional body indicating a level of competence in the relevant field. For example, a person registered under the Fenestration Self-Assessment Scheme (FENSA) would be authorised to carry out works including the installation of replacement windows, and a CORGI registered gas fitter could install a heating or hot water system connected to a heat-producing gas appliance. The installer must, within thirty days of completion of the work, give to the occupier of the building, and deposit with the council, a certificate that the work complies with the applicable requirements of the Building Regulations. A notice to the effect that the occupier has been served with the certificate, rather than a certificate itself, may be served on the authority.

Summary
Enquiry 1.1.(h) concerns certificates of compliance or notices relating to these minor works carried out under a self-certification scheme. If an inspection of the property reveals evidence of recent replacement windows, for example, or new sanitary ware, central heating or space heating appliances, the buyer will prefer to be supplied with copies of any certificate that relates to the work. The current owner of the property should be able to supply any certificate, as should the local authority.

How can copies of the above be obtained?

The register of planning applications and decisions, and the separate register of CLOPUDs, must be kept at the office of the local planning authority, that is, at the council offices. It is kept in addition to the register of enforcement and stop notices referred to in enquiry 3.9. Although parts of the register may be kept at different offices convenient to the areas of land to which they relate, in practice the register is kept at the council offices which accommodate the planning department.

Since decisions recorded on the register of planning applications and decisions, CLOPUDs, and listed building or conservation area decisions are of a public nature, the council normally supplies copies on request, but is not bound to do so free of charge. The council has a degree of copyright protection in respect of material generated pursuant to its statutory obligation to keep a register.

Copies of building regulation approvals and completion notices are not normally kept on a register as such, but again councils normally provide copies to *bona fide* enquirers on payment of a modest fee.

The Guidance Notes 2002 advised councils to add the following "informative statements" to the replies given to this enquiry:

(a) In all cases, "This reply does not cover other properties in the vicinity of the property."

(b) Where the council's records do not extend back before a certain date, the reply to the relevant part of the enquiry should state "The Council's records of [*specify the type of document*] do not extend back before [*insert date*] and this reply covers only the period since that date."

(c) Where computer records do not include records before a certain date, the following should be stated: "The Council's computerised records of [*specify the type of document*] do not extend back before [*insert date*] and this reply covers only the period since that date. Prior records would have to be searched manually at additional cost."

(d) Where the practice of issuing the particular type of document does not extend back before a certain date, the reply to the relevant part should state "The Council did not issue [*specify the type of document*] before [*insert date*]."

(e) If the building control function for the property is administered by an outside body (for example, the National House-Building Council for new residential property), this fact should be highlighted in the reply and, unless the council is administering the building control function or holds copies of all relevant consents and certificates, the following should be added: "The seller or developer should be asked to provide evidence of compliance with building regulations".

Enquiry 1.2: Planning Designations and Proposals

The second part of enquiry 1, entitled "Planning Designations and Proposals", relates to the strategic and local land use designations or proposals, if any, for the property, which are contained in existing or proposed "development plans". For the purpose of this enquiry, "development plans" is defined, by section 38 of the Planning and Compulsory Purchase Act 2004, to mean, when adopted, the new regional spatial strategy (spatial development strategy in Greater London) and, in both cases, the development plan documents adopted and approved for the area. For the time being, they may be taken to include the statutory structure, unitary and local plans prepared and adopted by local planning authorities under the Town and Country Planning Act, as well as non-statutory plans. While the Planning and Compulsory Purchase Act 2004 has made fundamental changes to the two-tier structure of structure plans and local plans, creating a new system of regional spatial strategies which are to be prepared at regional level, the old structure is likely to continue to be relevant to this enquiry for some time to come, at least until the new strategies and local development frameworks have been adopted.

Structure Plans

Structure plans were the responsibility of the county councils, and set the planning scene county-wide. They are broad general statements of principles relating to matters such as housing policies, shopping policies, transport, industry, commerce, the green belt; and cover a wide variety of economic, ecological, environmental and other issues. Under the Town and Country Planning Act, every county council was required to carry out a survey of its area to examine all those matters which might affect the development of the county from a town planning point of view. The matters which were to be examined, and kept under review by the county councils include:
  (i)   the physical and economic characteristics of the area, including the main purposes for which land is used, e.g., agricultural, industrial, commercial, residential;
  (ii)   population size, distribution and constitution;
  (iii) communications, transport and traffic;
  (iv)   projected changes in any of the above.
Having conducted the survey, the county council then prepared a structure plan covering the above matters. The structure plan is more than just a map. In fact it is principally a written document detailing the county policies and proposals in respect of development and land use within the area of the plan, including proposals for improvement of the environment. It is illustrated by diagrams and maps and accompanied by an "explanatory memorandum" summarising and explaining the policies.

Once formulated, the structure plan was then adopted by the county council, after first being advertised and placed on deposit at the council's offices for public inspection; opportunity for objections to be made by the public or interested bodies had to be given.

Before being formally adopted, the plan proposals were examined at an "examination in public", unless the Secretary of State otherwise directed. An examination in public was an in-depth discussion between the chairman and other members of a panel appointed by the Secretary of State for the purpose, representatives of the county council, and any others invited by the panel to take part. It is not a public local inquiry and no person had a right to be heard or to cross-examine. The plan proposals could be modified in accordance with the panel's findings.

Eventually the structure plan was approved by the county council with or without modifications.

Approved structure plans were in place for all of England and Wales, and the procedures contained in the Town and Country Planning Act 1990 were latterly relevant only in connection with the alteration, repeal or replacement of the existing structure plans.

In relation to Greater London, the structure plan was called the Greater London Development Plan and this structure plan continued in force, notwithstanding the abolition of the Greater London Council, until such time as a unitary development plan for a particular borough became operative. Once such a unitary development plan was approved by the Secretary of State, he could by order revoke that part of the Greater London Development Plan as was covered by the new unitary development plan, or that part of it which had come into force.

At any time after the structure plan had come into operation, the county council could submit proposals to the Secretary of State for its alteration or replacement. All such proposals had to go through a procedure similar to that for the original structure plan, except that sometimes the examination in public could be dispensed with.

Local Plans

As structure plans were the responsibility of the county councils and set out broad trends of policy, so local plans were the responsibility of district councils and had more specific and detailed provisions. It was from the local plan, rather than the structure plan, that a buyer would learn what effect the local council's planning proposals may have on the property being bought.

Action area plans were also prepared by the district council. These would be local plans prepared for part of the area of the local authority selected for comprehensive treatment by development, redevelopment or improvement.

The local plan was prepared generally in conformity with the broad principles of the structure plan, but it was prepared by the district council and, in so doing, the district council could take into account the survey conducted by the county council in connection with the structure plan.

The local plan consists of a map and a written statement, and may be accompanied by diagrams and other descriptive matter. It includes policies for housing, employment, industry, shopping, the green belt and other details of permitted land use and development in the district council's area.

The preparation of a local plan featured a number of steps. These may be summarised as follows:

(i)   formulation by the district council of its proposals;

(ii)   consultation with prescribed bodies and individuals;

(iii) service of the proposals on the county council (in a non-metropolitan area) for a statement by the county council of whether the proposals were in general conformity with the structure plan;

(iv) placement on deposit for public inspection and objection;

(v)   a public local inquiry into any objections, unless all objectors indicated that they did not wish to be heard;

(vi) a report by the inquiry inspector to the district council and the council's consideration of it. A statement of the council's intended action, and reasons for it, was to be made available for public inspection;

(vii) the Secretary of State could direct modifications to be made at this stage;

(viii) a list of proposed or directed modifications was prepared and notified to the public. Objections to the proposed modifications were considered; a further inquiry could be held;

(ix) public notice of intention to adopt the plan, with or without modifications, was given;

(x)   the Secretary of State could call in the plan for his approval at this stage;

(xi) the Secretary of State could direct the district council to consider further modifications;

(xii) approval or rejection by the Secretary of State, with or without modifications, if the plan was called in;

(xiii) adoption by the district council if the plan was not called in.

The district council could from time to time make proposals for altering or replacing a local plan, the procedure being similar to that for the preparation of a local plan.

"Old Style Development Plan"

The procedure for the preparation and adoption of structure plans and local plans was introduced by the Town and Country Planning Act 1971. Previously, the requirement was for the county council to carry out its survey and produce what is now called an "old style development plan". Some of these plans still survive.

A development plan under the old style procedure indicated both the manner in which the land covered by the plan was to be used, and the stages in which that development was to be carried out. Development plans consist of a basic map, written statement and other illustrative maps or plans, including, sometimes:

(i)   town maps indicating particular proposals for a town;

(ii)   comprehensive development area maps indicating proposals for complete redevelopment of particular areas; and

(iii) a programme map showing the stages by which the proposals contained in the written statement should be carried out.

Development plans may allocate specific areas for agricultural, residential, industrial or other purposes; define sites for proposed roads, buildings, airfields, parks, nature reserves and pleasure gardens; and define areas of comprehensive development.

London and the Metropolitan and Unitary Authorities

On 1 April 1986 the Greater London Council was abolished by the Local Government Act 1985, and the London borough councils became the local planning authorities for their respective boroughs. Schedule 1 to the Local Government Act 1985 applied to the local planning authorities (London borough councils) for the purposes of the preparation of development plans, instead of part II of the Town and Country Planning Act 1971 which applied to local planning authorities in the rest of the country. The Town and Country Planning Act 1990 provided for the system of unitary development plans, introduced by the Local Government Act 1985, and applicable to development plans within Greater London, the metropolitan authorities and the new unitary authorities introduced by the Local Government Act 1992.

In London and the metropolitan areas the council, as local planning authority, had a duty to keep under review matters affecting the planning and development of its area, and could institute surveys of the area for this purpose. The matters for survey and review by the council included:

(i) the physical and economic characteristics of the area, including principal land uses;

(ii) the size, composition and distribution of the population;

(iii) communications, transport and traffic;

(iv) projected changes in any of the above.

Within a time prescribed by the Secretary of State, the council had to prepare for its area a "unitary development plan". Unitary development plans comprised two parts:

- Part I: a written statement formulating the council's general development and land use policies for the area (including traffic management and environmental improvement provisions);
- Part II: detailed proposals for development or land use in the area; a map showing the proposals on a geographical basis; a reasoned justification of the policies and proposals; diagrams, illustrations and descriptive or explanatory matter.

The proposals in Part II had to be in general conformity with the general policy in Part I.

In preparing the unitary development plan as outlined above, and before finally determining its contents, the council had to secure that publicity was given to the proposals and that the public and interested bodies had an opportunity to make representations on them. Any representations made were to be considered by the council. Once the plan was prepared, but before it was adopted by the council as local planning authority, copies had to be made available for inspection at its offices and time given for objections to be made.

A copy of the unitary development plan as published was to be sent to the Secretary of State, together with a statement of the steps taken to publicise it and of the consultations which had taken place and the views of interested parties. The Secretary of State could require the council to conduct further consultation.

After the period for objections had expired and any objections had been considered by the council, the council could adopt the plan by resolution, either as originally prepared or as modified to take account of objections and representations. The plan became operational on the date of this resolution.

The council, as local planning authority, could hold a local inquiry to hear and debate objections made to the proposals contained in the unitary development plan before it was adopted. The inquiry was presided over by the Secretary of State or, in certain circumstances, by a person appointed by the council.

At any time before the plan was formally adopted by the council, the Secretary of State could "call it in" for his approval, and if he did, the council could take no further steps in its adoption until the Secretary of State had reached a decision. The Secretary of State could, in the event, approve the plan with or without modification, or reject it, giving reasons. If it was approved, the council could then adopt it, having made any appropriate modifications as directed by the Secretary of State. The Secretary of State could decide to call a public local inquiry into objections before approving the plan for adoption by the council.

Until a unitary development plan was approved for the area, existing local plans and any old development plans in existence remained relevant when considering the uses and developments for which planning permission would be granted.

Unitary development plans could be subject to alteration from time to time either on proposals made by the council as local planning authority or by the Secretary of State. Any alterations to a plan which were approved by the Secretary of State had to go through the complete publicity, objection, inquiry and adoption procedure outlined above.

Non-Statutory Plans

Structure plans, local plans, unitary plans and old style development plans are all "statutory plans", since the requirement to prepare them was imposed on councils by statute, namely the Town and Country Planning Act. Councils responsible for town planning could, however, make, on their own initiative, "non-statutory plans", that is, plans covering particular areas or particular issues. For instance, town plans might be prepared covering detailed proposals for development within particular towns. The public would be invited to participate in the plan-making process and interested bodies asked for their comments. Eventually, after having passed through a process similar to that for the preparation of statutory plans (but without submission to the Secretary of State), the council would adopt the final plan as planning policy for the area it covers. Such plans do not have the same status as statutory plans, but could be relied upon at public local inquiries into refusals of planning permission, since they have been subject to a public consultation process and finally adopted by a body of elected councillors.

Primary Uses of Land

The written statement or the proposals map which formed part of the local plan would indicate, by different notations, the primary uses to which certain areas were to be put, and might, exceptionally, make particular reference to individual properties or groups of properties. For example, the plan might identify prime industrial or shopping areas, land earmarked for public open space, agricultural priority areas or areas of archaeological importance. These notations meant that preference would be given to developments of the types conforming to those notations in the areas which they covered.

A unitary development plan indicates, by reference to the written statement and proposals map (on a geographical basis), primary uses to which particular areas of land should be put, and in respect of which there is a presumption in favour of granting planning permission. It may also indicate specific proposals for particular property within the area. Part II of the plan may designate any part of the area to which it relates as an "action area", that is, an area selected for comprehensive treatment by development, redevelopment or improvement, and the plan contains a detailed description of the proposed treatment of these action areas.

Non-statutory plans may also identify primary uses and particular proposals for properties within the area.

Summary

Enquiry 1.2 concerns, in relation to any development plan as defined, the primary use or zoning indicated for the area or property in question. While the system of structure, local and unitary development plans has technically been abolished, to be replaced over time by the structure of regional spatial strategies and, in London, its spatial development strategy, and the local development frameworks, in practice and for the foreseeable future the old system continues to be relevant. Local authorities are expected to provide details of all special policies applying to the property or its immediate area which do not apply generally to the whole area administered by the authority. The answer is important to the buyer as it might affect the intended use of the property, and the availability or otherwise of planning permission for that use. If no primary uses or designations are revealed, the buyer may assume that his intentions for the property should not be unusually hampered by the planning process.

The enquiry should also produce details of any specific proposal included in the plans for the property. The reply to this part of this enquiry may be decisive as to whether the buyer decides to proceed with the purchase.

The Guidance Notes 2002 advised councils that the reply to this part of the enquiry should state the development plan in which the relevant policy or proposal is contained and include a summary of the policy or proposal and how to obtain more details. The reply should also, according to the Guidance Notes, include the following statement: "This reply reflects policies or proposals in any existing development plan and in any formally proposed alteration or replacement plan, but does not include policies contained in planning guidance notes." ("Planning guidance notes" are policy and procedure notes issued by central government from time to time to guide the planning process for local planning authorities, and are of general application.)

Enquiry 2: Roadways, Footways and Footpaths

"Which of the roads, footways and footpaths named in the application for this search (via boxes B and C) are:
 (a) highways maintainable at public expense
 (b) subject to adoption and supported by a bond or bond waiver
 (c) to be made up by a local authority who will reclaim the cost from the frontagers
 (d) to be adopted by a local authority without reclaiming the cost from the frontagers"

Enquiry 2.(a): The Maintenance of Highways

This enquiry deals with the liabilities of the property owner and the council for the maintenance of highways.

The principal piece of legislation concerned with the classification, creation, maintenance and improvement of highways is the Highways Act 1980.

A "road" is not defined in the Act, but may be taken to be that portion of the highway over which vehicles travel, defined in the Act as the "carriageway". A "footway" is defined as "a way comprised in a highway which also comprises a carriageway, being a way over which the public have a right of way on foot only". A "footpath" is defined as "a highway over which the public have a right of way on foot only, not being a footway".

Thus a highway, for the purposes of this enquiry, normally consists either of a carriageway, with or without footway, or of a public footpath. Footpaths, as such, are more often than not unmade and they often cross or border on open fields. Footways, on the other hand, exist only in conjunction with a "carriageway".

Highways, as defined above, are either maintainable at the public expense, or not so maintainable.

Maintainable highways (generally called "adopted highways") are the responsibility of the highway authority, and it is the highway authority for the particular highway which bears the cost of maintenance and repair.

Highways which are not maintainable at the public expense (so-called "unadopted roads") are still highways and may be used by the public as carriageways or footpaths (or bridleways). Maintenance of their surface, however, is the responsibility of the owner of the land over which they run.

Summary
The purpose of enquiry 2.(a) is to seek information as to responsibility for the maintenance of highways described in the "description of the property" appearing on the front of Con 29R: *Enquiries of Local Authority*. The buyer usually hopes for a reply indicating that the highways are adopted and therefore maintainable at public expense. If the reply indicates private responsibility, the prospective buyer may be required to contribute towards the costs of highway maintenance, which could be considerable. When completing Con 29R, the enquirer should take particular care to ensure that all roads or parts of roads abutting on or leading to the property are accurately described in boxes B and C on the form.

The Guidance Notes 2002 advised that, where none of the roads described in boxes B and C is maintainable at public expense, councils should give as detailed a response as possible, specifying where possible the nearest road which is so maintainable. The reply is required by the Guidance Notes 2002 to contain a statement as follows: "If a road, footpath or footway is not a highway, there may be no right to use it. The Council cannot express an opinion, without seeing the title plan of the property and carrying out an inspection, whether or not any existing or proposed highway directly abuts the boundary of the property."

Enquiry 2.(b): Agreements for Adoption

Under section 38 of the Highways Act 1980, a developer who wishes to construct a new road or roads to service a new development (generally residential) may enter into an agreement with the council whereby the developer agrees to make up the roads, footways, etc., and to provide drainage and lighting, to adoption standard. The council, in the same agreement, agrees to adopt the roads and footways as highways maintainable at the public expense. In this way the developer divests himself of future responsibility for maintenance. These agreements are commonly called section 38 agreements.

If a section 38 agreement has been entered into by a developer, it is normally supported by a bond. A bond is a financial commitment entered into by a financial institution such as a bank or insurance company, whereby the financial institution agrees to pay to the council a specified sum of money in the event that the developer fails, for whatever reason, to make the road up to adoption standard. The sum of money should be sufficient to pay for any outstanding works necessary to bring the road up to adoption standard. As works proceed on the road, the bond sum will probably be reduced, with the consent of the council, to such sum as remains adequate to carry out the outstanding works.

Summary
Enquiry 2.(b) is designed to reveal whether such an agreement has been entered into. An affirmative reply indicates to the buyer that the road will, subject to its being made up to adoption standard by the developer, be adopted, and the buyer will have no future responsibility for its maintenance. The buyer will be looking for an affirmative reply if the reply to enquiry 2.(a)

was in the negative in respect of the roads serving the property. A prudent enquirer may also seek confirmation that the provisions of any such agreement have been complied with.

Enquiry 2.(b) is aimed at eliciting whether there is in existence a bond supporting any section 38 agreement referred to in the reply. If the reply is in the affirmative, the buyer should check, by inquiry and inspection, the adequacy of the amount of the bond to secure completion of any outstanding road works under the agreement. If there is a section 38 agreement but no bond, the buyer is put on notice that there is a possibility that the road will not be adopted, or at least not without expense to the buyer. Most local highway authorities will, on request, confirm the adequacy or otherwise of an outstanding bond.

It is quite common for the local authority to agree to waive the requirement for a bond, if it can be satisfied that the developer is of sufficient standing and reputation. If there is evidence of bond waiver, a prudent buyer might be well advised to make further enquiries of the local authority, to ascertain why the requirement for a bond was waived.

Enquiry 2.(c): Making up at Expense of Frontagers
The Highways Act contains a private street works code which provides for the making-up of private streets by the highway authority. Where the highway authority has inspected a private street and it is not, to its satisfaction, "sewered levelled paved metalled flagged channelled made good and lighted", the authority may decide to carry out street works and recover the cost of those works from the owners of premises fronting the street.

Summary
Enquiry 2.(c) concerns whether the council has decided to use its powers under the code to make up private roads, footpaths or footways at the cost of the frontagers. The buyer of the property usually hopes for a negative reply, but if an affirmative reply is given, the prospective owner will want to know the likely cost of the proposed works and the proportion he will be expected to bear.

Enquiry 2.(d): Adoption Without Cost to Frontagers
Where street works have been carried out in a private street, the council, if it is satisfied with those works, may adopt the private street as a highway maintainable at the public expense, and take over responsibility for its maintenance. This it may do simply by posting a notice in a prominent position in the highway, declaring the highway to be maintainable at public expense, unless the majority of the owners of the highway, within one month, object to its being adopted.

Summary
Enquiry 2.(d) is intended to elicit whether the council has agreed to adopt a private street when the works have been completed, at no further cost to the frontagers. A buyer who discovers that the property in contemplation lies in a private street will be delighted to find that it is to be made up and adopted at

no cost to the buyer; the hope will therefore be for an affirmative reply to this part of the question if the reply to enquiry 2.(a) indicates private responsibility for the frontage road.

Enquiry 3: Other Matters

Having dealt with the general planning and highways position of the property in enquiries 1 and 2, the 2007 edition of Con 29R: *Enquiries of Local Authority* treats all other issues of concern to a standard prospective buyer under the general heading of "Other Matters". These matters, the subject of the following thirteen parts of this book, may be dealt with by exception by the responding council, that is, the council need respond only in respect of those "matters" which have some implications for the property in respect of which the enquiries are submitted.

Matters which already appear in the register of local land charges are not revealed in response to this enquiry; rather they should appear in reply to the official search on form LLC 1.

Copies of any relevant documents are normally in the possession of the responding council, which will also supply photocopies on payment of a reasonable fee.

Enquiry 3.1: Land Required for Public Purposes

"Is the property included in land required for public purposes?"

The Town and Country Planning Act 1990 provides that where land is affected by provisions of statutory structure and local plans which provide for the land to be protected from development in the interests of the future needs of the government or council, or a statutory undertaker (gas, water, electricity, telecommunications etc.), so that its value for sale is affected, an owner may serve a "blight notice" on the council requiring the council to purchase the whole of the land concerned. If, for instance, land is protected from development by the plans because it will be required at some time in the future for laying new mains, this obviously affects its value since a buyer would be deterred from buying it.

Paragraphs 5 and 6 of schedule 13 to the Town and Country Planning Act extend these provisions to include any proposals contained in non-statutory plans.

Summary
Enquiry 3.1 is relevant if the property or any part of it is affected by provisions of a non-statutory plan which effectively prohibit development in the interests of preserving the council's plans for the future. A buyer will require a negative response, and an affirmative response will almost certainly deter the buyer from proceeding to acquire the property.

Enquiry 3.2: Land to be Acquired for Road Works

"Is the property included in land to be acquired for road works?"

This part of enquiry 3 is designed to elicit information relating to any approved schemes of highway construction or improvement that involve the acquisition by the competent highway authority of part or all of the property the subject of the search. As will be seen in respect of enquiry 3.4 (nearby road schemes), major schemes of highway construction and improvement take months and often years of consultation and examination, often in public, before final approval. Enquiry 3.2 is, however, concerned with definite action on the part of a highway authority that is almost certain to take place, having been approved after consultation and modification. Further, while enquiry 3.4 deals with nearby road schemes which may or may not have an environmental impact on the property to be acquired, enquiry 3.2 is directly concerned with acquisition of the property itself (or part of it) to enable the road scheme to proceed.

If there are proposals, either by the Secretary of State or the council, for the construction of a new road or for the improvement of an existing road, these often involve the acquisition of land by the Secretary of State or the council, as appropriate. The Secretary of State or the council may be able to acquire the land by agreement, but failing this the use of compulsory purchase powers would be necessary. Under sections 239 to 246 of the Highways Act 1980, both the Secretary of State and the council acting as highway authority have extensive powers of compulsory acquisition of land for highway construction and improvement.

Summary
Enquiry 3.2 is concerned with any road proposals approved by the council or notified to the council by the Secretary of State which involve the acquisition of the property or any part of it. The buyer usually prefers a negative reply, for although compensation would be due for the loss of the land, the precise amount of land to be lost, or the compensation to be paid for it, may be unclear for a considerable time. A prudent buyer will seek precise information on these two points before deciding whether or not to proceed with a purchase of land subject to acquisition for road improvement.

Enquiry 3.3: Drainage Agreements and Consents

"Do either of the following exist in relation to the property?
   (a) an agreement to drain buildings in combination into an existing sewer by means of a private sewer
   (b) an agreement or consent for (i) a building, or (ii) extension to a building on the property to be built over, or in the vicinity of a drain, sewer or disposal main"

Enquiry 3.3.(a): Combined Drainage

The general position relating to the drainage of property is dealt with in Part III of this work. Enquiry 3.3.(a) is concerned with the Building Act 1984 and the provisions of that Act on the combined drainage of buildings.

Section 22 of the Building Act 1984 provides that, when the drains of buildings are first being laid, if it appears to the local authority that those buildings may be drained more economically or advantageously in combination into an existing sewer by means of a private sewer, the authority may require this to be done, either by those constructing the buildings or by the authority on their behalf. The authority then determines the proportion of the expense of constructing and maintaining the private sewer to be borne by the owners; or, where the distance of the existing sewer from the site of any of the buildings in question is more than 100 feet (or 30.48 metres), the authority may agree to accept responsibility for part of the cost.

Summary
Enquiry 3.3.(a) is about whether an agreement under section 22 of the Building Act (formerly section 38 of the Public Health Act 1936) is in force which affects the property. A buyer normally prefers a negative reply, the usual preference being for the premises to drain directly to a public sewer. Maintenance of private sewers, even if shared, can be an expensive business and there are often arguments between landowners as to when a private sewer requires maintenance.

Enquiry 3.3.(b): Building over Drains and Sewers

Sewerage undertakers have special statutory powers to protect the structure and integrity of public sewers. By section 18 of the Building Act 1984, where building plans were deposited for approval with the local authority and they disclosed that a new structure was to be erected over a drain, sewer or disposal main (or would interfere with use of such pipes), the local authority was obliged to reject the plans, unless in the particular circumstances it was considered that consent could be granted. If the new structure would be over or would interfere with a drain, sewer or disposal main which was vested in a sewerage undertaker, the undertaker had to be notified of the proposed works. The undertaker could then require the local authority to refuse consent or make consent subject to conditions based upon the type of development involved.

The provisions of section 18 have been repealed and effectively replaced by an amendment to the Building Regulations 2000. Part H4 of the regulations now provides that the erection or extension of a building shall be carried out in a way that is not detrimental to the building or extension or to the continued maintenance of the drain, sewer or disposal main. The sewerage undertaker must be consulted by the local authority as soon as practicable after plans have been deposited with it and before issuing any completion certificate in relation to the building work where any proposal to build over sewers is made.

Buildings or extensions erected in contravention of building controls may have to be removed or altered as required by a notice served under section 36 of the Building Act 1984, and if the notice is not complied with, the authority may carry out any necessary works in default.

Summary
Enquiry 3.3.(b) concerns whether there is in force an agreement or consent under section 18 of the Building Act 1984 for a building or extension over or near a drain, sewer or disposal main or any building consent issued relating to Part H4 works involving building over a sewer. A buyer ideally prefers a negative response; if an affirmative one is forthcoming, a buyer should request full details of the agreement or consent, and confirmation that the conditions of any such agreement or consent have been complied with to date.

The sewerage undertaker for the area should ideally be asked the same question if there is any possibility at all of the existence of structures erected over drains. The sewerage undertaker's records are likely to prove, over time, more reliable than those of the council, but for the time being a prudent buyer should make enquiry of both authorities. If the searcher is making enquiries of the sewerage undertaker, the matter is covered in the drainage and water enquiries (dealt with in Part III of this book). The Guidance Notes 2002 advised the enquirer that "Enquiries about drainage should also be made of the local sewerage undertaker".

Enquiry 3.4: Nearby Road Schemes

"Is the property (or will it be) within 200 metres of any of the following?
  (a) the centre line of a new trunk road or special road specified in any order, draft order or scheme
  (b) the centre line of a proposed alteration or improvement to an existing road involving construction of a subway, underpass, flyover, footbridge, elevated road or dual carriageway
  (c) the outer limits of construction works for a proposed alteration or improvement to an existing road involving (i) construction of a roundabout (other than a mini roundabout), or (ii) widening by construction of one or more additional traffic lanes
  (d) the outer limits of (i) construction of a new road to be built by a local authority, (ii) an approved alteration or improvement to an existing road involving construction of a subway, underpass, flyover, footbridge, elevated road or dual carriageway, (iii) construction of a roundabout (other than a mini roundabout), or widening by construction of one or more additional traffic lanes;
  (e) the centre line of the proposed route of a new road under proposals published for public consultation
  (f) the outer limits of (i) construction of a proposed alteration or improvement to an existing road involving construction of a subway, underpass, flyover, footbridge, elevated road or dual carriageway, (ii) construction of a roundabout (other than a mini roundabout), (iii) widening by construction of one or more additional traffic lanes, under proposals published for public consultation"

[Note: A mini-roundabout is defined as a roundabout consisting of a level or raised circular marking of a diameter of four metres or less.]

Enquiry 3.4.(a): New Trunk Roads or Special Roads

Enquiry 3.4.(a) deals with proposals to construct new roads (or to alter or improve existing roads) which may affect the property in question in the future, but do not necessarily involve acquisition of any part of the property itself.

"Special roads" are roads reserved for particular classes of traffic. "Trunk roads" are major roads which generally stretch over considerable distances through several districts and counties. They are the responsibility of the Secretary of State for Transport, that is, central government.

Before constructing a new trunk road, the Secretary of State must make an order defining the route of the proposed new road. If there are any objections to the proposals, these must generally be subjected to examination at a public local inquiry before the order can be confirmed. The Secretary of State is obliged to notify the council in advance of his proposals for new roads. If the proposal is to construct a new road the centre line of which will be within 200 metres of the property to be purchased, the buyer will want to know full details of the proposals.

Enquiry 3.4.(a) concerns any published proposals for a new trunk or special road the centre line of which, if the proposal is adopted, would be within 200 metres of any part of the property. Ideally the buyer will be looking for a negative reply to this part of the question since, although compensation from the government may be available if the proposal is adopted, the existence of a new trunk road less than 200 metres away from a property may deter a future buyer.

Enquiries 3.4.(b) and (c): Alterations and Improvements

Enquiry 3.4.(b) makes a similar enquiry regarding proposals for the alteration or improvement of an existing trunk or special road, where such alteration or improvement would involve the construction of a subway, underpass, flyover, footbridge, elevated road or dual carriageway. Again, the 200 metres is to be taken from the centre line of the proposed subway, underpass, flyover etc., to the nearest part of the property affected.

Enquiry 3.4.(c) repeats the enquiry in connection with any proposals to construct a roundabout (other than a mini roundabout), or the widening of an existing trunk or special road by the provision of additional lanes. Here the 200 metres is to be taken from the outer limits of construction of the roundabout or additional lanes to the nearest part of the property affected.

Most buyers, again, prefer a negative response.

Enquiry 3.4.(d): Other New Roads

New roads other than trunk roads may be constructed by the council or the county council, generally as part of a development scheme involving a new housing project, or as a road which does not have national importance in the same way as a trunk road, but nevertheless is of such significance as to cross the boundaries of more than one council.

Enquiry 3.4.(d) is intended to reveal whether the council (or any county council or unitary council as highway authority) has approved any proposals for the construction of new roads, the outer limits of construction of which would lie within 200 metres of any part of the property searched against. It goes on to make a similar enquiry regarding proposals for the alteration or improvement of existing roads, involving the construction of a subway, underpass, flyover, footbridge, elevated road, dual carriageway, roundabout (other than mini roundabout as defined) or additional traffic lanes. The 200 metres is to be taken from the limits of construction of the proposed improvement to the nearest part of the property affected.

This part of enquiry 3.4 relates only to proposals of a council, not to those of other bodies or companies, which the council, in its capacity as local planning authority, may be asked to approve.

Most buyers prefer a negative response to part (d) and a prudent buyer who has any suspicion at all regarding impending road proposals of this nature would be wise to raise optional enquiry 4, "Road Proposals by Private Bodies" (see below).

Enquiry 3.4.(e) and (f): Proposals Published for Public Consultation

Before the preparation and formal submission for confirmation of orders made by the Secretary of State or the council for new road schemes, there is a lengthy period of consultation with interested parties and the public. Full details of proposals are published for inspection by the public, and the public is invited to comment on them. This takes place at an early stage in the process, the intention being to test public reaction to the proposals before the formal orders are adopted. Objections to the proposals may be tested at a public inquiry.

Enquiry 3.4.(e) is designed to elicit whether this preliminary consultation stage has been reached in connection with any road proposals which indicate that the centre line of the possible route of a proposed new road lies within 200 metres of the property enquired about. In this case the proposal is indicated by a line or series of lines on a map, and if any part of the property lies within 200 metres of that line this question is answered in the affirmative.

Enquiry 3.4.(f) concerns similar information on the consultation stage for proposals to alter or improve an existing road where the proposals include the construction of a subway, underpass, flyover, footbridge, elevated road, dual carriageway, roundabout (other than mini roundabout) or additional traffic lanes. Here the 200 metres is to be taken from the outer limits of construction of the subway, underpass etc., to the nearest part of the property affected. Clearly an intending buyer normally prefers a negative response to both parts (e) and (f) of enquiry 3.4.

Enquiry 3.5: Nearby Railway Schemes

"Is the property (or will it be) within 200 metres of the centre line of a proposed railway, tramway, light railway or monorail?"

This enquiry relates to proposals notified to or approved by the council for the construction of railways, either under special Act of Parliament or by virtue of an order made under the Transport and Works Act 1992.

A "railway" means a system of transport employing parallel rails which provide support and guidance for vehicles carried on flanged wheels and form a track which is either of a gauge of at least 350 millimetres or crosses a carriageway (whether of not on the same level), but does not include a tramway.

A "tramway" means a system of transport used wholly or mainly for the carriage of passengers and employing parallel rails which supply support and guidance for vehicles carried on flanged wheels and are laid wholly or mainly along a street or in any other place to which the public has access (including a place to which the public has access only on making a payment).

Railways

Any person may construct a railway on his or her own land, and no statutory authority is necessary beyond the normal requirement for planning permission in respect of the operational development entailed in its construction. However, since the construction of a railway usually involves the acquisition of land and interference with the private rights of other landowners, a special Act has in the past normally been necessary for the purposes of conferring compulsory purchase and other powers on a railway undertaker.

The authorisation and construction of almost all the public railway system in Great Britain were dealt with in the Railways Clauses Consolidation Act 1845 and the Railways Clauses Act 1863. Provisions are made in these enactments for the construction of works; the occupation of land in connection with construction; the protection of adjacent land; the crossing of roads and construction of bridges; and the operational requirements of railway undertakers.

Responsibility for the control of the public railway system, and for certain other railway and light railway undertakings, vested for many years in the British Railways Board and London Regional Transport. A few independent railway undertakings do survive and their functions and powers are contained in their own special Acts. By virtue of section 84 of the Railways Act 1993, which Act concerned the reorganisation of the railways, the British Railways Board could form companies for the purpose of facilitating the disposal of its undertaking, and this Act paved the way for privatisation. Later developments, particularly the disastrous rail crash at Hatfield in 2000, and the dismantling of Railtrack as one of these companies, suggested a need for re-evaluating the structure of the public railway system, and this took place in 2005. The functions of the franchising director, introduced by the 1993 Act, were transferred to the Strategic Rail Authority which was established by the Transport Act 2000. The Railways Act 2005 now provides for the transfer, by "transfer scheme", of functions from the Strategic Rail Authority to the Secretary of State.

British Railways and London Transport and the bodies that replace them have power to acquire land for the purposes of their operations, and compulsory purchase powers are available by order of the Secretary of State. Development of operational land (that is, land used for the purposes of carrying on the undertaking) by these bodies has the benefit of permitted development rights under the Town and Country Planning General Development Order (see the commentary on enquiry 3.9). Hence planning permission for development of their operational land is not required. Independent railway undertakers derive authority for the acquisition of land and construction works from their special Acts.

When a Bill is promoted for the construction of a railway, a plan in duplicate, together with a book of reference and a section of the works proposed, must be deposited with the council of the county(ies) in or through which the railway is to be constructed. An ordnance map showing the proposed line of the railway must also be deposited. Publicity must be given to the proposals and prescribed notices must be served, in particular upon the owners of land required by the undertaker for construction of the railway. Any interested person is entitled to inspect the plans and sections (and any altered plans and sections) and to make copies of them.

In constructing the railway the undertaker may deviate from the line shown on the deposited plans within the limits specified for such deviation, but by not more than ten yards from the delineated line when passing through built-up areas, and elsewhere by not more than one hundred yards. In deviating from the delineated line, the undertaker may not extend the railway construction into the land of any person whose name is not mentioned in the book of reference, without that person's consent.

In constructing the railway, the undertaker has extensive powers to build tunnels, embankments, aqueducts, bridges, arches, cuttings and fences; to alter the course of non-navigable rivers; build houses, warehouses, offices and other buildings, yards, stations, wharfs, machinery and such apparatus as is deemed necessary for the efficient operation of a railway undertaking.

The undertaker may take temporary possession of land (except domestic gardens) within two hundred yards of the centre of the line delineated on the plans for so long as may be necessary for the construction of the railway or associated works. This power to take temporary possession is exercisable without prior payment, but three weeks' written notice must be given to the owners and occupiers of the land (except in the case of accident to the railway requiring immediate repair). During the period of temporary occupation, the undertaker may take earth or soil by side cuttings from the land, may deposit soil on the land, and may take materials for repair or construction of the railway. The undertaker must pay compensation to the occupier of the land within one month of entry, calculated in accordance with the value of any crop or dressing on the land together with full compensation for other damage of a temporary nature. The undertaker must also pay compensation in respect of all permanent loss or damage within six months of completion of the works of construction.

Tramways, Light Railways and Monorails

In the past, the construction of tramways, light railways and monorails was authorised by order of the Secretary of State for Transport under the provisions contained in the Light Railways Act 1896. Applications for orders could be made by county, district and London borough councils, by private promoters (individuals, corporations or companies), or jointly by a council and a private promoter. Advertisement of the application was published in a local newspaper for two consecutive weeks and in the *London Gazette*, and notices were served on persons affected. The line of the railway and its termini, the proposed gauge and motive power of the railway and the land proposed to be taken for construction had to be described. The notice specified a place at which plans and sections of the proposed railway and of the land required for construction could be inspected at all reasonable hours, and copies of the draft order were made available on payment of the specified fee.

The notice and draft order, plans, sections, books of reference, estimate of expenses of the light railway and an ordnance map showing the line of the whole railway were deposited for inspection by the public with every county, London borough, district and parish council through whose area the line was proposed to be constructed. Objections and representations could be made in writing to the Secretary of State for Transport (and copied to the promoters of the order or their solicitors).

On receiving the application for a light railway order, the Secretary of State for Transport had to be satisfied that the local authorities through whose area the railway was intended to pass had been consulted, and the owners and occupiers of land proposed to be taken had been notified. A local public inquiry into the application could be conducted and the Secretary of State had to be satisfied as to the safety of the public and other material considerations, including the utility of the proposed railway, its advantage to the public, the nature and extent of opposition to the application and the probable effect on existing railways of the competition.

If the Secretary of State agreed to grant an application for a light railway order, he was to ensure that all matters necessary for the construction and working of the railway were inserted in the order, including provisions for the safety of the public and particulars of the land proposed to be taken.

Provisions of the Railways Clauses Consolidation Acts could be incorporated, conferring compulsory purchase powers on the promoters of the railway.

The Transport and Works Act 1992 introduced a new regime of procedures for the authorisation of major transport projects which is to replace the light railways order procedures. By virtue of this Act, which is fleshed out by detailed rules and regulations, the Secretary of State is empowered, by order, to make provision for the construction of railway, tramway, trolley vehicle and other guided transport systems and inland waterways. Orders made by the Secretary of State under the Act may include provisions for:

- the construction, alteration, repair, maintenance, demolition or removal of railways;
- the carrying out of civil engineering works;
- the acquisition of land by compulsory purchase powers;
- the creation and extinguishment of rights over land;
- the protection of property;
- the payment of compensation;
- the making of by-laws.

Detailed rules as to the procedure for making these orders, the form of application, the documents which must be submitted with it, the publication of notices, and other steps to be taken, have been made. There is a formal procedure for making objections and an inquiry process for dealing with any objections duly made.

Once an order under this Act has been made, the Secretary of State is obliged to publish a notice giving details of the order in the *London Gazette*.

Orders under the Transport and Works Act 1992 are normally applied for by transport undertakers or railway promoters. In limited circumstances, however, the Secretary of State may make an order himself without application. This may be done only:

- in relation to certain defence works and operations;
- on safety grounds;
- to repeal or revoke spent provisions in other orders made under the Act.

Applications for schemes which, in the opinion of the Secretary of State, are of national significance, are not approved until notice has been published in the *London Gazette* identifying the application and proposals, and all objectors have been notified. These schemes must then be approved by a special parliamentary procedure, going through both Houses of Parliament on a motion moved by a Minister of the Crown.

Summary

Enquiry 3.5 is drafted to elicit whether the property in question lies within 200 metres of the centre line of a proposed railway, tramway, light railway or monorail. A buyer notified of outline proposals in reply to this enquiry would be well advised to secure a copy of any plans, sections and relevant extracts from the books of reference, which should be on deposit at the offices either of the county (or London borough) council or, in the case of light railways, the district (or London borough) council. A buyer of property within 200 yards of the centre line of a proposed railway may be subjected to the rights of temporary occupation by the railway operator during the course of construction. Buyers of property which is close to the route of a proposed railway line should be aware that, during the course of construction, the line may deviate, within prescribed limits, from the line shown on the deposited plans.

Enquiry 3.6: Traffic Schemes

"Has a local authority approved but not yet implemented any of the following for the roads, footways and footpaths (named in Box B) which abut the boundaries of the property?
  (a) permanent stopping up or diversion
  (b) waiting or loading restrictions
  (c) one way driving
  (d) prohibition of driving
  (e) pedestrianisation
  (f) vehicle width or weight restriction
  (g) traffic calming works including road humps
  (h) residents parking controls
  (i) minor road widening or improvement
  (j) pedestrian crossings
  (k) cycle tracks
  (l) bridge building"

This enquiry relates to a host of highways and traffic management measures which the council, as highway authority, may have approved under highways or traffic regulation legislation, but not yet undertaken. The searcher is reminded that proper and full description in boxes B and C of all roads, footways and footpaths which service the property in question is crucial if a full picture of the traffic management situation is to be obtained. Most of the measures with which enquiry 3.6 is concerned are apparent from a physical inspection of the streets and footpaths themselves once the measures have been implemented, as appropriate signage is normally required by the relevant legislation and regulations. The purpose of enquiry 3.6 is to identify measures which have been approved but not yet implemented.

Enquiry 3.6.(a): Permanent Stopping up or Diversion
This part of enquiry 3.6 relates to proposals for the stopping up or diversion of roads or footpaths which are referred to in the description of the property appearing on the front of Con 29R: *Enquiries of Local Authority*.

A council which wishes to stop up or divert a highway (that is, a road or a footpath) has a number of statutory powers available and these are to be found in various Acts of Parliament, depending on the reasons for which the stopping up is sought.

Magistrates' Court Order

Under section 116 of the Highways Act 1980, the council may apply to a magistrates' court for an order stopping up or diverting a road on the grounds that the road is unnecessary or that it can be diverted so as to make it nearer or "more commodious" to the public. This provision is used at the request of the landowner over whose land the road runs, and indeed it is the only power which can be invoked by a landowner, provided that he can persuade the council to take action on his behalf.

Notices must first be given by the council to the owners of all land adjoining the highway, the statutory undertakers concerned, the parish council and the Secretary of State in the case of a classified road. A notice must be displayed at each end of the highway to be stopped up and notices must appear in the *London Gazette* and local newspapers. All these notices must be served or published at least twenty-eight days before the application to the magistrates is made, and any person on whom a notice has been served has the right to be heard by the magistrates before an order is made.

The magistrates may decide to inspect the highway themselves before making the order. The order, when made, may stop up the highway for all purposes, or reserve rights of way for pedestrians, or bridleway rights.

While a landowner may request the council to make this application on his behalf, if the council refuses to do so, the landowner cannot apply to the magistrates on his own initiative.

Stopping up of Public Footpaths and Bridleways

Under section 118 of the Highways Act, a special procedure is provided for the stopping up of public footpaths and bridleways. An order extinguishing the public path or bridleway may be made by the council where the council considers it expedient that it should be stopped up as it is not needed for public use. If the council decides to make such an order, notice of intention to make it must first be published, and at least twenty-eight days must be given to the public to lodge objections to the extinguishment order. Notices must be served on the owner of the land over which the path passes and must be posted at each end of the footpath concerned. If there are no objections to the making of the order, the council may then make it. If there are objections, the order must be confirmed by the Secretary of State, who may confirm it only after he has held a public local inquiry, to allow objectors to make their representations.

There are further special powers for councils to apply for the extinguishment of public rights of way (footpaths and bridleways) under section 118B in the interests of crime prevention or reduction. Further powers are bestowed by section 118ZA on owners of agricultural and forestry land, and by section 118C on proprietors of schools.

Public Path Diversion Orders

Under section 119 of the Highways Act, the council may make a "public path diversion order" if requested by the owner of land crossed by a public path. Here the owner of the land has to show that it is expedient that the path be diverted in the interests of the owner or in the public interest. These diversion orders may be proposed purely in the interests of agricultural management and good husbandry, but the Secretary of State, before confirming such an order, must be satisfied on the evidence that the path, when diverted, "will not be substantially less convenient to the public". Otherwise the procedure for making and confirming diversion orders is similar to that for extinguishment orders.

Stopping up and Diversion of Footpaths and Bridleways

Sections 118A and 119A of the Highways Act 1980 make provision for the stopping up and diversion, respectively, of footpaths and bridleways crossing railways (otherwise than by tunnel or bridge) in the interests of public safety. Orders under these sections may be confirmed, by the council or by the Secretary of State, only upon being satisfied that it is reasonably practicable to make the crossing safe for public use and that appropriate barriers and signs will be erected and maintained. The procedures for making these orders are similar to those outlined above.

Temporary Diversion of a Highway

Section 122 of the Highways Act gives the council, as highway authority, power to divert a highway temporarily where it is about to repair or widen it. The diversion may be onto any land adjoining the highway, even without the owner's consent, but the owner is entitled to compensation for any damage.

Stopping up or Diversion to Facilitate Development

Under section 247 of the Town and Country Planning Act, an order may be made authorising the stopping up or diversion of a highway where necessary to enable development to be carried out under a planning permission which has been granted. Similar provisions in section 257 of this Act authorise the making of an order stopping up a public footpath where it is necessary to do so to enable development to proceed. In both cases it is necessary to show to the council, and to the Secretary of State in the event of objections to the order and a subsequent public local inquiry, that planning permission for the development has been obtained and that it is not possible to carry out the development unless the road or footpath is stopped up. If, by the time the public local inquiry into objections is held, the development has been completed, it is unlikely that the order will be confirmed by the Secretary of State. The developer will then find himself in breach of the Highways Act 1980 for obstruction of a highway by his development, and may be prosecuted for this offence or even forced, by proceedings for an injunction at the suit of the highway authority, to remove it.

Summary

The above is an outline of some of the provisions which may be used to effect a stopping up or diversion of roads or footpaths. It is not exhaustive.

Enquiry 3.6.(a) is intended to establish whether the council has considered and approved any proposals for the stopping up or diversion of roads or footpaths referred to in the description of the property. A buyer wanting a reply to this enquiry must be careful to name or describe all those roads or footpaths enquired about, and it would be prudent to attach a plan showing them. The desirable reply depends on the wishes of the buyer. A buyer does not normally want the road fronting on the property to be stopped up or diverted, but may be quite happy to find that the council proposes to stop up a footpath crossing the property. Of course an affirmative reply does not necessarily mean that the road or footpath will be stopped up or diverted. It means only that the council has approved proposals to stop up or divert. Most of the orders discussed above require the confirmation of the Secretary of State.

The Guidance Notes 2002 recommend that councils add the following informative statement to replies: "In some circumstances, road closure orders can be obtained by third parties from magistrates' courts or can be made by the Secretary of State for Transport, without involving the Council."

Enquiries 3.6.(b) to (f): Restrictions on the Movement of Traffic

These parts of enquiry 3.6 ((b) waiting or loading restrictions; (c) one way driving; (d) prohibition of driving; (e) pedestrianisation; (f) vehicle width or weight restriction) refer to restrictions on the movement of traffic (or certain classes of traffic including pedestrian traffic) to be imposed by the council under the Road Traffic Regulation Act 1984 and other legislation.

The duty of the local authority in exercising its functions under the 1984 Act is to secure the expeditious, convenient and safe movement of vehicular traffic and pedestrians and the provision of suitable and adequate parking facilities on and off the highway. The local authority's functions are exercised under the Act largely by way of traffic regulation orders.

Outside Greater London

Outside Greater London, traffic regulation orders may be made by the local highway authority in respect of roads other than trunk roads, and by the Secretary of State for Transport in respect of trunk roads. The highway authority for these purposes is the county council (or metropolitan district council), but in practice, in many areas the district council makes traffic regulation orders on behalf of the relevant county council under agency arrangements.

The making of a permanent traffic regulation order under section 1 of the Act must be shown to meet one of the following purposes:

(i)   avoiding or preventing danger to persons or traffic;

(ii)   preventing damage to roads or buildings;

(iii) facilitating the passage of traffic (including pedestrians);

(iv) preventing the use of the road by vehicular traffic which is unsuitable having regard to the character of the road or adjoining property;

(v)   preserving the character of a road which is specially suitable for use by persons on horseback or on foot;

(vi) preserving or improving the amenities of the area;

(vii) maintaining or managing the quality of air.

Provisions which may be imposed in traffic regulation orders include prohibitions or restrictions regulating the use of a road, or any part of the width of a road, by vehicular traffic of any class specified in the order; the order may also specify exemptions, and times of the day or days of the week during which the prohibitions or restrictions apply.

Examples of restrictions that may be imposed by traffic regulation orders outside Greater London include:

- one-way traffic;
- the provision of bus or taxi lanes;
- the prohibition of waiting or loading and unloading;
- the prohibition of through traffic;
- restrictions on overtaking;
- pedestrian precincts;
- pedestrian bans;
- through routes for, or prohibition of, heavy commercial vehicles.

The scope of the provisions which may be made by traffic regulation orders is not limited to these examples, but speed restrictions may not be imposed in this way.

A traffic regulation order may not be made so as to prevent access by pedestrians to premises which can be accessed only from the road to which the order relates, or to prevent such access by vehicles for more than eight hours in twenty-four, except in special circumstances.

Once a traffic regulation order has been made, traffic signs must be placed by the authority on or near the road to which it relates, giving sufficient information of the effect of the order to persons using the road. It is an offence to contravene the provisions of a traffic regulation order, but it has been held that if signs conforming to the requirements of the Act have not been duly erected, the order is invalid and contravention is not punishable by fine or otherwise.

In Greater London

Within Greater London, traffic regulation is achieved in respect of non-trunk roads by order of the appropriate London borough council, or the Common Council of the City of London, and in respect of trunk roads by the Secretary of State or, with his consent, by the appropriate London borough council (or Common Council of the City of London). Orders, which for Greater London are made under section 6 of the Act, may be made for one of the purposes outlined in (i) to (vii) above; in addition a further twenty-two purposes are prescribed in schedule 1 to the Act. These include:

- prescribed routes to be followed by all or any class of traffic;
- the prohibition of U-turns;
- the maximum number, size and weight of trailers;
- conditions upon which horses, cattle and sheep may be driven on streets in London;
- the control of broken-down vehicles;
- restrictions on the use of vehicles, animals and sandwich men or women for advertisement purposes;
- the lighting and guarding of streetworks.

Orders in respect of Greater London may be made so as to apply to the whole area of the relevant local authority, or to particular parts of it, and may apply throughout the day or during particular periods or on special occasions only.

As with orders made outside Greater London, the regulation of speed by orders under section 6 of the Act is not permitted.

Experimental Traffic Orders

Experimental traffic orders may be made both within and outside Greater London for similar purposes and subject to the same restrictions as are outlined above. Experimental orders continue in force for a maximum period of eighteen months, but may be continued for a further period of six months by the Secretary of State. Experimental schemes may also be introduced for limited purposes, in Greater London, by the Commissioner of Police. The consent of the appropriate local authority is required. Such schemes may continue in force for a maximum of six months in the first instance, subject to extension by up to a further six months with the consent of the local authority.

Special Cases

There are further provisions in the 1984 Act in relation to traffic regulations on special roads; one-way traffic on trunk roads; the use of highways by public service vehicles; special areas in the countryside (national parks, areas of outstanding natural beauty etc.); school crossings; street play-grounds; on- and off-street parking; and general traffic schemes.

Procedure

Before making a traffic regulation order, the local authority must consult the police authority and give public notification of its intentions. There are detailed provisions relating to the procedures for making orders, the publicity which must be given to them, and the consideration which must be given to objections; in the case of permanent orders, there are provisions for holding public inquiries into objections.

Summary

Parts (b) to (f) of enquiry 3.6 are intended to reveal details of proposals approved by the council, but not yet put into operation, in respect of traffic schemes affecting the roads specified by the enquirer. The enquiry relates particularly to waiting and loading; one-way driving; the prohibition of driving; pedestrianisation (see further below); and weight and width restrictions. Before the detailed procedures contained in the Act are put into effect, the local authority must have considered the proposals and adopted them by formal resolution. A buyer receiving an outline of the proposals should press for full details of the approved proposals, including a date when it is intended to bring the restrictions into force, and the full implications of such restrictions. The buyer will also be concerned to know whether any restrictions are to be of a temporary or permanent nature.

Enquiry 3.6.(e): Pedestrian Planning Orders

The local planning authority (as opposed to the highway authority) may apply to the Secretary of State for an order – a pedestrianisation order –

extinguishing the right to use vehicles on a highway. These orders are made with the principal purpose of improving the amenities of an area, and are promoted under powers contained in section 249 of the Town and Country Planning Act 1990.

Pedestrian planning orders have the effect of excluding vehicular traffic from the roads to which they apply. The emergency services (fire, police and ambulance) and statutory undertakers (water, gas, electricity, tele-communications etc.) are excluded from the operation of these orders, and further exclusions may provide for access to premises by, for example, vehicles driven by disabled drivers, Post Office vehicles, and service vehicles. The procedure for making pedestrian planning orders provides for public notice of the proposals; consultation with highway authorities, the police and the statutory undertakers; consideration of objections; and the holding of public inquiries into such objections.

When a pedestrian planning order comes into force, compensation for depreciation in the value of property is due to any person with an interest in land with access to highways to which the order relates. Compensation is calculated in accordance with the principles applicable to compulsory purchase compensation and is payable by the local planning authority.

Once a pedestrian planning order has been made, the authority is invested with powers contained in the Highways Act 1980 to erect structures on the highway to improve its amenity for pedestrians. Seating, lighting, landscaping and small information kiosks are permitted by these provisions to be erected on the pedestrianised highway.

Summary

Enquiry 3.6.(e) specifically concerns approved pedestrianisation schemes. Although modest pedestrian schemes can be achieved by way of a traffic regulation order, the powers contained in the Town and Country Planning Act are generally used for the more ambitious town centre improvement schemes. A buyer of property affected by a pedestrianisation scheme will be concerned to have full details of the proposals approved by the council, including the extent of the scheme's operation, and details of any classes of traffic which will be entitled to continue to use the road in question despite pedestrianisation. A buyer may become entitled to compensation from the local planning authority if the purchase is completed before the order comes into force.

Enquiry 3.6.(g): Traffic Calming Works

The highway authority may (by virtue of section 90A of the Highways Act 1980) construct road humps on certain roads with the purpose of "calming" traffic movements. Humps may be constructed only on roads subject to a statutory speed limit of thirty miles per hour or less, unless specially authorised by the Secretary of State. The Secretary of State may, with the consent of the highway authority, construct road humps in roads for which he is not the highway authority, and may enter into agreements with the highway authority for their installation and future maintenance.

Before road humps are constructed, the highway authority (including the Secretary of State) must consult the chief officer of police, the district council, bus operators and representative organisations. Twenty-one days' notice of the proposal to install road humps must also be published in local newspapers and posted at appropriate locations in the highway. Any objections received must be considered and a public local inquiry into them may be convened.

Road humps must be constructed in accordance with regulations stipulating their dimensions, location and spacing, the placing of signage and the carrying out of ancillary or consequential works. Once constructed, the highway authority becomes responsible for future maintenance.

Other traffic calming works may be installed by the highway authority under section 90G of the 1980 Act. These include:

- "build-outs" – effectively narrowing the highway;
- "chicanes" – two or more build-outs on alternate sides of the highway;
- "gateways" – structures indicating the existence of traffic calming measures;
- "islands" – again, effectively narrowing the width of available highway;
- "overrun areas" – textured or coloured material in the highway which appears to narrow it;
- "pinch points" – build-outs constructed on both sides opposite one another;
- "rumble devices" – use of materials which generate noise or vibration in a vehicle passing over them.

Summary

Part (g) of enquiry 3.6 concerns any proposals which have been approved to install any of the traffic calming measures mentioned above. Generally, a buyer is advantaged by their existence, since they should have the effect of calming traffic otherwise speeding through a residential area. A prudent buyer might not be too pleased, however, to have a "hump" immediately outside the premises in question, and detailed investigation of the approved proposals may be necessary.

Enquiry 3.6.(h): Residents Parking Controls

Residents parking schemes may be introduced by local authorities under powers contained in part IV of the Road Traffic Regulation Act 1984. Where, for the purpose of relieving or preventing congestion of traffic, it appears necessary to provide suitable parking places for vehicles, the authority may by order authorise any part of a road to be used as a parking place. The order may provide for the vehicles or classes of vehicle which are entitled to use the parking place; the conditions under which it may be used; and the removal from it of vehicles left in contravention of the order. Contravention of the provisions of a parking places order is an offence.

There are detailed provisions relating to the making of these orders, including requirements on consultation, publication of proposals, dealing with objections, the holding of a public inquiry, and the publication of the effect of the order, if made, in the local newspaper.

Summary
Part (h) of enquiry 3.6 concerns approved residents parking schemes, yet to be implemented, in respect of the roads mentioned in boxes B and C of Con 29R. If the property to be purchased is residential, and situated in a busy town road, the buyer is normally pleased to find that a residents parking scheme is to be implemented. It would, however, be prudent to ascertain the residents' precise qualifications and entitlement to park.

Enquiry 3.6.(i): Minor Road Widening or Improvement
Temporary orders under the Road Traffic Regulation Act 1984 (section 14) may be made within and outside Greater London for the purpose of restricting or prohibiting traffic or pedestrians on roads where works are to be carried out, and restriction is necessary to prevent danger to the public or serious damage to the highway. In cases of emergency, similar restrictions and prohibitions may be imposed by the highway authority by notice, if it is necessary that they come into force without delay. Temporary orders and notices may also make provision for temporary speed restriction.

Temporary orders may continue in force for a maximum of eighteen months, although they may be extended by consent of the Secretary of State. This limitation does not apply to orders made in Greater London, or by the Secretary of State. Notices imposing temporary restrictions in cases of emergency may not continue in force for more than twenty-one days.

Summary
Part (i) of enquiry 3.6 relates to minor road widening or improvement. A buyer normally prefers a negative response to this part, but if the response is in the affirmative, the prudent buyer will want to know whether the "minor road widening or improvement" will directly affect the property in contemplation, and if so how much, if any, land is to be taken. The buyer will also be interested to know the expected duration of any works, and the nature of any temporary highway use restrictions imposed by an order made under section 14. Temporary road closure is, or can be, severe in its effects on the business community and those who depend on the highway for their own, or their customers', convenient access to premises.

Enquiry 3.6.(j): Pedestrian Crossings
Pedestrian crossings are established under powers contained in section 23 of the Road Traffic Regulation Act (non-trunk roads, by the council) and section 24 (trunk roads, by the Secretary of State). They come in several zoological varieties, notably the zebra crossing, which is uncontrolled, and the pelican and puffin, which are push-button controlled.

Before executing any works to establish a pedestrian crossing, the council, as local traffic authority, must consult the chief officer of police about the proposal, give public notice of the proposal, and inform the Secretary of State in writing. There are no provisions on considering any objection to such a proposal, or for a public local inquiry. The local traffic authority is empowered, by section 23, and the Secretary of State by section 24, to execute the necessary works, including the placing, erection, maintenance, alteration and removal of marks and traffic signs.

Summary
The purpose of enquiry 3.6 part (j) is to find out about any approved proposals, not yet implemented, to site a pedestrian crossing in the road or roads enquired about. Whether the buyer will favour a negative or affirmative response largely depends on the buyer's individual circumstances. A prudent buyer is, however, normally concerned to know just how close to the property to be purchased the crossing will be.

Enquiry 3.6.(k): Cycle Tracks
Section 65 of the Highways Act 1980 confers the power on the council as highway authority to construct, in or by the side of a maintainable highway, a cycle track. The track, which may be illuminated, remains part of the highway and maintainable as such. However, the public's right to use it, otherwise than on a cycle, is prohibited. The Cycle Tracks Act 1984 removed the right of the public to ride motor cycles and mopeds on cycle tracks.

Cycle track orders, which are the subject of this part of enquiry 3.6, are made by the council after consultation with other local authorities and relevant parish councils through whose areas the track will run, the statutory undertakers whose operational land will be crossed, and the chief officer of police.

In the time-honoured fashion, the council must publish notices in a local newspaper circulating in the locality and give a period of twenty-eight days for objections. Notices must be displayed at each end of the proposed track, and all consultees must be notified. Objections to a proposed order may be considered at a public local inquiry, unless the Secretary of State is of the opinion that such an inquiry can be dispensed with.

If an order is made, the council must give due notice, describing its general effect and naming a place where the order may be inspected. Notices must similarly be sent to all interested persons, that is, normally, all those who appeared at any inquiry into objections.

The effect of the order is as outlined above. It removes the public's right to use that part of the highway designated as a cycle track, otherwise than on a pedal cycle.

Summary
Enquiry 3.6.(k) deals with approved cycle ways. Whether a buyer is likely to prefer a negative or an affirmative response largely depends on the degree of the buyer's enthusiasm for cycling.

Enquiry 3.6.(1): Bridge Building

The general power of the council as highway authority to construct a bridge to carry a highway maintainable at the public expense is contained in section 91 of the Highways Act 1980. In addition, section 92 confers the power to reconstruct a bridge which is already carrying a maintainable highway, either on the same site or on a new site within 200 yards of the old one.

Section 93 confers a power for the local highway authority to maintain and improve privately owned bridges, and to adopt them for future maintenance. Orders made by the Secretary of State under this latter provision may require significant works of reconstruction or improvement; determine who will in future be responsible for maintenance of the bridge and its approaches; provide for vesting the ownership of the bridge in the highway authority; and, in the case of a swing bridge, direct how and by whom it is to be operated. The order may also incorporate compulsory purchase powers in respect of land adjoining the bridge, if necessary to put the scheme into effect.

Summary

Part (1) of enquiry 3.6 concerns any approved but as yet unimplemented proposals for bridge construction affecting the roads in question. Clearly a buyer will want to know full details of any such approved proposals, and the degree to which they may affect ownership of land comprised in the property to be purchased; or, operationally and in the short to medium term, what disruption to traffic in the street is likely. Few buyers will relish responsibility for the future maintenance of a bridge, or its mechanical operation.

Enquiry 3.7: Outstanding Notices

"Do any statutory notices which relate to the following matters subsist in relation to the property other than those revealed in a response to any other enquiry in this form?
  (a) building works
  (b) environment
  (c) health and safety
  (d) housing
  (e) highways
  (f) public health"

Enquiry 3.7 relates to notices in respect of the property issued by the council by virtue of the council's wide range of statutory and regulatory powers. Such notices are issued principally under public health, environmental, housing or highways legislation. The enquiry is not concerned with any of the following:
  (i)   notices shown in the official certificate of search, since they create a local land charge and will be registered as such;
  (ii)   notices issued under powers contained in the Town and Country Planning Act and dealt with by enquiry 3.9 (see below);
  (iii) notices served on owners of land after a compulsory purchase order has been made. These are notices to treat and as such are normally registrable as local land charges. They invite the owner concerned, whose land is subject to a compulsory purchase order, to put in a claim for compensation. Enquiry 3.11 concerns resolutions to make compulsory purchase orders;
  (iv) notices relating to matters covered by other paragraphs of enquiry 3.
  Notices served on the property which this enquiry is designed to reveal may be served under numerous Acts, the most important of which are the Public Health Act 1936, the Housing Acts and the Highways Act 1980. Examples under each heading are as follows:

Public Health Act
  (i)   Notice requiring the carrying out of works to remedy an overflowing cesspool (section 50).
  (ii) Notice requiring owner to remedy the condition of filthy or verminous premises by cleaning and disinfecting them (section 83).

Housing Acts
    (i)   Improvement notice requiring the carrying out of remedial action in respect of hazards in residential premises (sections 11 and 12, Housing Act 2004).
    (ii)   Notice of emergency remedial action that has been or is to be taken by the local housing authority to remove the imminent risk of serious harm to health or safety.
    (iii) Notice requiring the abatement of overcrowding of a house (section 338, Housing Act 1985).

Highways Act
    (i)   Notice requiring occupier of a building to remove or alter a porch, shed, projecting window, wall or fence which has been erected against or in front of the building and is an obstruction to safe or convenient passage along the street (section 152).
    (ii)   Notice requiring occupier of land to lop or cut a hedge, tree or shrub where it overhangs the highway so as to cause a danger or obstruction (section 154).
    (iii) Notice requiring removal of barbed wire from a fence where it is a nuisance to the highway users (section 164).
    (iv) Notice requiring owners of premises fronting a private street to carry out urgent repairs to the street to prevent danger to traffic (section 230).

Examples of notices affecting property which a council has power to issue under environmental and safety legislation include:

Health and Safety at Work Act 1974
    (i)   Improvement notice issued by a health and safety inspector in respect of contraventions of statutory provisions relating to health and safety. Such notices identify the breach of safety requirements and require remedial action to be taken (section 21).
    (ii)   Prohibition notice issued by an inspector in respect of activities being carried out involving a serious risk of personal injury. These notices direct the activities complained of to cease with immediate effect (section 22).

Environmental Protection Act 1990
Notices requiring the abatement of a statutory nuisance, for example, premises in such a state as to be prejudicial to health, animals kept in such a place as to be a nuisance, accumulations or deposits of refuse, dust etc. (section 80).

(There are numerous other notices which may be served under environmental and control of pollution legislation, and which may be revealed in reply to optional enquiry 19 (see below)).

Building Act
    (i)   Notice requiring owner of building to pull down or remove work to which the Building Regulations are applicable and which contravenes the regulations, or to effect alterations to make the work comply (section 36).

(ii)   Notice to the effect that the premises are in such a state as to be prejudicial to health or a nuisance and stating that the local authority intends to remedy the defective state and specifying what the defects are (section 76).

(iii)   Notice requiring owner to execute works of repair or restoration or to demolish a building which is, by reason of its ruinous or dilapidated condition, seriously detrimental to the amenities of the neighbourhood (section 79).

The London Building Acts, with the exception of the provisions relating to the naming and numbering of streets, apply only to the inner London boroughs. Within those boroughs the construction of buildings was formerly governed by the London Building Acts and supplementary by-laws made by the now defunct Greater London Council. District surveyors employed by the Greater London Council supervised building works in much the same way as do building control officers elsewhere.

The Greater London Council also had duties under the London Building Acts relating to building near dangerous and noxious businesses, dwellings on low-lying land and means of fire escape.

In inner London, the London borough councils and the Corporation of the City of London had responsibility for the control of dangerous and neglected structures.

When the Greater London Council was abolished in 1985, its functions under the London Building Acts and the duties of the district surveyors were transferred to the inner London boroughs and the Corporation of the City of London in respect of their areas.

The Building Regulations 2000 (see the commentary on enquiry 1.1 above) now also apply to the inner London boroughs, and considerable amendment has been necessary to what remains of the London Building Acts.

The London Building Acts, however, remain in force in respect of the inner London boroughs which have regulatory functions and duties under those Acts in relation to the naming and numbering of streets and buildings, and the construction of buildings (including roof drainage, fire precautions and the "uniting of two buildings into one").

Examples of the "current notices relating to the property" which may have been issued by an inner London borough council and which might be expected to be revealed in response to this enquiry are as follows:

(i)   Section 35, London Building Acts (Amendment) Act 1939: Notice requiring owner of an old building occupied by a number of families or as a boarding house to provide proper and sufficient means of escape in the event of fire.

(ii)   Section 62, London Building Acts (Amendment) Act 1939: Notice requiring owner or occupier of a certified dangerous structure to take it down or to repair or secure it.

(iii)   Section 88, London Building Acts (Amendment) Act 1939: Notice of irregularity served by district surveyor in respect of a building or structure which is being erected or constructed in contravention of the provisions of the Act, requiring the builder to amend the irregularity within forty-eight hours.

The following is a list of the London borough councils (together with the City of London Corporation), divided into inner and outer status:

- *Inner London authorities:* City of London; Camden; Greenwich; Hackney; Hammersmith and Fulham; Islington; Kensington and Chelsea; Lambeth; Lewisham; Southwark; Tower Hamlets; Wandsworth; Westminster.
- *Outer London authorities:* Barking and Dagenham; Barnet; Bexley; Brent; Bromley; Croydon; Ealing; Enfield; Haringey; Harrow; Havering; Hillingdon; Hounslow; Kingston-upon-Thames; Merton; Newham; Redbridge; Richmond-upon-Thames; Sutton; Waltham Forest.

Summary

Enquiry 3.7 is intended to reveal whether there are any current notices relating to the property under the legislation. A buyer will obviously prefer a negative response. The prudent buyer in any doubt would be wise to raise optional enquiry 19 (see below). The reply to enquiry 3.6 is unlikely to elicit information as to spent notices, that is, notices that have been complied with, withdrawn or quashed by a court of competent jurisdiction.

Enquiry 3.8: Contravention of Building Regulations

"Has a local authority authorised in relation to the property any proceedings for the contravention of any provision contained in Building Regulations?"

An outline of the provisions of the Building Regulations 2000 is given in the commentary on enquiry 1.1.(f) (see above). That enquiry is concerned with applications for building regulation approvals and (at enquiry 1.1.(g)) completion certificates. Enquiry 3.8 is concerned with contravention of the Building Regulations in respect of the property, and proceedings authorised by the council for any such contraventions.

Breach of the Building Regulations 2000 is dealt with by sections 35 to 38 of the Building Act 1984. Section 35 in particular provides that if any person contravenes any provision contained in the Building Regulations, he is liable on summary conviction to a substantial fine (level 5 on the standard scale) and to a further fine of up to £50 for each day on which the default continues after conviction.

Section 36 of the 1984 Act provides for the removal or alteration of offending work, that is, work to which the Building Regulations apply but which has been carried out in breach of them. Without prejudice to the right to take proceedings under section 35, the council may, under section 36, serve a notice requiring the owner of the premises to pull down or remove the offending work, or make such alterations as may be necessary to make it comply with the regulations. If such a notice is served, and not complied with within twenty-eight days, the council may pull down the offending work or make the necessary alterations, and recover any expenses reasonably incurred in doing so.

Section 36 notices must be served within twelve months of completion of the works in question.

Summary
Enquiry 3.8 concerns any proceedings authorised by the council for infringement of the Building Regulations. Clearly, an intending buyer would prefer a negative response. Any alleged breach of the Building Regulations indicates a possible problem with the property, and the safety or even stability of the building may be in doubt. An owner of property usually escapes

prosecution for a breach of the regulations, as it is the builder who is normally responsible for contravention. Nevertheless, an owner may be required to effect remedial works if served with a section 36 notice. A prudent buyer receiving an affirmative response to this enquiry is well advised to obtain full details of the alleged breach; when it is anticipated the proceedings will be taken; and whether remedial works have been or will be required to be undertaken by the owner.

Enquiry 3.9: Notices, Orders, Directions and Proceedings under Planning Acts

"Do any of the following subsist in relation to the property, or has a local authority decided to issue, serve, make or commence any of the following?

(a) an enforcement notice

(b) a stop notice

(c) a listed building enforcement notice

(d) a breach of condition notice

(e) a planning contravention notice

(f) another notice relating to breach of planning control

(g) a listed building repairs notice

(h) in the case of a listed building deliberately allowed to fall into disrepair, a compulsory purchase order with a direction for minimum compensation

(i) a building preservation notice

(j) a direction restricting permitted development

(k) an order revoking or modifying planning permission

(l) an order requiring discontinuance of use or alteration or removal of building or works

(m) a tree preservation order

(n) proceedings to enforce a planning agreement or planning contribution"

This enquiry relates to a range of breaches of planning control affecting the premises and action taken or proposed by the council. With regard to listed buildings, the enquiry is also concerned with the service of listed building enforcement notices; repairs notices; compulsory purchase orders by the council for lack of repair; and building preservation notices served by the council as an interim measure before the property becomes listed. Directions restricting permitted development, the revocation of planning permission and tree preservation orders are also covered.

Under the Town and Country Planning Act 1990, planning permission issued by the council is required for the carrying out of any development of land. Development, for these purposes, is defined to mean either:

(i) the carrying out of building, engineering, mining or other operations; or

(ii) the making of any material change in the use of any buildings or land.

Thus, for example, planning permission is required before any building or other structure can be erected. In addition, planning permission is required (with certain exceptions) before the use to which any existing building is put can be changed, so that, for example, change of use of a building from house to shop requires planning permission.

If application for planning permission is duly made, it may be granted by the council subject to conditions which must be complied with.

Enquiry 3.9.(a): Enforcement Notices

If a person carries out development, either by erecting a building or structure, or by changing the use of an existing building or structure, without first obtaining planning permission, the council may serve an enforcement notice on that person. The enforcement notice requires the person who has carried out the development, or any other owner of the land in question, to restore the land or buildings to the original condition, or to cease the unauthorised change of use. The notice also gives a prescribed time in which to comply with the requirements. Enforcement notices are served under section 172 of the Town and Country Planning Act.

The recipient of an enforcement notice may appeal against its requirements to the Secretary of State on a number of specified grounds; if an appeal is lodged, no further action can be taken by the council until the appeal is dealt with. If, at the appeal, the enforcement notice is upheld, the recipient of the notice must comply with it within the prescribed time, which may have been extended by the Secretary of State.

A notice may be quashed by the Secretary of State on appeal, in which case it is of no effect.

If the person on whom the notice was served fails to appeal or comply with it within the prescribed time, that person may be prosecuted in the magistrates' court or Crown Court, and may have to pay a substantial penalty (up to £20,000 on conviction in a magistrates' court, and an unlimited fine on conviction in the Crown Court).

In addition, the council has powers under the 1990 Act to carry out whatever work is necessary to remedy the breach of planning control and to charge the costs of so doing to the offender; this is in addition to the power to prosecute.

Enquiry 3.9.(b): Stop Notices

In certain circumstances it may be particularly important to stop the unauthorised development before the time allowed in an enforcement notice for compliance. In these cases the council may serve a stop notice prohibiting the unauthorised development, but must normally give at least three days' notice. There is no appeal against a stop notice but if the enforcement notice, which will have been served before or at the same time as the stop notice, is successfully appealed against, the council may have to pay compensation to the recipient of both notices. Service of a stop notice by a council is therefore rare and should be justifiable in the particular circumstances. Stop notices are served under section 183 of the Town and Country Planning Act. They may not be served so as to prohibit the use of a building as a dwelling house.

Enforcement notices, stop notices and breach of condition notices (see below) are normally shown in the official certificate of search, or in the register which the council is obliged to keep by virtue of section 188 of the Town and Country Planning Act.

A notice may be withdrawn at any time by the council if, for example, it has been complied with.

Summary

Enquiry 3.9.(a) and (b) concern whether there are any subsisting notices or any relevant entries of enforcement and stop notices in the register which the council is required to keep under section 188 of the Town and Country Planning Act, or whether the council has decided to issue any such. Obviously a buyer will desire a negative response, but if entries are revealed, full details, including effective dates for compliance with the requirements of any notices, will be required.

Under section 188 the register must be open for public inspection at all reasonable hours and is generally kept in the planning department of the council's offices. Since the register is public, copies of the notices should be made available to the enquirer on request, but the council may impose a charge for this service. The register does not reveal notices proposed to be served but not yet served, and the buyer should insist on copies of these, or information as to their likely content. Once served, they are in the public domain.

Enquiry 3.9.(c): Listed Building Enforcement Notices

As mentioned in the commentary on enquiry 1.1.(b), "listed building consents" (see above), the carrying out of works for the demolition or alteration of a listed building without listed building consent, or the carrying out of these works otherwise than in strict compliance with any conditions attached to such a consent, renders the person carrying out the works liable to a fine or imprisonment. However, prosecution does not of itself restore the listed building.

Under section 38 of the Planning (Listed Buildings and Conservation Areas) Act 1990, the council, as local planning authority, may in these circumstances, and if it feels it expedient to do so, issue and serve a listed building enforcement notice, specifying the contravention complained of, and requiring steps to be taken to restore the building to its former state. If such restoration would not be practicable, the council may specify other works which would alleviate the effect of the works which have been carried out.

A listed building enforcement notice may also be served to achieve compliance with conditions attached to a listed building consent.

The notice is served on the owner and the occupier of the building, and on any other person who has an interest in it.

The person on whom the notice is served may appeal to the Secretary of State against the notice on a number of grounds, including the ground that the works were urgently necessary in the interests of safety or health or the preservation of the building.

If an appeal is made, the effect of the notice is suspended until the Secretary of State has held an inquiry into the matter and reached his decision.

If no appeal is brought, or if an appeal is brought and is unsuccessful (that is, the listed building enforcement notice is confirmed), failure to comply with the requirements in the notice is an offence and the person who is then the owner of the property may be prosecuted, and, if convicted, fined.

Enforcement notices, listed building enforcement notices, stop notices and breach of condition notices (see below) are issued by the council after a report has been made to the relevant committee and a resolution has been passed to take appropriate action.

Summary
Enquiry 3.9.(c) concerns subsisting listed building enforcement notices served in respect of the property, or any which the council has decided to issue and serve. A buyer will clearly prefer a negative response. An affirmative response indicates not only that there are significant problems with the property from the local planning authority's point of view, but that the proposed buyer could become liable to prosecution. Full details of the outstanding works to be carried out in respect of the listed building should, at the very least, be sought by an intending buyer. This part of the enquiry is not of course relevant if the property does not consist of or comprise a listed building.

Enquiry 3.9.(d): Breach of Condition Notices
A breach of condition notice may be served under section 187A of the Town and Country Planning Act. Where there has been a failure to comply with a condition attached to a planning permission, the council, as local planning authority, may serve such a notice on any person carrying out (or who has carried out) the development, or on any person having control of the land in question. The notice must specify the steps which ought to be taken to secure compliance with the planning condition which has been breached, and give at least twenty-eight days for compliance. If the specified steps are not taken within the period given for compliance, the notice is breached and the person responsible is guilty of an offence and may be prosecuted; if convicted, a fine may be imposed. There is no appeal against a breach of condition notice.

Summary
The purpose of enquiry 3.9.(d) is to find out whether there are any subsisting breach of condition notices, or whether the council has decided to issue any, in connection with the property. A buyer will obviously prefer a negative response, but if an affirmative one is forthcoming, the buyer would be wise to require full details. The purported breach might be readily and cheaply remedied. On the

other hand, purchasing a property subject to a subsisting breach of condition notice could well involve the buyer in imminent criminal proceedings.

Note on Enquiry 3.9.(a) to (d)

Enquiry 3.9.(a), (b), (c) and (d) concern whether any enforcement notices, stop notices, listed building enforcement notices or breach of condition notices are subsisting or have been authorised for service by the council. The questions are designed to reveal to an intending buyer decisions made by the council to issue and serve these notices where they have not yet been served. Notices which have already been served should be shown in the official certificate of search and the register of enforcement and stop notices kept by the council under section 188 of the Town and Country Planning Act. In effect, while providing a double check on the contents of the register of local land charges and the section 188 register, these parts of enquiry 3.9 are directed at proposals or intentions to serve such notices. A buyer will always prefer a negative response to avoid being required to comply with notices subsequently served in respect of the property. Many buyers are deterred from buying a property if there is a likelihood that one of these notices will be served. Buyers are not, however, normally interested in notices which have been withdrawn or quashed.

If the breach of planning control complained of in a notice has been put right, that is, the offending building or structure has been demolished or the use has reverted to an authorised use, no further action is taken under the notice, but it may remain on the record. Notices may have already been served (and therefore should be revealed by the official certificate of search) but subsequently complied with to the satisfaction of the council. The notice may not, in these circumstances, have yet been removed from the register of local land charges, but proceedings under them for prosecution will not take place.

A buyer may not be deterred from buying the property if assured that any outstanding notices revealed have been complied with. A council normally gives such an assurance, however, only if its officers have had an opportunity to inspect the property since the notice was served. If a special inspection is required to enable the council to give an acceptable assurance, the council may ask the buyer to pay for it. If the council is prepared to confirm that any enforcement notice or listed building enforcement notice served in respect of the property has been duly complied with, it is possible for the council to withdraw the notice. An approach to the council, either before or after purchase of the property, would be advisable to enable any such notices to be removed from the record.

Enquiry 3.9.(e): Planning Contravention Notices

A planning contravention notice is served by the council, as local planning authority, under section 171C of the Town and Country Planning Act, where it appears that there may have been a breach of planning control. It is served on any owner or occupier of the land concerned (or anybody carrying out operations on it) and requires specified information to be provided. The information required may include details of the operations or other activities being carried out on the land, or the use to which the land is being put. The notice may specify a time and place at which the authority will consider an offer to apply for planning permission, to refrain from carrying out the activities, or to undertake remedial works.

Representations in respect of such a notice may be made in person. It is an offence to fail to comply with the requirements of the notice within twenty-one days of its service, or to make false or misleading statements in purporting to comply with it.

Planning contravention notices are primarily investigative in nature; they do not take the place of enforcement notices but may supplement their effectiveness and generally speed up enforcement procedures.

Summary
Enquiry 3.9.(e) concerns whether any planning contravention notices are subsisting in respect of the property, or whether the council has decided to serve any such notice. A buyer normally prefers a negative response. An affirmative response should not necessarily deter a keen buyer, however, as breach of one of these notices is an offence only if committed by the person on whom it was served. Certainly, a buyer should investigate the background to service or proposed service of a planning contravention notice, since such a notice at least indicates a measure of concern on the part of the local planning authority, and that a breach of planning control may have taken place. Planning contravention notices are normally served as a precursor to the more formal and draconian enforcement notice (see above).

Enquiry 3.9.(f): Other Notices Relating to Breach of Planning Control
This part of enquiry 3.9 is a catch-all provision, designed to elicit information as to any form of notice relating to a breach of planning control not covered by the other paragraphs of enquiry 3.9. The regime of planning control is highly regulatory, and many notices, of both a formal and an informal nature, may be served by local planning authorities in their efforts to enforce planning controls properly and fairly. While the other paragraphs of 3.9 are both comprehensive and realistic in their purpose of capturing the major types of notice that can or may be served, part (f) is designed to reveal the more minor or unusual notices. An example of a notice which might be revealed in response to this part is a notice of intended entry to inspect a building used as a dwelling house. By virtue of section 196A of the Town and Country Planning Act 1990, a duly authorised officer of the council (an enforcement officer) may at any reasonable hour enter land to ascertain whether a breach of planning control has taken place. If the land in question comprises a dwelling house, admission as of right cannot be demanded unless twenty-four hours' notice has been given to the occupier.

Long before the Planning and Compensation Act introduced section 187B into the Town and Country Planning Act, the courts had jurisdiction to issue injunctions in appropriate cases of planning enforcement. It was, however, normally necessary to show persistent breaches of planning control on the part of the defendant, or a flagrant disregard of the council's planning enforcement powers, to sustain an application for injunctive relief. Section 187B now confers a general power by which a local planning authority is entitled to apply to the court for an injunction restraining actual or potential breaches of planning control, whether or not other enforcement measures have been contemplated. The county court has jurisdiction to entertain applications for injunctions in these matters. While councils do not make extensive use of this power, it is clear that injunctions are available as a tool of planning enforcement. Breach of the provisions of an injunction can of course lead to imprisonment for contempt of court.

A letter before action under these provisions could constitute "another notice relating to breach of planning control" which is intended to be caught by part (f) of enquiry 3.9.

Summary
Enquiry 3.9.(f) is designed to elicit information in connection with some of the more unusual formal or informal notices that may be subsisting or proposed and which are not covered by the other paragraphs of enquiry 3.9. In view of the comprehensive nature of the other paragraphs in enquiry 3.9, paragraph (f) is unlikely to elicit an affirmative response. But it is submitted that it should also reveal any intention to institute proceedings for an injunction or other proceedings (including prosecution for breach of an enforcement notice). An intending buyer would clearly prefer a negative response, but should request full details if an affirmative reply is given.

Enquiry 3.9.(g): Listed Building Repairs Notices
Part (g) of enquiry 3.9 relates to the service of repairs notices on owners of listed buildings and the compulsory purchase of such buildings by the council for lack of repair. This part of enquiry 3.9 is relevant only if the property enquired about is revealed to be listed, and a survey of the property has shown it to be in a bad state of repair.

The Town and Country Planning Act does not impose obligations on an owner of property, even the owner of a listed building, to maintain it in good repair. However, the council, as local planning authority, does have the following powers (now contained in sections 47 to 56 of the Planning (Listed Buildings and Conservation Areas) Act 1990) in relation to listed buildings which have been allowed to fall into a state of disrepair:

(i)   power to carry out works urgently necessary for the preservation of an unoccupied listed building on giving at least seven days' prior notification to the owner (section 54);

(ii)   power to acquire, using compulsory purchase powers if necessary, any listed building in need of repair, subject, in the case of buildings which have been allowed to fall into disrepair deliberately for the purpose of justifying demolition and redevelopment of the site, to the payment of "minimum compensation", calculated on the basis that neither planning permission nor listed building consent would be granted except for maintaining the building in a proper state of repair (sections 47 and 50).

The procedure contained in sections 47 and 48 of the Planning (Listed Buildings and Conservation Areas) Act 1990 enables a council compulsorily to acquire listed buildings in need of repair. The procedures are primarily designed to encourage preservation of these buildings, and compulsory acquisition by the council is invoked only as a last resort.

The first step is the service of a repairs notice under section 48. The compulsory purchase of a listed building under section 47 (discussed below) cannot proceed unless this notice has been served. It must be served on the owner of a listed building at least two months before section 47 compulsory purchase powers are invoked. The repairs notice must specify the works which it is considered are reasonably necessary for the proper preservation of the building in question. The notice may not require the complete restoration of the building with all its features of architectural and historic interest (it may not have been in this condition for many years). Only those works reasonably necessary to preserve the building may be required.

The repairs notice must also explain to the owner the effect of the provisions of the Act relating to compulsory purchase. Thus, the notice gives the owner an opportunity to put the building into a state of repair before the council goes one step further and commences the compulsory purchase procedure.

The compulsory purchase of listed buildings in disrepair may be pursued by the council as local planning authority, or by the Secretary of State who originally compiles the lists of listed building; or, if the building is in Greater London, by the Historic Buildings and Monuments Commission. Each of these may serve a listed building repairs notice under section 48.

Summary

Enquiry 3.9.(g) concerns whether the council is aware of any listed building repairs notices which have been issued or which the appropriate authority has decided to issue. It should therefore reveal not merely notices that have been served by the council, but also notices which the council, the Secretary of State or the Historic Buildings and Monuments Commission has decided to serve. The council should be aware of any such notices it has itself authorised to be served but may not yet be aware of any authorised to be served by the Secretary of State or the Commission. A buyer obviously prefers a negative response; otherwise there is a likelihood that the property will be compulsorily purchased if it is not put into order without delay. A prudent buyer should make further enquiries of the Secretary of State or the Commission if the property is listed and in a state of disrepair, since a negative response to this enquiry does not necessarily mean that no such notices have been authorised to be served, merely that the council is not aware of any.

Enquiry 3.9.(h): Order for Compulsory Acquisition of a Listed Building with a Minimum Compensation Provision

Once a repairs notice has been served, if it appears to the Secretary of State that reasonable steps are still not being taken for properly preserving the property, he may authorise the council for the district in which the property is situated (or the Historic Buildings and Monuments Commission if the property is in London) to acquire compulsorily the property and any land adjacent to it which is considered necessary for preserving the building or its amenities. The council makes and submits to the Secretary of State a compulsory purchase order, and if the Secretary of State is satisfied that this is a necessary course of action to provide for the preservation of the building, he confirms the order.

Any owner or other person having an interest in the building may apply to a magistrates' court for an order staying proceedings under the compulsory purchase order. If the court is satisfied that reasonable steps have been taken for properly preserving the building, the court may make an order staying the proceedings.

Compensation is due and payable to the owner of a listed building by the council if it uses these compulsory purchase powers, and the compensation generally amounts to the market value of the property concerned. Under section 49 of the Act, in assessing the compensation, any depreciation in value attributable to the possible restriction on alteration or extension of the building due to its being listed must be disregarded. Thus, the owner should generally obtain open market value (bearing in mind the property's state of disrepair) without regard to the restrictions which listing imposes.

However, by virtue of section 50, where the council proposing to exercise these compulsory purchase powers is satisfied that the building has been deliberately allowed to fall into disrepair to justify demolition and redevelopment, the council may include in the compulsory purchase order a direction for "minimum compensation". The possibility of such a direction is aimed at discouraging owners of listed buildings from deliberately allowing the buildings to fall into disrepair so that the property can be demolished and redeveloped. The effect of a "minimum compensation" direction is that compensation payable for the building on its compulsory purchase is assessed on the basis that neither planning permission nor listed building consent would be granted for any works except to restore the building to a proper state of repair and so maintain it. Such a direction would obviously have a considerable effect on the compensation which the owner would recover, and this can be seen as a form of punishment for deliberately allowing the property to deteriorate.

There is a right of appeal against the decision to insert a "minimum compensation" provision in the compulsory purchase order. The appeal is to the magistrates' court, and if it can be shown to the court that the building has not been allowed to fall into disrepair deliberately, the magistrates may order the provision not to be included so that full compensation will be paid. Further appeal on these issues lies to the Crown Court.

Summary
Enquiry 3.9.(h) is intended to reveal whether a "minimum compensation" provision has been, or is intended to be, included in a compulsory purchase order authorised to be made by the council in respect of the property. A buyer who has not been dissuaded from buying the property by the fact that it is to be subjected to compulsory purchase will prefer a negative response to this part of the enquiry, so that he may expect full compensation to be payable. An

affirmative reply would substantially affect the price a buyer would be willing to pay.

Enquiry 3.9.(i): Building Preservation Notices

Enquiry 3.9.(i) relates to any building preservation notice served by the council as an interim measure before the property becomes a listed building.

A brief resumé of the criteria for listing buildings was given in the commentary on enquiry 1.1.(b) (see above).

Listed buildings are buildings of special architectural or historic interest which appear on lists compiled by the Secretary of State and deposited with the relevant council(s). Once the lists are deposited with the council, they are local land charges and any building on the list will appear in the register as a listed building. The fact that a building is listed therefore appears in the official certificate of search.

Buildings are listed either on account of their own architectural or historic merit, or because of their relationship to other such buildings, and there may be particular features or characteristics which make a building worth listing either for itself or as part of a group of buildings.

Once listed, any object or structure fixed to the building or forming part of the curtilage must be treated as part of the building, so that, for instance, a garden wall surrounding a listed building is also protected by the listing (provided it was in existence on 1 July 1948).

Although the owner and occupier of a building which is listed must be informed of the fact, he need not be consulted. The Secretary of State is obliged to consult persons with special knowledge of, or interest in, such buildings, but is not obliged to consult the owner.

The Secretary of State must keep the lists open and available for public inspection, and the council must also keep available for public inspection any portion of the lists relating to properties in its area.

The consequences of a building's being listed are, briefly:

(i)   Any person causing damage to the building may be prosecuted for this offence and, if convicted, ordered to pay a fine. Failure, after having been convicted, to prevent further damage may result in a daily penalty being imposed by the court.

(ii)   Listed building consent is required for the demolition or alteration of the building. These were discussed in the commentary on enquiry 1.1.(b) above.

(iii) Special listed building enforcement notices may be served by the council. These were also discussed earlier in this commentary (see above).

It will be seen that the initiative to compile the lists of buildings of special architectural or historic importance is taken by the Secretary of State. The council cannot itself impose listed building status; it merely acts as a registering authority, receiving the lists, entering the details on the register of local land charges, notifying the owners and occupiers on behalf of the Secretary of State, and revealing the entries in the replies to official searches of the register.

However, where a building is not listed by the Secretary of State, but it appears to the council as local planning authority that, due to its special architectural or historic interest, it ought to be listed and it is threatened with demolition or alteration, the council may serve on the owner and occupier a building preservation notice under section 3 of the Planning (Listed Buildings and Conservation Areas) Act 1990. This has the effect of imposing the same protection as listed building status for a maximum period of six months.

The notice must either be served on the owner and occupier or, in a case of urgency, by fixing it conspicuously to the building.

The conditions which must be fulfilled before the council may serve a building preservation notice are as follows:
(i)   the building must not already be listed (otherwise the listed building protection would apply anyway);
(ii) the building must, in the opinion of the council as local planning authority, be of special architectural or historic interest;
(iii) the building must be threatened with demolition or alteration. If it appears to the council that a building of special architectural or historic interest is about to be demolished, it must act quickly with the service of a building preservation notice.

During the period of six months through which the building preservation notice lasts, the council may request the Secretary of State to include the building concerned in one of the lists of listed buildings. If the Secretary of State agrees to do so, or notifies the council that he does not intend to include it, then the building preservation notice ceases to have any effect. Thus the temporary protection afforded by the notice ceases once the Secretary of State has made his decision. The building then either has the protection of full listed building status, if the Secretary of State has included it in a list, or ceases to have any special protection at all, if the Secretary of State has decided not to include it in a list.

If the Secretary of State decides not to include the building in a list, a further building preservation notice cannot be served for at least twelve months. Furthermore, the council may have to pay the owner compensation for any loss or damage caused by service of the building preservation notice if it has been unsuccessful, that is, if the council's attempts to have the building listed have failed. This may occur, for example, if the owner has entered into a contract with a demolition firm which then has to be breached by the owner since the owner is prevented from demolishing the building.

In London, the Historic Buildings and Monuments Commission for England has the same powers to issue building preservation notices as has a London borough council. For the purposes of such notices the Commission has the same functions as a London borough council acting as local planning authority.

If the property is situated in a London borough, it may be the subject of a building preservation notice issued by the Historic Buildings and Monuments Commission, and since a reply given by the council does not necessarily reveal such a notice, a prudent buyer should make separate enquiries of the Commission if there is any likelihood that such a notice has been issued.

Summary
Enquiry 3.9.(i) is intended to reveal whether there are any subsisting building preservation notices, or any intended to be served in respect of the property, that is, whether the council has decided to attempt to have the building listed and to protect it in the meantime.

A buyer normally prefers a negative response; otherwise, unless the building can be demolished or any desired alteration carried out before the notice is actually served (and it may be served, in urgent cases, by affixing it to the property), there is a possibility that the building will be listed and the owner will then be substantially prevented from interfering with the property in the future. If the owner does demolish the building in contravention of the building preservation notice, the owner is liable to be prosecuted and, if convicted, fined.

The Guidance Notes 2002 advise London borough councils to insert an informative statement in their reply to this enquiry, as follows: "The Historic Buildings and Monuments Commission (also called English Heritage) also have power to issue building preservation notices for listed buildings in London Boroughs and enquiry should also be made of them if appropriate".

Enquiry 3.9.(j): Direction Restricting Permitted Development

This part of enquiry 3.9 relates to permitted development under the Town and Country Planning (General Permitted Development) Order 1995 and restriction of that development.

As mentioned earlier, under the Town and Country Planning Act, planning permission issued by the council is necessary before any development of land within the area of the council can take place. For these purposes "development" means the carrying out of building, engineering, mining or other operations, or the making of any material change in the use of buildings or land.

Exceptions to this general rule are set out in the Town and Country Planning (General Permitted Development) Order 1995, which lists classes of development which may be carried out as if permission had been granted by the council; that is to say, the specified classes of development have "permitted development rights", and application to the council for permission is not necessary.

The General Permitted Development Order is extremely detailed (schedule 2 runs to thirty-three complicated parts), but basically it defines some seventy-six classes of development which enjoy permitted development rights. Some of the more important or commonly used of these classes are as follows:

- Development within the curtilage of a dwellinghouse, e.g:
    (i)   the enlargement of a dwellinghouse by not more than seventy cubic metres (or fifteen per cent);
    (ii) the erection of a porch so long as the floor area is not more than three square metres;
    (iii) the installation of satellite antennae not exceeding one hundred centimetres in length;

    (iv) the provision of a building or enclosure with a height of not more than four metres for a purpose incidental to the enjoyment of the dwellinghouse;

    (v) the construction of hardstanding for vehicles;

    (vi) the erection of an oil storage tank for domestic heating not exceeding 3,500 litres.

- Minor operations, e.g:
  - (i) erection of fences, gates and walls not exceeding two metres (one metre if abutting a highway);
  - (ii) painting the exterior of a building.
- Temporary uses, e.g., the use of land for any purpose except as a caravan site for not more than twenty-eight days in any one year (fourteen days for markets, motor-car and motor-cycle racing).
- Agricultural buildings, e.g., the erection of agricultural buildings such as barns for use in agriculture on an agricultural unit of five hectares or more.
- Development by the local highway authority, e.g., the carrying out of works for the maintenance or improvement of highways.

Any of the above classes of development, and the many other classes mentioned in the General Permitted Development Order, do not need planning permission, provided they are carried out within the limitations imposed by the order. Permission has been granted generally for these classes by the order.

Under article 4 of the order, however, the council as local planning authority, or the Secretary of State, may effectively take away the permitted development rights within a specified area. This they do by making an article 4 direction. The direction is generally made by the council and approved or modified by the Secretary of State. Once in force, any property within the area specified in the direction no longer enjoys the permitted development rights granted by the General Permitted Development Order, so that development of the specified kind can proceed only once planning permission for it has been applied for and granted in the usual way. For example, the erection of a barn on an agricultural holding is normally permitted by the General Permitted Development Order. If, however, the council makes an article 4 direction removing, within a particular agricultural area, the permitted development rights granted in part 6 of the schedule to the order (agricultural buildings and operations), then the erection of such a barn does require specific planning permission, which of course the council may refuse to grant.

Article 4 directions, once made by the council and approved by the Secretary of State, are registrable as local land charges and therefore appear in the official certificate of search.

Before the direction can be made, the council must pass a resolution to do so.

Summary

Enquiry 3.9.(j) concerns whether the council has made or decided to make an article 4 direction removing permitted development rights of any particular class in the area which includes the property. The reply may reveal decisions to make such orders which have not yet been made. A buyer normally prefers a negative reply, but if the reply is affirmative the buyer would certainly want to know whether the proposed direction would affect the use intended for the property, or any development in contemplation.

Enquiry 3.9.(k): Orders Revoking or Modifying a Planning Permission

Enquiry 3.9.(k) concerns the council's powers under the Town and Country Planning Act to revoke or modify planning permissions (section 97).

Once planning permission has been granted by the council for a development, whether it be for the erection of buildings or for a change of use of existing land or buildings, that planning permission attaches to the land and subsists for the benefit of any person who is for the time being the owner of the land or building. It is often the case that the planning permission is not exercised by the original applicant. Land or buildings may be sold with the benefit of the planning permission once granted.

In exceptional circumstances, however, the council may make an order revoking or modifying planning permission after it has been granted. If the planning permission is revoked in this way it is no longer of any effect and the buildings can no longer be erected or the change of use be put into effect. Orders made by the council must normally be confirmed by the Secretary of State unless they are unopposed. More usually, however, they are opposed and can be confirmed by the Secretary of State only after he has held a public local inquiry into the objections.

A council can make an order revoking or modifying a planning permission only before building operations authorised by the planning permission have been completed, or before any change of use authorised by the planning permission has taken place.

Two further points on revocation or modification orders are that:

(i) compensation may be payable to the owner of the land affected by the order for loss of the planning permission, and this may amount to a considerable sum; and

(ii) in certain circumstances the owner of the land or building may be able to serve on the council a purchase notice requiring the council to buy the land the subject of the revocation or modification order.

Councils use the power to revoke or modify planning permission only in exceptional circumstances, since the consequences may be very expensive.

Summary

Enquiry 3.9(k) seeks information on any subsisting or proposed revocations or modifications of planning permissions which affect the property. Orders for the revocation or modification of planning permission which have been made should appear on the official certificate of search. Clearly, a buyer will prefer a negative response to this part of the enquiry, confirming effectively that the planning position of the land and buildings is secure. If a subsisting or an intended revocation or modification order is revealed, the buyer should seek full details.

Enquiry 3.9.(l): Orders Requiring Discontinuance of Use or Alteration or Removal of Buildings or Works

The power under section 97 (revocation or modification orders, above) relates to existing planning permissions and must be used by the council *before* the building operations have been completed or the change of use has taken place. A council also has power to make a discontinuance order under section 102, requiring the discontinuance of any use of land (or the imposition of conditions on its future use for any particular purpose), or indeed the removal or alteration of any buildings, even after they have been completed and may have been used or occupied quite lawfully for many years.

If it appears to the council, as local planning authority, that it is in the best interests of the proper planning of the area, including the best interests of public amenity, the council may make a discontinuance order under section 102.

Once again, these orders must be confirmed by the Secretary of State and if there are objections, as there almost always are, a public local inquiry must be held to enable the objectors to be heard.

If people are, as a result of an order under this section, required to leave their homes, the council must normally rehouse them.

Compensation must be paid to the owner of the land if a discontinuance order is made, of an amount equal to the sum by which the value of the land has depreciated as a result of the order.

It is an offence to breach the terms of a discontinuance order and any person who does so may be prosecuted for this offence and may be liable to a substantial fine.

Summary

Enquiry 3.9.(l) concerns whether there are any subsisting or proposed discontinuance orders which, when made, will affect the land or buildings which are the subject of the enquiries. Orders which have already been made are revealed by the official certificate of search. A buyer will prefer a negative reply, confirming that there is no doubt that the buyer may use the land and buildings for the purposes intended. If this part of the enquiry reveals a subsisting order, or an intention by the council to make an order, the buyer should seek full details.

Enquiry 3.9.(m): Tree Preservation Orders

Councils have powers to preserve and protect trees or woodlands in their areas, and in particular they may make orders, under section 198 of the Town and Country Planning Act, prohibiting the cutting down, topping, lopping, uprooting of, or causing wilful damage to, particular trees or woodlands. An order made by the council may require any person who wishes to interfere with protected trees to obtain consent from the council before so doing.

These orders are made by the council, and although notice is first served on the owner of the land on which the trees grow, and objections must be taken into account before the order is confirmed, the Secretary of State's approval is no longer required, so that the making of these orders (TPOs) is completely within the control of the council. Orders may be made in respect of (i) single trees; (ii) a group of trees; (iii) an area; or (iv) a woodland, territorially defined. Hedgerows, however, are protected by their own regulations, made in 1997, and discussed below (see optional enquiry 21).

Trees which are dying or dead or which have become dangerous may be uprooted without consent, but with this exception, where any tree protected by a tree preservation order is removed or uprooted or destroyed, the person causing the damage or removing or destroying the tree may be prosecuted in the magistrates' court and fined up to £20,000, or in the Crown Court, where there is no limit on the fine which may be imposed. Furthermore, the owner of the land may be required to plant another tree of an appropriate size and species as soon as reasonably practicable.

Summary
Enquiry 3.9.(m) concerns whether the council has made or decided to make any tree preservation orders which (when made) would affect the land or buildings which are the subject of the enquiries. A buyer will prefer a negative reply, normally preferring not to be burdened with the obligation to preserve trees. If an affirmative response is given, the buyer should request full details of the trees proposed to be protected by the order; a physical inspection of the property is advisable to check on the existence and condition of the trees in question.

Enquiry 3.9.(n): Proceedings to Enforce a Planning Agreement or Planning Contribution

Section 106 of the Town and Country Planning Act 1990 facilitates the making of agreements between developers and others owning land, and the council as local planning authority. These agreements are now called "planning obligations", and they are useful to local planning authorities in enabling them to restrict the development or use of land in ways not possible by the application of conditions to a planning permission. They can facilitate development which might not be enabled by the use of traditional planning application and permission procedures.

Agreements (or obligations) under section 106 of the Act may impose restrictions or requirements of an indefinite nature. They may (unlike conditions attached to a planning permission) require sums of money to be paid to the council for, for instance, the commutation of car parking places, or for other works of benefit to the area or the community to be funded.

These agreements, which must be entered into by a person with a legal interest in the land in question, are then enforceable against any subsequent owner of the land deriving title under that person. Thus they are as enforceable as a planning permission, but they may achieve more of positive benefit to the development and to the community than mere restrictive conditions attached to a permission.

Most commonly, section 106 agreements (or obligations) are negotiated with developers at the time of application for planning permission for developments of significant size. New housing estates, industrial and commercial complexes and the larger leisure developments are facilitated in this way. The agreement is generally entered into just before, and in consideration of, the issue of formal planning permission.

Section 106 agreements are registrable as local land charges.

Restrictions or other requirements imposed in a section 106 agreement are not enforceable by means of an enforcement or breach of condition notice. Rather, they are enforceable as any other agreement, by injunction at the suit of the council as local planning authority. There are further powers of enforcement within section 106 itself. Breach of a requirement in a section 106 planning agreement to carry out certain operations (for example, to install a tree planting scheme, or provide car parking places to serve a development) can lead to the council's itself entering the land, carrying out the works and recovering the costs and expenses from the owner. This power of entry is exercisable after twenty-one days' notice has been served on any person responsible for complying with the agreement, such as the owner of the land. Wilful obstruction of the council carrying out these powers is a serious offence and may lead to prosecution.

Section 106 agreements could be modified and the obligations required in them discharged, either by agreement at any time, or by an application to the local planning authority (if no earlier date was specified in the agreement itself) at the expiry of five years from the date the agreement was entered into.

Section 106 planning obligations are to be abolished by the Planning and Compulsory Purchase Act 2004, and replaced by "planning contributions" which will be made pursuant to regulations promulgated under that Act. Under the new, and yet to emerge, provisions, local planning authorities will be permitted to negotiate with developers to secure "contributions", in money or in kind, towards off-setting the impact of proposed developments. These contributions may be towards off-site infrastructure, such as highway or other works in order to accommodate the new development, or social infrastructure such as educational establishments and nursery facilities. Until now, the means of securing such contributions has been the planning obligation or planning agreement. Quite how existing planning obligations and the new regime of planning contributions will interrelate will no doubt be fleshed out in the regulations yet to be made. The enforcement of the payment of "contributions" is also, as yet, unclear. Developers may be required to part with their contributions before planning permission is granted, or may be required to put in place security for payment. Failure to pay a due contribution may be made the subject of criminal sanction. At the time of going to press the position is uncertain.

Summary

Enquiry 3.9.(m) is intended to elicit whether there are any subsisting or intended proceedings for breach of a section 106 agreement (or obligation). Any prospective buyer should be advised of the implications, for the buyer and the property, of any subsisting section 106 agreement. If proceedings (either already commenced or projected) for breach of such an agreement are revealed in response to this part of enquiry 3.9, full details of the implications, especially for owners of the original site or parts of it, should be sought by a prudent buyer, before proceeding with the purchase. The buyer will become bound by the terms of any section 106 agreement, and therefore potentially affected by any proceedings for its breach, at least during the period of ownership.

If proceedings for the enforcement of a planning contribution under the emerging provisions have been commenced, or are in contemplation, a prudent buyer will require to know just how much is expected by way of contribution, if in money terms, and the consequences of failure to make the contribution, whether in money or in kind. Outstanding or contemplated proceedings for breach of a section 106 obligation or failure to make a due contribution are likely to deter a buyer from proceeding with the transaction.

Enquiry 3.10: Conservation Area

"Do the following apply in relation to the property?
  (a) the making of the area a conservation area before 31st August 1974
  (b) an unimplemented resolution to designate the area a conservation area"

Enquiry 3.10 relates to conservation areas designated before 31 August 1974. Conservation areas designated after that date are local land charges and are revealed in the official certificate of search. The enquiry also relates to areas designated by resolution of the council as conservation areas but which have not, as yet, been registered in the register of local land charges.

Conservation areas are designated by councils as local planning authorities (and, in London, by the Historic Buildings and Monuments Commission). They are areas of special architectural or historic interest, the character or appearance of which the council or Commission considers it desirable to preserve or enhance. It is the preservation of areas, as distinct from individual buildings, which section 69 of the Planning (Listed Buildings and Conservation Areas) Act 1990 regulates.

Conservation areas may be enlarged or reduced by the council from time to time, and whenever a council designates a conservation area or enlarges or reduces it, it must notify the Secretary of State. The council must also publicise the making or alteration of a conservation area in the *London Gazette* and the local newspaper.

The consequences of the fact that a property is within a designated conservation area can be summarised as follows:

(i)   In general no building within the conservation area may be demolished without the consent of the council; consent for the demolition of buildings (other than listed buildings) not lying within conservation areas is generally not required.

(ii) Trees in conservation areas are protected in much the same way as those covered by tree preservation orders, so that they cannot be cut down, uprooted, topped, lopped or destroyed or damaged without the consent of the council; and any person who does damage such a tree may be prosecuted and, if convicted, fined (see enquiry 3.9.(m) above).

(iii)   The council is under a duty to consider and publish proposals for the preservation and enhancement of the area.

(iv)   Any applications for planning permission for development in the area which would affect the character or appearance of the conservation area must be given special publicity. Any objections to the proposed development must be taken into account by the council before the application can be properly determined and permission given.

(v)   Permitted development rights under the General Permitted Development Order (see enquiry 3.9.(j)) and the right to display certain types of illuminated advertisement under the Town and Country Planning (Control of Advertisements) Regulations (see optional enquiry 6 below) are either limited or excluded.

Summary

Enquiry 3.10 concerns whether the property lies within one of these conservation areas, either recently designated by resolution of the council and not yet registered in the local land charges register, or designated before 31 August 1974. If the property is within a conservation area designated later than that date, this should be revealed in the official certificate of search since such designations are local land charges.

A buyer will want to know whether or not the property lies within a conservation area, but whether a negative or an affirmative reply is to be preferred depends on the circumstances. The fact that a property lies within such an area has advantages – the area will be preserved and possibly enhanced in its architectural or historic context. Grants and loans may be available towards expenditure incurred in the preservation or enhancement of the character or appearance of the area. There are also disadvantages – demolition and many classes of alteration of premises may not be allowed, and these may be important to a prospective developer.

Enquiry 3.11: Compulsory Purchase

"Has any enforceable order or decision been made to compulsorily purchase or acquire the property?"

This enquiry relates to the use by councils of their compulsory purchase powers.

As a statutory authority charged with the performance of a wide variety of functions, a council has the power to purchase property compulsorily under a range of enactments for different purposes.

The procedure for compulsory purchase is contained largely in the Acquisition of Land Act 1981, the Compulsory Purchase Act 1965 and the Land Compensation Acts, but the actual power to purchase land compulsorily for a particular purpose is to be found in the legislation relevant to that purpose, for example, Housing Acts, Highways Acts, the Town and Country Planning Act and the Planning and Compulsory Purchase Act 2004, which makes significant changes to all of the above.

In brief, the procedure is that the council must first pass a resolution to acquire land for a specific purpose. The council must then draft a compulsory purchase order and advertise it. The compulsory purchase order is then made (that is, sealed and dated) and forwarded to the Secretary of State for confirmation. If there are no objections, the Secretary of State may confirm the order as unopposed. If there are objections, the Secretary of State must generally arrange for a public local inquiry into those objections, at which the case for the council and the case for the objectors are put. In due course the Secretary of State decides whether or not the compulsory purchase order should be confirmed.

If the order is confirmed, the council serves on the owners of the land in question a notice to treat, that is, a notice inviting the owners to submit a claim for compensation based on the value of the land to be purchased. Alternatively, the council may make a vesting declaration which passes ownership of the land direct to the council, subject to appropriate compensation being paid. Notices to treat and the like are registrable in the register of local land charges. Somewhat surprisingly, a confirmed order for compulsory purchase, even if relating to a single identifiable property only, is not.

A person making enquiries should perhaps be aware that other authorities have compulsory purchase powers and should be consulted if there is any possibility that compulsory purchase may be a threat to the property.

Authorities other than district (or London borough) councils having compulsory purchase powers include the following:

- central government departments;
- statutory undertakers;
- railway authorities;
- road and transport authorities;
- county councils;
- water transport authorities;
- electricity, gas or hydraulic power undertakers;
- the British Airports Authority;
- the Civil Aviation Authority;
- the Post Office;
- British Telecom.

Summary
Enquiry 3.11 is designed to reveal whether any enforceable compulsory purchase order has been made by the council, or whether the council has passed any resolution to make such an order in respect of the property or any part of it. A buyer normally prefers a negative reply, and indeed an affirmative reply usually deters a buyer from proceeding with the purchase. An affirmative reply is given in any case where any part of the premises concerned is the subject of a proposed or actual compulsory purchase order.

Enquiry 3.12: Contaminated Land

"Do any of the following apply (including any relating to the land adjacent to or adjoining the property which has been identified as contaminated land because it is in such a condition that harm or pollution of controlled waters might be caused on the property)?
  (a) a contaminated land notice
  (b) in relation to a register maintained under section 78R of the Environmental Protection Act 1990
    (i)   a decision to make an entry
    (ii) an entry
  (c) consultation with the owner or occupier of the property conducted under section 78G(3) of the Environmental Protection Act 1990 before the service of a remediation notice"

This enquiry concerns entries in the registers of contaminated land and notices in respect of remediation of contaminated land. It is normally relevant only in respect of undeveloped land where there is some history of the site's having been used in connection with an industrial process or, perhaps, as a landfill site. Local authorities are required to maintain registers for these purposes by virtue of section 78R of the Environmental Protection Act 1990.

The Environmental Protection Act is a radical and wide-ranging statute containing powers and duties for local authorities to deal with a host of issues. The Act includes provisions on the following:

- control of industrial and air pollution;
- the collection and disposal of controlled waste;
- statutory nuisances and clean air;
- litter control;
- abandoned shopping trolleys;
- the control of genetically modified organisms;
- potentially hazardous substances;
- oil pollution from ships;
- identification and control of dogs;
- burning of crop residues.

Part IIA of the Act imposes a duty on the local authority, as respects land in its area which appears to be subject to contamination, to take certain measures including the maintenance of a register containing specified

83

particulars of the action taken in relation to that land. The local authority charged with this duty is the district council or other unitary authority and, in the city of London, the Common Council of the City.

"Contaminated land" is land which appears to the council to be in such a condition, by reason of substances in, on or under it, that significant harm is being caused (or there is a significant possibility of such harm being caused), or pollution of controlled waters is being, or is likely to be, caused.

"Harm" means harm to the health of living organisms or other interference with ecological systems, and includes harm to property.

"Remediation" means doing things for the purpose of assessing the condition of the land or any controlled waters or land adjoining it; doing actual works for the purpose of preventing or minimising the harm or pollution or restoring the land and water to its former state; and making subsequent inspections.

The council has a duty under this regime to inspect its area from time to time to identify contaminated land. If it does identify contaminated land in its area, it must give notice to the Environment Agency (in Scotland, the Scottish Environmental Protection Agency). The owner of the land in question must also be notified, as must any person in actual occupation of any part of the land. Other persons ("appropriate persons") must also be notified if they are deemed to bear responsibility for the contamination.

Where the council identifies contaminated land, remediation notices must be served on those responsible for the land or its contamination, specifying what must be done by way of remediation, and the period in which those measures are to be taken. Different remediation notices may be served on different persons requiring different works to be carried out in respect of different contaminative substances.

Only steps which are reasonable may be required by a remediation notice, having regard to the costs likely to be involved, and the seriousness of the harm (or pollution to controlled waters) in question.

Before serving a remediation notice, the council is obliged to endeavour to consult every person who appears to the council to be an owner or occupier of the land (or waters) or any part of them, and anyone who appears to be a person who might be required to grant rights of way or wayleaves to enable the remedial works to be undertaken. The requirement to consult does not preclude the service of a remediation notice if, in the opinion of the council, the land is in such a condition as to be in imminent danger of causing serious harm or pollution. Adjoining owners, or anyone whose consent is required to enable the works to be undertaken, are obliged to grant such rights as will enable compliance with the terms of the remediation notice by the person on whom it has been served. These people are of course entitled to compensation.

There are rights of appeal against remediation notices. The appeal must be lodged with the magistrates' court (in Scotland, the sheriff) within twenty-one days of service of the notice. An appeal against a notice served by the Environment Agency (in Scotland, the Environmental Protection Agency) in the case of a special site under the Act, is to the Secretary of State. Whoever is the appellate authority in respect of the notice may either confirm, quash or modify its requirements.

Failure to comply with the requirements of a remediation notice by a person on whom one has been served constitutes a serious criminal offence. A fine may be levied for each day on which the failure continues after conviction. In addition, the council and the Environment Agency (in Scotland, the Environmental Protection Agency) have power to carry out the necessary remedial works in default and to recover their costs of so doing.

Section 78R of the 1990 Act requires the council to maintain registers containing prescribed particulars relating to, *inter alia*:

- remediation notices it has served;
- appeals against remediation notices;
- appeals against charging notices in respect of costs to be recovered by the enforcing authority;
- convictions for offences of breach of remediation notices;
- other matters not specified above.

Enquiry 3.12.(a): Contaminated Land Notices

This part of the enquiry should produce copies of notices of identification of contaminated land which have been served under section 78B(3) of the 1990 Act, or which the council has resolved to serve.. A buyer will prefer a negative response. The fact that the land in question has been identified as contaminated would certainly affect its value, and the buyer in receipt of an affirmative response to this part would be concerned to ascertain whether the enforcing authority (the council or the Environment Agency) is considering the service of a remediation notice, and if so, what remedial works are likely to be required.

Enquiry 3.12.(b): Entry in the Register under Section 78R(1)

This part of enquiry 3.12 is intended to elicit information as to, and copies of, any remediation notices, appeals, charging notice appeals, convictions and other matters appearing in the register. Clearly, a buyer will prefer a negative response (although such a response does not, of itself, mean that the land is uncontaminated). If the response is affirmative, the buyer will certainly wish to have full details of any subsisting notices and appeals. If, on enquiry, it can be ascertained that all remediation works have been carried out to the enforcing authority's satisfaction, the buyer may well be content to proceed.

Enquiry 3.12.(c): Consultations under Section 78G(3)

This part of the enquiry is intended to reveal consultations which have taken place with owners and occupiers of land which is contaminated (including controlled waters affected by that land) and land adjoining contaminated land, before the service of a remediation notice. Such adjoining owners and occupiers might be required to grant rights of access, and to suffer work being done on their land, even if their own land is not itself contaminated. A buyer will not necessarily be put off purchasing land adjoining contaminated land, but if an affirmative response is received to this part of enquiry 3.12, the buyer will want to know what negotiations have taken place and what measures are proposed on the land to be purchased in order to remedy the contamination of the neighbouring land. The buyer would also be concerned to know what measure of compensation might be due.

The Guidance Notes 2002 advise councils to add the following informative statement when replying to this enquiry: "A negative reply does not imply that the property or any adjoining or adjacent land is free from contamination or from the risk of it, and the reply may not disclose steps taken by another council in whose area adjacent or adjoining land is situated."

Summary
Enquiry 3.12 is unusual in that it asks for full details of contaminated land notices, remediation notices, appeals, charging notice appeals and anything else that might be revealed not only in relation to the land to be purchased, but also in connection with land adjacent to or adjoining it, which has been identified as contaminated, because its condition might harm the land to be purchased. It is suggested that the greatest care should be taken, if there is any suggestion of land contamination in the area, to investigate the records (and perhaps historical records) of significantly sized parcels of adjoining or adjacent land.

Enquiry 3.13: Radon Gas

"Do records indicate that the property is in a 'Radon Affected Area' as identified by the Health Protection Agency?"

This enquiry concerns whether the property is situated in an area which may be affected by the presence of radon gas.

Radon gas is a naturally occurring, tasteless, colourless and odourless gas which is given off in the course of the radioactive decay of uranium. Uranium is found in small quantities in most soils and rocks, but it is particularly associated with granite. The radon gas given off in the decay process rises to the surface where it normally dissipates harmlessly into the atmosphere. However, where the gas enters enclosed spaces, such as houses, it can, given the right atmospheric and other conditions, reach high concentration.

It is possible for air from soil and rock containing radon to enter into a house through small cracks in the substructure, and, the air pressure inside houses being generally slightly lower than that in the soil because of atmospheric conditions, air may be drawn from the ground into the house. Indoor radon levels that are high enough to give any cause for concern are normally caused by this seepage of radon from the soil.

There is some evidence that exposure to radon and its inhalation over a prolonged period can give rise to damage to lung tissue and in extreme cases it may be a contributory cause of lung cancer, although the risk estimates in this area were originally derived from studies of lung cancer rates in uranium miners, who work under conditions very different from those of the average house dweller.

Radon levels inside a house may vary according to the time of day, from day to day and in accordance with seasonal conditions. There is a recommended level for existing homes, above which action should be taken to remedy the situation. There is a number of methods of reducing indoor radon levels.

The National Radiological Protection Board (which has since merged with the Health Protection Agency) recommended that radiological surveillance be carried out to identify areas at greater risk so that priority may be accorded them in the monitoring of radon emissions and the taking of measures to minimise its ingress into homes and other buildings.

The Health Protection Agency (HPA) advises that areas where one per cent or more of homes exceed the stipulated action level (200 becquerels per cubic metre, the average level in UK houses being twenty Bq/m^3) should be regarded as action areas, and prioritised in respect of radon precautions. Areas identified by the Agency have been duly designated by the Department of the Environment as radon-affected, in accordance with these recommended criteria. These areas are in Devon, Cornwall, Derbyshire, Northamptonshire, Somerset and, now, in many other counties. The Health Protection Agency publishes, on behalf of the government, maps of radon-affected areas, and councils will be aware of any such areas within their administrative areas.

The Building Regulations 2000, schedule 1, part C, requires, in respect of new buildings, that precautions be taken to avoid danger to health and safety caused by substances found on or in the ground to be covered by the building. The Building Research Establishment has issued guidance in support of the regulations, entitled *Radon: Guidance on Protective Measures for New Dwellings*, which should be followed by developers and others responsible for the construction of new buildings, extensions and conversions in areas where there may be "elevated radon emissions".

While there is as yet no compulsory code of precautions to be taken in connection with existing dwellings, the Building Research Establishment has issued guidance, entitled *The Householder's Guide to Radon*, which is designed to encourage householders in affected regions to have measurements made and take suitable precautions.

Non-domestic buildings are not yet covered by the requirements. However, employers of staff within such buildings would undoubtedly have a duty of care towards their employees under general health and safety legislation and should not take advisory radon precautions lightly.

Radon Precautions

Radon gas is known to enter houses by a number of routes – through cracks in solid floors, via construction joints, through cracks in walls above or below ground level, by way of wall cavities and through gaps in suspended floors and around service pipes.

A variety of methods or precautions may be taken to minimise or eliminate the ingress of gas. Installation of a radon sump incorporating air extraction (in the case of solid floors) is effective in reducing the level to one-tenth of the existing level in most cases. Floor sealants may be applied to prevent radon ingress. Additional air bricks may be installed below floor level to increase the flow of air under the floor. The house may be pressurised with a fan drawing air from the loft space. Inventive methods of ventilating the property may be effective to avoid drawing air and radon through the floor. All these methods are successful to a greater or lesser degree and at moderate cost. The level of precautions taken in respect of existing dwellings is largely a matter for the owner and would depend upon factors including the measured level of radon gas within the property, the nature of its occupation and the type of its construction. Measurement of radon levels in a property is carried out by the Health Protection Agency and other bodies at a reasonable cost, but accurate tests can take up to three months to conduct. Grants may be available from the council to fund the necessary works, and a prospective buyer may care to investigate these.

The precautions to be considered in respect of new dwellings and extensions in radon-affected areas, and outside those areas where elevated radon emissions have been shown to exist, are constantly under review.

Current guidance (and this was referred to in the Guidance Notes 2002) is contained in BR211: *Guidance on Protective Measures for New Dwellings*. This provides for two levels of protection, basic and full. Basic protection is recommended where there is a three per cent or greater probability of exceeding action level, and comprises a barrier across the ground floor. Where radon levels may significantly exceed action level, full protection should be provided, incorporating sub-floor depressurisation or ventilation in addition to the barrier, and a sump may also be required where there is a ground-bearing slab.

Summary
Enquiry 3.13 is intended to reveal whether the property is situated in a radon affected area as identified by the Health Protection Agency. Generally, the buyer will prefer a negative response. If the reply is in the affirmative, any new dwelling or extension may be required to be constructed taking into account the necessary radon precautions. Buyers of existing dwellings would be well advised to investigate further the need to take the precautions recommended by the Health Protection Agency and the Building Research Establishment. Buyers should not be unduly discouraged by an affirmative response, however, since the cost of any precautions is likely to be modest. Radon precautions can be easily and cheaply installed and very effective. An assessment can be obtained of the need for precautions and their cost. This can be done prior to purchase, if time permits, or after completion and occupation, with some acknowledgement of the cost of necessary works being incorporated in the price. A radon bond may be considered as a solution to this problem, and has proved popular with sellers and buyers. The seller and buyer agree on a likely sum of money which would be enough to cover typical radon reduction costs. The money is deducted from the purchase price and held by a third party, as stakeholder, until the outcome of any tests is known, and reduction measures have been put in place. Contracts are then exchanged, and completion proceeds on the basis that, if the tests show that there is no real radon problem, the bond money is returned to the seller. If the test shows a problem to exist, the reduction measures are put in hand and the work is paid for from the bond money, the excess being returned to the seller.

As mentioned above, radon precautions may not be excessively expensive or complicated, and the prospective buyer should not be unduly concerned by the need for them. Further advice and assistance on radon can be obtained from the Health Protection Agency's extensive website at www.hpa.org.uk/radiation and from the environmental health department of the local council.

The Guidance Notes 2002 advise councils, if the reply is affirmative, to provide in the reply the following informative note:

"Radon Affected Areas are designated by the National Radiological Protection Board. It is recommended that the level of radon gas should be measured in all properties within Radon Affected Areas. The present owner or (for a new property) the builder should be asked whether protective measures were incorporated in the construction of the property; whether radon levels have been measured in the property; whether the results were at or above the Action Level (prescribed by the NRPB) and if so whether remedial measures were installed and whether the radon levels were re-tested and confirmed the effectiveness of the measures.

A guide containing further information about Radon Affected Areas is available free from DEFRA Warehouse Publications, Admail 6000, London SW1A 2XX (tel 08459 556000, fax 020 8957 5012) or from DEFRA Radioactive Substances Division, Zone 4/E7, Ashdown House, 123 Victoria Street, London SW1E."

Part II: Optional Enquiries

The optional enquiries now appear on a separate form – Con 29O, *Optional Enquiries of Local Authority*. The council will reply only to those optional enquiries which the enquirer has indicated by placing a tick in the appropriate box on the front of the form. A charge is made for answering each individual enquiry.

Optional Enquiry 4: Road Proposals by Private Bodies

"What proposals by others, still capable of being implemented, have the Council approved for any of the following, the limits of construction of which are within 200 metres of the property?
  (a) the construction of a new road
  (b) the alteration or improvement of an existing road, involving the construction, whether or not within existing highway limits, of a subway, underpass, flyover, footbridge, elevated road, dual carriageway, the construction of a roundabout (other than a mini roundabout) or the widening of an existing road by the construction of one or more additional traffic lanes

This enquiry refers to proposals by bodies or companies (such as private developers) other than the Council (and where appropriate the County Council) or the Secretary of State.
A mini roundabout is a roundabout having a one-way circulatory carriageway around a flush or slightly raised circular marking less than 4 metres in diameter and with or without flared approaches."

This optional enquiry is designed to elicit information in connection with road construction, alteration or improvement within 200 metres of the property the subject of the enquiry. Whereas standard enquiry 3.4 (see above) dealt with major road proposals of the Secretary of State or the council itself as highway authority, this enquiry deals with proposals by "others", such as private developers. The note to the enquiry contains an attempt to elucidate.

Proposals by private developers for road construction are normally associated with the development of the land in question for residential, commercial or industrial purposes, the scheme being the subject of an application for planning permission to the council as local planning authority. The application is dealt with in accordance with the procedures detailed in the Planning Acts, and owners of land adjoining that to be developed should be made aware of what is being proposed, by means of the neighbour notification procedures.

The construction by a developer of a road which is not associated with any development also requires planning permission, since road construction involves engineering operations in, over or under land, which constitutes "development" as defined in the Town and Country Planning Act. Even a purely internal access road therefore requires planning permission.

Private developers may, by virtue of section 38 of the Highways Act 1980, enter into agreements with the council, as local highway authority, for the future maintenance of a road. If the council, as highway authority, is satisfied that the road in question has been constructed in accordance with the agreement to appropriate standards, then, on completion of the construction, the council adopts the road as a highway maintainable at the public expense. The developer can in this way divest himself of future maintenance responsibilities.

Summary

Optional enquiry 4.(a) concerns whether the council has approved any proposals made otherwise than by the traditional highways authorities for a new road where the limits of construction fall within 200 metres of any part of the property searched against.

Optional enquiry 4.(b) is a similar enquiry regarding proposals for the alteration or improvement of existing roads, involving the construction of a subway, underpass, flyover, roundabout etc. (but not a mini roundabout, which is defined for these purposes in the note to this enquiry). The 200 metres are to be taken from the limits of construction of the proposed improvement to the nearest part of the property affected.

The desired reply to this enquiry entirely depends upon the buyer's intentions in respect of the property. New or improved roads may well entail increased traffic flow in the vicinity of the property. On the other hand, improved road conditions can alleviate traffic congestion.

Optional Enquiry 5: Public Paths or Byways

"5.1. Is any footpath, bridleway, restricted byway or byway open to all traffic which abuts on, or crosses the property, shown in a definitive map or revised definitive map prepared under Part IV of the National Parks and Access to the Countryside Act 1949 or Part III of the Wildlife and Countryside Act 1981?

5.2. If so, please mark its approximate route on the attached plan."

This optional enquiry relates to public rights of way which may cross or abut on the property. It is normally asked only where the property to be purchased consists of open fields or cleared development sites, or where a physical inspection of the property has revealed a path which appears to be used by the public.

Public rights of way are rights for the public at large to walk, ride or drive over defined paths or byways crossing land which is otherwise in private ownership. They generally fall into three categories, as follows:

- a "footpath", defined as a highway over which the public has a right of way on foot only, other than a highway at the side of a public road (called a "footway");
- a "bridleway", defined as a highway over which the public has the right of way on foot and a right of way on horseback or leading a horse. There may also be a right to drive other animals along a bridleway;
- a "byway open to all traffic" (BOAT), defined as a highway over which the public has a right of way for vehicles and other traffic but is used by the public mainly for the purpose for which footpaths and bridleways are used.

A "restricted byway", introduced by the Countryside and Rights of Way Act 2000 to replace the old "road used as a public path" (RUPP), means a highway over which the public has restricted byway rights, with or without a right to drive animals of any description along the highway, but no other rights of way. "Restricted byway rights" means a right of way on foot, on horseback, or leading a horse, and a right of way for vehicles other than mechanically propelled vehicles.

The Wildlife and Countryside Act 1981, and in particular part III thereof, introduced a new code for the preparation and revision of definitive maps relating to public rights of way in the countryside. The new code replaced provisions formerly contained in the National Parks and Access to the Countryside Act 1949 and the Countryside Act 1968. Those provisions were cumbersome; and, since the revision of the maps did not take effect until all objections and representations had been resolved, decisions took many years to be implemented.

The new definitive map and statement procedure provides for continuous review. It has been modified extensively by the Countryside and Rights of Way Act 2000.

It is the responsibility of the surveying authority (generally the county council or, in London, the London borough council) to keep under review the definitive map showing all public rights of way in its area; to make modifications to it in the event of such rights of way being stopped up, widened or diverted, upgraded or downgraded (for example, bridleway to footpath, BOAT to bridleway); and to add rights of way to the map where new rights are shown to exist.

Any person may apply to the surveying authority for an order making modifications to the map if it can be shown, for example, that a right of way that actually exists is not shown on the map, or that a right of way shown on the map as a right of a particular description ought to be shown as of a different description (for instance, that a right shown as a footpath should be a bridleway).

There is a formal procedure under the Wildlife and Countryside Act 1981 (schedule 14) for applying for these orders. In particular, an applicant must show documentary evidence, including statements of witnesses, which supports the application. The applicant must notify the owner of the land to which the application relates. The council then investigates the application and decides whether or not to make the order. There is a right of appeal to the Secretary of State if the council refuses to make the order.

Many of these public rights of way, as defined in the definitive map and statement, are highways maintainable at the public expense (that is, by the council as highway authority on behalf of the payers of council tax), but the council is not obliged to provide a metalled carriageway, and in practice many public paths are difficult to negotiate during periods of wet weather. Many public rights of way are privately maintainable notwithstanding the public right to use them.

Once a right of way appears on the definitive map, it is conclusive evidence of the fact of its existence and the public is entitled to demand its right to pass on foot, on horseback or in motor vehicles, as appropriate to the description of the right of way in question. It is an offence, even for the owner of the land in question, punishable in the magistrates' court, to obstruct the right of the public to pass.

A copy of the definitive map and all modification orders must be kept available for public inspection free of charge at all reasonable times in each district to which the map relates (usually at the district council offices).

There are two other particular restrictions arising by virtue of the existence of a public right of way:

(i)   Prohibition on keeping bulls – any occupier of a field crossed by a public right of way, for example a farmer, may not permit a bull to be "at large", that is, free to roam in that field. An occupier failing to comply with the prohibition may be fined up to £1,000 in the magistrates' court.

       The prohibition does not, however, apply if the bull is under the age of ten months or is not a recognised dairy breed and is accompanied by cows or heifers. A recognised dairy breed means Ayrshire, British Friesian, British Holstein, Dairy Shorthorn, Guernsey, Jersey or Kerry.

(ii)   Restrictions on ploughing – farmers may be fined for ploughing up rights of way over their land, and may be required to reinstate them and restore the surface to a reasonable condition.

Summary

Optional enquiry 5.1 concerns whether there are any public rights of way over the property or abutting on it which are shown in the definitive map or any revision of the map. A buyer normally prefers a negative answer, to avoid being inhibited in the use to which the land may be put. A buyer intending to farm the land in question will be particularly interested in, and may need to make special provision for, the security of beasts and crops. It is not an offence to fence the path off, but it is an offence to obstruct it, otherwise than by, for example, a stile for pedestrians (provided the right is not a BOAT or bridleway). Developers of cleared sites also need to ensure that their proposed developments will not obstruct the footpath.

Optional enquiry 5.2 presupposes the attachment of a plan if this enquiry is raised. The buyer should always supply a plan with the application for search if a reply to this enquiry is sought. The council is asked to mark the approximate route of the right of way on the plan supplied.

The Guidance Notes 2002 advise councils to include the following informative statement in any reply to this enquiry: "The definitive map does not show every public footpath or byway."

Optional Enquiry 6: Advertisements

"Entries in the register

6.1. Please list any entries in the register of applications, directions and decisions relating to consent for the display of advertisements.

6.2. If there are any entries, where can that register be inspected?

Notices, proceedings and orders

6.3. Except as shown in the official certificate of search:

- (a) has any notice been given by the Secretary of State or served in respect of a direction or proposed direction restricting deemed consent for any class of advertisement
- (b) have the Council resolved to serve a notice requiring the display of any advertisement to be discontinued
- (c) if a discontinuance notice has been served, has it been complied with to the satisfaction of the Council
- (d) have the Council resolved to serve any other notice or proceedings relating to a contravention of the control of advertisements
- (e) have the Council resolved to make an order for the special control of advertisements for the area"

This optional enquiry relates to the special code of advertisement control contained in the Town and Country Planning (Control of Advertisements) Regulations and how it may affect the property. It is normally asked by buyers of commercial properties who are concerned to know whether there are any restrictions on the advertisements that may be displayed.

The current regulations are the Town and Country Planning (Control of Advertisements) Regulations 1992.

Optional Enquiries 6.1 and 6.2: Entries in the Register

The regulations confer powers on the council, as local planning authority, to control the display of advertisements in the interests of amenity and public safety.

An "advertisement" is defined by section 336(1) of the Town and Country Planning Act 1990, for the purposes of the regulations, as any word, letter, model, sign, placard, board, notice, awning, blind, device or representation whether illuminated or not, in the nature of, and employed wholly or partly for the purposes of advertisement, announcement or direction. The present definition specifically excludes memorials and railway signals, but hoardings and balloons are included.

By virtue of regulation 3, the regulations apply to the display of all advertisements except the ten classes of advertisement specified in schedule 2, which are broadly as follows:

(i) those displayed on enclosed land and not readily visible from land outside that enclosure;

(ii) those displayed within a building and not visible from outside;

(iii) those displayed on vehicles;

(iv) those displayed on balloons flown at a height of not more than sixty metres above ground level for a maximum of ten days in a calendar year;

(v) those actually forming the fabric of a building, e.g., incised stonework lettering;

(vi) those displayed on an article for sale or on its container, provided they are not illuminated and do not exceed 0.1 square metres in area;

(vii) those relating to Parliamentary, European or local government elections up to fourteen days after close of the poll;

(viii) those required by statute;

(ix) traffic signs;

(x) national flags flown on a single vertical flagstaff without added inscriptions beyond the approved design of the national flag.

Generally, under the regulations, no advertisement except as above may be displayed without the consent of the council as local planning authority. In giving such consent the council must have regard, in the interests of amenity, to the suitability of the use of a site for the display of advertisements, taking into account the general characteristics of the locality, including any features of historic, architectural, cultural and similar interest; and, in the interests of public safety, to the safety of persons using any roads, railways, waterways, docks, harbours or airfields. In having regard to safety aspects the council must consider whether any display is likely to obscure or hinder road signs, railway signals or water navigational aids.

Any person displaying an advertisement without the consent of the council is liable to prosecution and, on conviction, to a fine.

Application for consent under the regulations is made on a form issued by the council. The application must be accompanied by full particulars of the proposed advertisement and plans and the prescribed fee. The council must consult neighbouring local planning authorities which may be affected by the advertisement; the Secretary of State for Transport if the advertisement may affect the safety of users of a trunk road; and other authorities, notably statutory undertakers. Those consulted must be given fourteen days to make their observations. The council may then grant the application subject to conditions relating to cleanliness and safety. Advertisement consents generally last for a maximum of five years.

The council must notify the applicant of its decision within eight weeks of the application. There is a right of appeal to the Secretary of State against refusal of consent or against conditions imposed on the grant of consent.

Once granted, whether by the council on application or by the Secretary of State on appeal, the consent runs with the land and may be exercised by any owner of the land for the time being (unless it is revoked or modified by the council) until it expires – normally after five years.

The council, as local planning authority, must keep a register containing details of all applications for advertisement consent, including the name and address of the applicant; the date of application; details of the advertisement; and the decision of the council (that is, grant or refusal) or of the Secretary of State on appeal. The register must be indexed for the assistance of the public inspecting it, and must be kept at the offices of the council. Entries in the register must be made within fourteen days of the receipt of application.

Summary
Optional enquiry 6.1 is intended to elicit a list of any entries relating to the property contained in the statutory register. A buyer making this enquiry will be interested to know what, if any, applications have been made and granted or refused; whether those granted are subject to any special conditions; and how long the consents granted are to last. Optional enquiry 6.2 concerns the location at which the register of advertisement consents can be inspected.

If the reply to optional enquiry 6.1 is in the affirmative, and lists relevant entries, the buyer may wish to inspect the register. It is kept at the council's offices, generally in the planning department, and must be open to public inspection at all reasonable hours.

Optional Enquiry 6.3.(a): Restriction of Deemed Consent

Regulation 6 provides deemed consent for the fourteen classes of advertisement specified in schedule 3 to the regulations, so that advertisements within these categories may be displayed without express consent, subject to the council's power to require discontinuance. The fourteen classes are as follows:

- Class 1: functional advertisements of local authorities, statutory undertakers and public transport undertakers (e.g. "Bus Stop", "To The Library");
- Class 2: miscellaneous advertisements relating to premises on which they are displayed (e.g. "Dentist", "Solicitor", "Community Centre");
- Class 3: certain advertisements of a temporary nature (e.g. advertising property or livestock for sale or the carrying on of building works or local cultural events, travelling circuses and fairs);
- Class 4: illuminated advertisements on business premises displayed on the frontage of premises within a retail park and overlooking a communal car park, where the advertisement refers to the goods

sold and services provided, the business carried on and the name and qualifications of the person carrying it on;

- Class 5: advertisements on business premises (e.g. nature of the business carried on or goods or services provided), other than illuminated advertisements;
- Class 6: advertisements on the forecourts of business premises (e.g. as in Class 5 above);
- Class 7: flag advertisements (e.g. on a flagstaff and showing the name or emblem of the person occupying the building, or on a residential development site where the houses are still being sold);
- Class 8: certain advertisements displayed on hoardings (e.g. hoardings enclosing building sites);
- Class 9: advertisements on highway structures designed to accommodate panel displays;
- Class 10: advertisements for neighbourhood watch schemes;
- Class 11: directional advertisements: house building sites (e.g. advertisements directing potential buyers to a site where residential development is taking place);
- Class 12: advertisements displayed inside buildings;
- Class 13: advertisements displayed on a site used for the display of advertisements without express consent ever since 1 April 1974;
- Class 14: advertisements displayed with express consent after the consent has expired, unless a renewal of consent has been applied for and refused.

The above is only a summary of the fourteen classes. There are detailed requirements for each class and a maximum size for each class of advertisement.

Normally, then, express consent is not required for these fourteen specified classes of advertisement, within the strict limitations detailed in schedule 3. They have "deemed consent" under the regulation. The Secretary of State may, however, by direction, order that the provisions of deemed consent be removed from a particular area or in a particular case, so that application for express consent has to be made to the council.

Before making such a direction, the Secretary of State publishes notice of his intention in the local newspaper and the *London Gazette*; notifies the owner of any land involved; and considers objections. If the direction is made, the council must publish the effect of it in the local newspaper, specifying the date the direction comes into force and, thereafter, application for advertisement consent has to be made before advertisements of any of the fourteen classes specified in the direction can be displayed.

These directions of the Secretary of State are made under regulation 7 of the current regulations and are very similar in effect to directions made under article 4 of the General Permitted Development Order restricting permitted development (see the commentary on enquiry 3.9.(j)).

Summary

Optional enquiry 6.3.(a) concerns whether the Secretary of State is proposing to make a direction removing "deemed consent" for any of the schedule 3 classes of advertisement. If a direction has already been made, it will appear in the official certificate of search. A buyer will prefer a negative reply since an affirmative reply may mean having to apply for consent for an advertisement in respect of which "deemed consent" could otherwise be claimed, and the consent of the council may not be forthcoming.

Optional Enquiry 6.3.(b): Discontinuance Notices

Under regulation 8, the council, as local planning authority, may serve a discontinuance notice requiring the discontinuance of the display of an advertisement displayed under the "deemed consent" provisions of regulation 6 and schedule 3. The council may do this only if it is satisfied that substantial injury to amenity or danger to the public is being caused by the advertisement.

A discontinuance notice is served on the advertiser, owner and occupier of the site, and any other person displaying the advertisement. It must give a specified time (not less than eight weeks) for the advertisement to be removed, and explain the reasons (amenity or public safety) why it is being served. There is a right of appeal against service of a discontinuance notice to the Secretary of State. If the discontinuance notice is not complied with (and if any appeal against its service has been unsuccessful), it is an offence punishable by fine to continue to display the advertisement.

Summary

Optional enquiry 6.3.(b) is designed to elicit whether the council has decided to serve a discontinuance notice. If one has already been served, it will appear in the official certificate of search. A buyer generally prefers a negative reply since an affirmative one would mean an obligation to remove the advertisement complained of.

Optional Enquiry 6.3.(c): Compliance with a Discontinuance Notice

As mentioned above, if a discontinuance notice has been served, it will be revealed by the official certificate of search. In these circumstances a buyer will want to know whether the requirements of the notice have been complied with.

This part of the enquiry is answered only if the site has already been inspected by the council's officers. If a special inspection is required to confirm the position, the buyer may be asked to pay for it.

Summary

Optional enquiry 6.3.(c) is intended to reveal whether any discontinuance notice served on the property has been complied with to the satisfaction of the council. The buyer would obviously prefer a reply confirming compliance.

Optional Enquiry 6.3.(d): Proceedings for Contravention

Section 224 of the Town and Country Planning Act makes it a criminal offence, punishable by fine (and a daily fine for a continuing offence following conviction), to display advertisements in contravention of the 1992 regulations.

Furthermore, a person is deemed to display an advertisement if he is the owner or occupier of the land on which it is displayed, or the advertisement gives publicity to his goods, trade or business (unless he can show that the advertisement was displayed without his knowledge or consent). The council has, under section 225 of the Act, power to remove or obliterate unauthorised advertisements (placards and posters), but must first give written notice of its intention so to do unless, of course, the placard or poster does not identify the name of the person who displayed it.

Summary
Optional enquiry 6.3.(d) concerns whether the council has resolved to serve any other notices or proceedings relating to the control of advertisements. Clearly, a buyer prefers a negative reply. If the reply is in the affirmative, the buyer will require full details of the alleged contravention of advertisement control since, on completion, the buyer could find himself in breach of section 224.

Optional Enquiry 6.3.(e): Special Control of Advertisements

Regulation 18 of the 1992 regulations provides for the council to define areas of special control for advertisement purposes. In these areas, only the following advertisements may be displayed:

- nine of the ten schedule 2 classes of advertisement exempted in general from the operation of the regulations by virtue of regulation 3 (see page 99). The exception is balloon advertisements flown at not more than sixty metres above ground level on not more than ten days in a calendar year – these may not be displayed in areas of special control;
- twelve of the fourteen schedule 3 "deemed consent" classes of advertisement. The exceptions here are classes 4 (illuminated advertisements on business premises) and 8 (advertisements on hoardings) which may not be displayed in areas of special control;
- advertisements with express consent of the council relating to local events, activities, entertainments, for public safety, or for announcement or direction in relation to buildings in the locality.

Areas of special control are made by order of the council and have to be approved by the Secretary of State. The proposal to make an order defining such an area must be published in the *London Gazette* and a local newspaper, and an opportunity (at least twenty-eight days) for representations or objections must be given. If there are objections, the Secretary of State may, and in certain circumstances must, hold a public local inquiry before confirming the order, with or without modifications.

Once the order is made, further press publicity must be given.

In these areas of special control, there are considerable restrictions on the nature of advertisements that may be displayed.

Summary

Optional enquiry 6.3.(e) is designed to reveal whether the council has decided to make an order defining an area of special control. If such an order has already been made which affects the property, it will appear in the official certificate of search. The buyer will want to know of proposals to define an area of special control if the buyer's business undertaking depends to any extent on the types of advertising discussed here. An affirmative reply to this part of the enquiry may inhibit a commercial buyer's operation.

Optional Enquiry 7: Completion Notices

"Which of the planning permissions in force have the Council resolved to terminate by means of a completion notice under s. 94 of the Town & Country Planning Act 1990?"

This optional enquiry relates to the duration of planning permissions granted under the Town and Country Planning Act, and the circumstances in which such planning permissions may be brought to an end. It is normally asked where a buyer has agreed to buy a property with the benefit of planning permission and it is particularly important to the buyer that the planning permission can still be implemented.

Once planning permission for a particular development has been granted, be it for development consisting of building operations or for a change of use, the permission granted attaches to the land and may be implemented by whoever is, for the time being, the owner of the land. Land can thus be sold with the benefit of the planning permission which may then be implemented by the buyer.

However, the Town and Country Planning Act recognises that it is undesirable to have an accumulation of unimplemented planning permissions and encourages early implementation and the bringing of the land into effective use. While there is no rule that planning permissions automatically lapse after a given time, the Act does establish a procedure whereby unimplemented planning permissions can be terminated.

Section 91 of the Act provides that, with certain exceptions, every planning permission granted shall be deemed to be granted subject to a condition that the development permitted must be begun within three years, or such longer or shorter defined period as the council, as local planning authority, shall impose. If no period is specified, the three-year rule applies. If development is not begun within the specified period, then the planning permission lapses and any attempt to begin the development after the end of the specified period is a breach of planning control, that is, the development is not permitted and the council may serve an enforcement notice on the person purporting to implement the permission which has lapsed.

Section 56 of the same Act goes on to define what must be done to show that development has begun within the specified period. If one of the following operations has been carried out on the land within the specified period for commencement of implementation of the planning permission, the permission does not lapse automatically and the developer can at least show that he has complied with the commencement provisions. The operations are:

- any work of construction in the course of erection of the building, or in the course of its demolition;
- the digging of a trench which is to contain the foundations of the building;
- the laying of underground mains or pipes;
- the laying out or construction of a road;
- any change in the use of the land, where that change constitutes a material development.

By carrying out one of the above operations within the specified period (that is, normally within three years of the grant of permission) the developer is normally able to keep the permission "alive". In fact, very little need be done to prevent a planning permission lapsing for non-implementation, provided that what is done is genuinely done for the purpose of carrying out the development.

What if development is begun within the time limit specified in the planning permission, or the three-year period if no other time limit is specified, but the development is not completed? Clearly it would be most unsatisfactory for uncompleted developments to proliferate and for the country to be littered with half-finished building sites. It is for this reason that section 94 of the Act provides a procedure for the termination of planning permissions where development has commenced but has not been completed.

Section 94 provides that where the development permitted by the planning permission has been begun within the time limit specified for its commencement, but has not been completed within that time, the council may serve a completion notice, stating that the planning permission will be terminated at the end of a further specified period, which must be at least twelve months after the notice takes effect, so that the owner of the land has at least one further year to complete the development.

The completion notice is served on the person who is the owner and occupier of the land at the time the notice is served. The notice must be confirmed by the Secretary of State and takes effect only after it has been so confirmed. The Secretary of State may extend the period given by the council for completion of the development, and if the landowner so requests, a public local inquiry into the notice will have to be held so that the owner and the council may present their arguments on whether the notice should be confirmed or quashed.

If the completion notice is served and is confirmed by the Secretary of State, the planning permission is invalid except in so far as it authorises any development carried out up to the end of the period specified in the notice for completion of the development. It is therefore a very definite encouragement for the owner of the land to ensure that the development is completed within the time specified in the notice. Any development taking place after the expiry of the time specified in the notice does not have the benefit of planning permission and the council may take enforcement action for a breach of planning control.

The Secretary of State may himself serve a completion notice; this has the same effect on a planning permission as if it had been served by the council as local planning authority. The Secretary of State must, however, consult the local planning authority before serving such a notice.

Summary
Optional enquiry 7 concerns whether the council has decided to serve a completion notice under section 94 terminating any planning permission(s) in force in respect of the property. A buyer will prefer a negative reply, wishing to buy the property with the benefit of any existing planning permissions and without the threat of any termination of permission. If the reply is affirmative, the buyer will want to know which planning permission(s) it is proposed to terminate, and what period of time will be allowed under the proposed completion notice to complete the development before the planning permission lapses.

Optional Enquiry 8: Parks and Countryside

"Areas of outstanding natural beauty

8.1. Has any order under s. 82 of the Countryside and Rights of Way Act 2000 been made?

National Parks

8.2. Is the property within a National Park designated under s. 7 of the National Parks and Access to the Countryside Act 1949?"

This optional enquiry concerns areas of outstanding natural beauty and national parks designated by the Countryside Agency (or, in Wales, the Countryside Council), which may affect the property. It is normally asked by a buyer who is concerned that any proposals for development of the property may be hampered by such a designation.

The Countryside Agency (formerly the Countryside Commission and originally the National Parks Commission) was established by the National Parks and Access to the Countryside Act 1949 with the functions of:

(i) encouraging the preservation and enhancement of natural beauty in England and Wales, and particularly in those areas designated as national parks or areas of outstanding natural beauty; and

(ii) encouraging the provision or improvement, for persons resorting to national parks, of facilities for the enjoyment thereof, and for the enjoyment of the opportunities for open-air recreation and the study of nature.

These functions are now performed in England by the Agency and in Wales by the Countryside Council, established under provisions contained in the Environmental Protection Act 1990. References in this commentary to "the Commission" should be taken to include the Countryside Council for Wales.

Optional Enquiry 8.1: Areas of Outstanding Natural Beauty

An area of outstanding natural beauty is not a national park. The terms are mutually exclusive. Under section 82 of the Countryside and Rights of Way Act 2000, the Agency may make orders designating areas of outstanding natural beauty, if it is felt desirable in the interests of preserving that beauty. These powers are derived from provisions originally contained in section 87 of the National Parks and Access to the Countryside Act 1949 under which most existing areas of outstanding natural beauty were established.

Before making an order designating an area of outstanding natural beauty, the Agency must consult all councils whose areas include any part of the area to which the order is to relate. Then it must publish notice of intention to make the order in the *London Gazette* and the local newspapers circulating in the areas affected. This gives the public the opportunity to make representations or objections.

The order must then be submitted to and confirmed by the Secretary of State (in Wales, the National Assembly for Wales), who must be supplied with copies of all observations made by each affected council and the public. The Secretary of State or Assembly may then confirm the order, modify it or refuse to confirm it.

Copies of the order must be kept by each council whose area includes part of the area designated, and must be available for inspection by the public at all reasonable times.

The Government encourages the Agency in its objectives of conserving natural beauty. It is generally considered that areas of outstanding natural beauty, when designated, should be used to meet the demand for recreation so far as this is consistent with the conservation of natural beauty and the needs of agriculture.

Once an area of outstanding natural beauty is confirmed by the Secretary of State or Assembly this may be taken as recognition by the Government of the national importance of the natural beauty of the area designated. Councils, as local planning authorities, should have regard to the existence of areas of outstanding natural beauty within or covering their areas, and take them into account in preparing their local plans, and in making decisions on planning applications.

The Government recognizes that in general it is inappropriate to permit the siting of major industrial and commercial development in areas of outstanding natural beauty, and that only "proven national interest and lack of alternative sites" justifies an exception. Applications for planning permission for such major industrial development in areas of outstanding natural beauty are unlikely to be successful.

Over forty areas of outstanding natural beauty have so far been designated, covering something over 20,000 sq km in area, ranging from the Scilly Isles (16 sq km) and Chichester Harbour (75 sq km) to the Cotswolds (2,038 sq km) and the North Wessex Downs (1,738 sq km), and including such areas as the Quantock Hills, the Malvern Hills, the Isle of Wight, the Chilterns, the Sussex Downs, the Wye Valley and the Northumberland Coast.

Broadly, the effects of designating an area as an area of outstanding natural beauty are that:

   (i)   the Countryside Agency advises the council on any development proposed within the area of outstanding natural beauty, if it is consulted by the council;

   (ii)   the council must consult the Countryside Agency when preparing its development plan (structure plan, local plan, regional spatial strategy etc.; see enquiry 1.2 above);

(iii) the council has power to preserve and enhance the natural beauty of the area;

(iv) the council may make by-laws regulating land owned by it in the area of outstanding natural beauty;

(v) the range of permitted development under the General Permitted Development Order (see enquiry 3.9(j) above) may be restricted.

Summary

Optional enquiry 8.1 concerns whether the property lies within an area of outstanding natural beauty. Whether an affirmative or negative reply is to be preferred depends on the buyer's circumstances, and on what the buyer wishes to do with the land or buildings. A buyer of residential property, for instance, may well be happy living in an area of outstanding natural beauty with the protection afforded to the area from adverse planning applications. A developer wishing to establish substantial industrial premises in the area is, however, likely to be disappointed by an affirmative reply to this enquiry, since a planning application for such a development is bound to be questionable. Small industries, though, may be received favourably by the council as local planning authority. Applications to use, for example, derelict or redundant farm buildings for small industrial concerns may be successful. Any new building in an area of outstanding natural beauty will be expected to be in harmony with the landscape and architecture of the area, and a prospective buyer must be prepared for this.

Optional Enquiry 8.2: National Parks

National parks are designated by the Agency under the provisions of section 7 of the National Parks and Access to the Countryside Act 1949 as part of the Agency's general duty to make provision for the preservation and enhancement of the natural beauty of the countryside, and its use and enjoyment. National parks are extensive tracts of country in England and Wales which, by reason of their natural beauty, and the opportunities they afford for open-air recreation (having regard to their character and position in relation to population centres), are especially worthy of preservation and enhancement.

The Agency's duty in relation to national parks is to determine (and keep under review) those tracts of country appropriate for designation and protection. Before making an order designating a national park, the Agency must consult all local planning authorities affected by the proposed designation. Designation is by way of an order which describes the area by reference to a map and other descriptive statement and notation. Orders made by the Agency have to be confirmed by the Secretary of State. Before submission for confirmation, notice of the effect of the order and the date upon which it was made must be published in the *London Gazette* and local newspapers. An opportunity must be given for the public to inspect the order and map over a period of at least twenty-eight days. If no objection or representation is lodged, the Secretary of State may confirm a national park order as unopposed, with or without modifications. If objections are lodged, the Secretary of State must convene a public local inquiry and afford objectors the opportunity of being heard by an inspector before a decision is taken to confirm the order. If confirmed, further publicity must be given to the order.

The Agency has a duty to secure that copies of confirmed orders relating to national parks are maintained at its offices and at the offices of each local authority, for inspection by the public at all reasonable times. The Agency may also determine that copies of the order and map be maintained in or near the national park itself.

The principal consequences of designation of an area as a national park may be summarised as follows:

(i)   the park is administered by a special National Park Authority;

(ii)   the National Park Authority is the local planning authority for all planning functions in the area of the national park;

(iii) there are restrictions on permitted development rights under the General Permitted Development Order (see the commentary on enquiry 3.9.(j) above);

(iv) the right to undertake certain types of agricultural and forestry development is subject to an obligation to notify (and sometimes to obtain the approval of) the local planning authority;

(v)   the Agency may give advice and make recommendations to the National Park Authority and the Secretary of State on planning issues associated with the national park, and must be consulted by the local planning authority in the preparation of development plans;

(vi) the National Park Authority itself has power to take action for the preservation and enhancement of natural beauty within the area, and must seek to foster the economic and social well-being of local communities within the park (without incurring significant expenditure);

(vii) the local planning authority may provide accommodation, meals and refreshments, camping sites and parking places, either in a national park or on land in its neighbourhood, and may use compulsory purchase powers to this end;

(viii) a local planning authority whose area includes a national park with a waterway (including one bounded by the sea) may provide public sailing, boating, bathing or fishing facilities, and other forms of recreation. The local planning authority may use compulsory purchase powers to this end.

Between 1950 and 1957 ten national parks were designated under the legislation. These range from the Pembrokeshire coast (583 sq km) and Exmoor (693 sq km) to Snowdonia (2,171 sq km) and the Lake District (2,292 sq km). The other designated national parks are the Peak District; Dartmoor; the North Yorkshire Moors; the Yorkshire Dales; Northumberland and the Brecon Beacons. No further parks have yet been designated, but Dartmoor was the subject of a National Park Variation Order in 1994.

Summary

Optional enquiry 8.2 concerns whether the property lies within a national park. Whether an affirmative or negative reply will be preferred by a buyer is again largely a matter of the buyer's plans for the property. There are obviously considerable attractions for a residential buyer in view of the limited forms of development which will attract planning permission. Developers intending to establish substantial industrial or commercial premises would not normally choose a national park in which to locate their enterprises. The restrictions on permitted development rights should be further investigated by the intending buyer of property in a national park. As the National Park Authority is the local planning authority for national parks, enquiry should be made of that authority as to the detailed planning position, except perhaps by the intending buyer of purely residential property.

Optional Enquiry 9: Pipe-lines

"Has a map been deposited under s. 35 of the Pipelines Act 1962, or Schedule 7 of the Gas Act 1986, showing a pipeline laid through, or within 100 feet (30.48 metres) of the property?"

This optional enquiry is designed to reveal pipe-lines laid or to be laid in close proximity to the property. It is likely to be asked by a buyer who is aware of the possible presence of such a pipe-line.

The Pipe-lines Act 1962

A "pipe-line", as defined in the Pipe-lines Act 1962, is a pipe or system of pipes for the conveyance of any thing other than air, water, water vapour or steam. A drain or a sewer is not a pipe-line.

The Pipe-lines Act 1962 was passed with the purpose of controlling, in the interests of the public, the construction and diversion of pipe-lines, and to regulate, in the interests of safety, their construction, operation and maintenance.

There are two main types of pipe-line:

- a "cross country pipe-line", the length of which exceeds, or will when constructed exceed, ten miles (from 1 January 1995, 16.093 kilometres);
- a "local pipe-line" – any other shorter pipe-line.

A cross country pipe-line cannot be constructed unless the Secretary of State has issued construction authorisation. It must be constructed along the route marked on the map annexed to such an authorisation. Works for the construction of the pipe-line must generally be commenced within twelve months of the grant of the authorisation.

There are detailed provisions for the procedure to be followed in applying for the authorisation, including the service of notices and plans specifying the points between which the pipe-line is to run, a statement of what is proposed to be conveyed in it, and the holding of an oral inquiry or an inquiry by written representations into any objections.

A local pipe-line did not need a construction authorisation, but at least sixteen weeks before works were commenced on its construction, notice of intention to commence works had to be given to the Secretary of State; the notice had to be accompanied by a plan showing the route of the pipe-line.

Once again, works on construction of the pipe-line then had to commence within twelve months of the notice of intention. The requirement to notify the Secretary of State in advance of constructing a local pipe-line was abolished with effect from 3 April 1999 by virtue of the Deregulation (Pipe-lines) Order 1999. But local pipe-lines must still be authorised by a planning permission under the normal planning system.

Further provisions in the Act controlling the construction of pipe-lines cover such matters as:

(i)   diversion of pipe-lines (similar authorisations have to be obtained if the diversion is to a cross-country pipe-line);

(ii) removal of works executed in contravention of an authorisation;

(iii) provisions for the avoidance of construction of superfluous pipe-lines;

(iv) preservation of amenity;

(v)   protection against water pollution;

(vi) obligation to restore agricultural land;

(vii) safety of pipe-lines.

As soon as the construction authorisation is granted (in the case of a cross country pipe-line), the person who has been granted the authorisation must deposit with each council through whose area the pipe-line is to be constructed a copy of the map annexed to the authorisation showing that part of the pipe-line which is to be constructed through the area of the council.

The requirements to deposit maps are contained in section 35 of the Pipe-lines Act. Failure to deposit them renders the person in default liable to prosecution, and, on conviction, to a fine.

The maps must be kept at the council offices and must be available for public inspection at all reasonable hours free of charge.

The Gas Act 1986

By virtue of section 58 of the Pipe-lines Act, the general provisions of that Act do not apply to pipe-lines laid for the supply of gas by a public gas supplier. However, certain of those provisions, namely those relating to the protection of pipe-lines imperilled by buildings, structures or deposits, did apply to gas pipe-lines other than those laid in a street, or service pipes, provided a map showing the route of these had been deposited with the council.

In brief, the provisions, which have now been repealed, were that, if the public gas supplier deposited a map with the council showing the route of the gas pipe-line (this map had also to be kept at the council offices and open to the public at all reasonable hours), then in certain circumstances buildings or structures erected close to the pipe-line could be ordered to be demolished. In particular, if a person so constructed a building that part of it was situated less than ten feet (from 1 January 1995, three metres) away from the pipe-line route, and the Minister was satisfied that the pipe-line might be damaged as a result, he could, after conducting an inquiry into the matter, order the building to be demolished or order other works to be carried out to the building so as to safeguard the pipe-line.

Similarly, if, without the consent of the Secretary of State, a person deposited earth, refuse or other materials within ten feet (from 1 January 1995, three metres) of a pipe-line route then, unless the materials were deposited in the course of agriculture or certain street works, the Secretary of State could have them removed and recover the expenses of so doing from the owner of the land on which they were deposited.

These provisions on the protection of pipe-lines relate to all pipe-lines, but applied to gas pipe-lines only if the map which was required to be deposited under paragraph 5(3) of schedule 7 to the Gas Act was duly deposited with the council.

Summary
Optional enquiry 9 concerns whether a pipe-line map has been deposited with the council (and is therefore open to public inspection) under section 35 of the Pipe-lines Act after authorisation for construction or diversion of a pipe-line has been obtained; or under schedule 7 to the Gas Act relating specifically to the pipe-line protection provisions which would thereby apply to a gas pipe-line in the area. The enquiry is aimed specifically at eliciting information regarding pipe-lines within 100 feet (or 30.48 metres) of the property (and this means within that distance of any part of the property). A buyer normally favours a negative reply, preferring not to purchase a property so close to a pipe-line. If the property to be purchased is in fact within ten feet (or three metres) of the route of a pipe-line, gas or otherwise, there is the possibility that the property may be the subject of a demolition order if it is subsequently found adversely to affect the condition or safety of the pipe-line.

Optional Enquiry 10: Houses in Multiple Occupation

"Is the property a house in multiple occupation, or is it designated or proposed to be designated for selective licensing of residential accommodation in accordance with the Housing Act 2004?"

This optional enquiry relates to houses in multiple occupation and their licensing, as provided for by the Housing Act 2004. It also relates to selective licensing of residential accommodation. The enquiry is normally raised by a buyer of a house which is already in multiple occupation or has been adapted for such use.

The provisions formerly contained in sections 346 and 347 of the Housing Act 1985 have been repealed and replaced by a new regime for houses in multiple occupation (HMOs) contained in the 2004 Act.

Definition of a House in Multiple Occupation

The basic definition of an HMO in the 1985 Act was "a house which is occupied by persons who do not form a single household". Further specific provision was made for flats in multiple occupation. The new definition, contained within sections 254 to 259 of the Housing Act 2004, is much more complex, but may be summarised as follows. To constitute an HMO, a building must satisfy one of the following:

- the standard test;
- the self-contained flat test; or
- the converted building test.

Alternatively, it must:

- be the subject of an HMO declaration; or
- be a converted block of flats to which section 257 applies.

Most HMOs are covered by the standard test and are, for example, bedsit accommodation or shared houses or hotels. The building must consist of one or more units of accommodation not consisting of self-contained flats. It must be occupied by persons who do not form a single household, and the occupiers must occupy the accommodation as their only or main residences. Occupation of the living accommodation by residential occupiers must constitute the only use of the accommodation. Rent must be payable, or the provision of services by way of payment must be due. Finally, there must be some element of sharing between households of one of more of the basic facilities (lavatory, personal washing facilities, cooking facilities), or one or more of these facilities must be lacking.

To satisfy the self-contained flat test, the premises, to constitute an HMO, must meet substantially the conditions of the standard test, but instead constitute a self-contained flat, which is also defined in section 254 of the Act.

The converted building test is concerned with buildings or parts of buildings that have been partly converted into self-contained flats. Conditions similar to those for the standard test apply.

HMO declarations are dealt with in section 255 of the Act, which provides a mechanism for the local housing authority to declare a building or part of a building to be an HMO, where one of the three tests above would apply, but the population of the building is so transient or fluctuating that the "sole use" condition of occupation cannot easily be shown to exist. For such a declaration to be made, the occupation of the premises by people who do not form a single household as their only or main residence must be a "significant use" of the relevant property.

To constitute an HMO as a converted block of flats, the building works which converted the building must have failed to comply with appropriate building standards at the time of conversion, and continue to fail to comply. Furthermore, fewer than two thirds of the flats must be owner-occupied. Accordingly, whether or not a converted block of flats is an HMO may well vary from time to time depending on whether the owners of the flats sub-let them.

Licensing of HMOs

Broadly speaking, a property is defined as an HMO if it fulfils one of the above five tests. The Housing Act 2004 introduced a mandatory scheme for the control of conditions in HMOs. While it is not envisaged that all HMOs should be licensed, and regulations to define the ambit of the mandatory scheme are to be made, the intention of the Government is that mandatory licensing will apply to HMOs with three or more storeys and five or more occupiers.

Where a property is an HMO as defined, it must have a licence, unless there is a temporary exemption notice in force in relation to it. The licence specifies the maximum number of households or persons who may occupy the house. Before granting a licence, the housing authority must be satisfied that the licence holder is a fit and proper person and that the HMO is being managed effectively. Certain licence conditions must be imposed on all licences, and the housing authority has discretion to impose further conditions. Failure to obtain a licence and breach of licence conditions are criminal offences. Furthermore, in certain circumstances, a landlord may be required to repay rent received during the period when the HMO was unlicensed. Where there is no prospect of an HMO being licensed, the housing authority may, to protect the health, safety and welfare of the occupiers or neighbours, assume control of an HMO by making a management order.

Licences may be varied by the local housing authority and they may be revoked for serious breach of licensing conditions, or because the authority considers that the licence holder is no longer a fit and proper person. Licences are not transferable.

Serious criminal offences are established in connection with HMO licensing. If an HMO is not licensed when it is subject to the mandatory scheme or a scheme for additional licensing, the person having control of the HMO commits an offence. Over-occupation of an HMO renders the manager or person having control liable to prosecution if that person can be shown to have knowingly allowed the house to be occupied by more households than is permitted. Failure to comply with a licence condition is also an offence. Although, historically, fines for offences in relation to HMOs have been relatively low, the 2004 Housing Act has substantially increased the level of fines for certain offences. Failure to licence, or permitting over-occupation, may attract a fine up to £20,000. Breach of a licence condition is punishable by a fine up to £5,000.

Selective Licensing of Other Residential Accommodation

Part 3 of the Housing Act 2004 introduced the concept of selective licensing by local authorities in the private rented sector. The rationale for this regime was said to be the problem with the management of the private rented sector in some areas of low housing demand, where the absence of owner occupiers wishing to live in the area has sometimes led to an influx of landlords speculating in property.

Part 3 licensing applies to a house if it is in an area for the time being designated under section 80 of the Act as subject to selective licensing, where the whole of the house is occupied either under a single tenancy, or under two or more tenancies in respect of different dwellings contained in it. Under section 80, a local housing authority may designate either its entire district, or a part of it, as subject to selective licensing, provided the authority is satisfied that the area is, or is likely to become, an area of low lousing demand and that making the designation will, when combined with other measures it intends to take, contribute to the improvement of the social and economic conditions in the area. To qualify for designation, the area in question must also be experiencing significant and persistent problems of anti-social behaviour, which are not being helped by the attitude of private sector landlords who have premises in the area.

Once designated (and the designation has to be confirmed by the Secretary of State or, in Wales, the National Assembly) the area's designation lasts up to five years from its inception, unless revoked by the licensing authority which introduced the designation.

All houses covered by a part 3 designation must be licensed, unless they are already HMOs (see above), or are the subject of temporary exemption or of a management order made by the local housing authority (effectively taking over control of the house because of its condition). The part 3 licence authorises occupation of the house under one or more tenancies. A licence is granted only if the authority is satisfied that the proposed licence-holder is a fit and proper person and the one most appropriate to hold a licence. The authority needs to be satisfied that the proposed manager is either the person having control of the house or his agent or employee, that the manager is also a fit and proper person, and that the proposed management arrangements for the house are otherwise satisfactory.

The licence itself may include such conditions as the housing authority considers appropriate, including restrictions or prohibitions on the use or occupation of particular parts of the house, and conditions requiring that reasonable steps be taken to prevent or reduce anti-social behaviour by occupiers or visitors to the house. Conditions requiring facilities or equipment to meet certain standards, obligations to keep it in repair and good working order, and time limits for carrying out necessary repairs, may be imposed.

Each part 3 house must have its own licence. They may not last for more than five years. They are not transferable, and they cease on the death of the licence-holder. Licences may be varied by the local housing authority and revoked for serious breach of condition.

A serious criminal offence may be committed by a person having control of or managing a house which is required to be licensed under part 3, but is not so licensed. The fine is a maximum of £20,000. Breach of a licensing condition can lead to a fine of £5,000. Other consequences of running an unlicensed house may include the requirement for the landlord to repay rent received during the unlicensed period, and the landlord may not be able to seek possession from a defaulting tenant.

Summary
Optional enquiry 10 concerns whether the property is an HMO, as defined, or whether it is included in an area, and is a type of house, covered by a designation (actual or proposed) for selective licensing of residential accommodation. A buyer of an HMO will want to know whether the property is regarded as such by the local housing authority. A buyer would also want to know whether it is currently licensed, and the details of the general mandatory, and any additional, licensing conditions, since these may affect the prospects of future licensing in respect of the property. The buyer will almost certainly need a copy of the licence conditions, which will be supplied to him by the council on request and on payment of a modest fee.

If the property is found to be in an area designated or proposed to be designated for selective licensing of residential accommodation under part 3, a prospective landlord would be well advised to investigate further the physical and social conditions pertaining to the area, and the likely licensing conditions that will be imposed. Further enquiries of the local housing authority in this respect would be appropriate.

Optional Enquiry 11: Noise Abatement

"Noise abatement zone

11.1. Have the Council made, or resolved to make, any noise abatement zone order under s. 63 of the Control of Pollution Act 1974 for the area?

Entries in register

11.2. Has any entry been recorded in the noise level register kept pursuant to s. 64 of the Control of Pollution Act 1974?

11.3. If there is any entry, how can copies be obtained and where can that register be inspected?"

This optional enquiry relates to noise abatement zone orders made, or proposed to be made, by the council. It may be asked by a buyer who intends to carry out on the property industrial or other operations which may cause above-average noise levels.

Part III of the Control of Pollution Act 1974 contains part of the code of statutory control of noise nuisance, other parts now being contained in the Environmental Protection Act 1990 and the Noise and Statutory Nuisance Act 1993. Councils may serve noise abatement notices on persons responsible for creating noise nuisances, or on the owners and occupiers of premises from which noise is emitted. These notices may require the abatement of the nuisance. Failure to comply with such a notice amounts to an offence punishable by fine. There are particular provisions for the control of noise on construction sites (noisy operations or machinery) and for the control of noise in streets (loudspeakers etc.).

Optional Enquiry 11.1: Noise Abatement Zones

Under section 63 of the Control of Pollution Act, the council may make an order, known as a noise abatement zone order, designating all or part of its area as a noise abatement zone. The order specifies the classes of premises to which it applies, and these classes of premises are subject to the noise control provisions of the Act once the order is made.

Before making an order, the council must serve a notice on owners and occupiers of all premises of the class which will be affected in the area to be covered. Notice must also be published in the *London Gazette* and the local newspapers. This notice must state the council's proposals to make the order and its general effect. It must also specify a place (normally the council offices) where a copy of the order and the accompanying map may be inspected free of charge at all reasonable times for at least six weeks. This notice gives those persons to be affected by the order an opportunity to object to it.

If objections to the order are made, the council must normally consider them, but since these orders no longer require the confirmation of the Secretary of State, they may come into force on a date specified in the order itself, or on such later date as the council may decide.

Although a council has a duty to inspect its area from time to time to decide how to exercise its powers concerning noise abatement zones, it has been held that there is no obligation to make such an inspection before making an order, and the fact that no inspection has been made does not invalidate a noise abatement zone order.

Summary
Optional enquiry 11.1 concerns whether the council has made, or decided to make, an order designating a noise abatement zone covering the area which includes the property. A buyer of industrial premises may be concerned if the processes he intends to carry out are of a noisy nature, and would therefore normally prefer a negative reply.

Optional Enquiries 11.2 and 11.3: Entries in the Register
Under section 64 of the Control of Pollution Act, a council which has designated a noise abatement zone by order in its area must measure the levels of noise emanating from premises within the zone (provided they are of a class of premises specified in the order) and record all measurements in a register, called the noise level register, which must be maintained by the council.

A copy of the recordings of measurements taken must be served on the owner and occupier of the premises, and that person may, within twenty-eight days, appeal to the Secretary of State against the record. The Secretary of State may issue directions to the council, and the council must comply with any such directions.

The noise level register is open to public inspection at the council offices at all reasonable times free of charge, and copies of the entries must be provided on request and on payment of a reasonable charge.

Once a noise level is registered for particular premises, that level must not be exceeded except with the consent of the council. The council may give consent subject to conditions as to the amount by which the level of noise may be increased, and the days and hours during which it may be increased. These conditions are recorded in the noise level register.

A person who applies for consent to exceed the registered noise level for particular premises, and is refused consent, may appeal to the Secretary of State within three months; the council must comply with the decision of the Secretary of State.

It is an offence to allow noise to be emitted from registered premises in excess of the registered noise level, and the magistrates' court may impose a fine for this offence. The court may also order the owner of the premises to carry out works to prevent the nuisance recurring, for example, to install noise insulation measures.

Where new buildings are to be erected which fall within a class of premises specified in a noise abatement zone order, or where a building is being converted into a class of building specified in such an order, the owner or any person who is negotiating to buy the land or building can ask the council to determine the noise level which will be acceptable as emanating from the premises when constructed or converted. Any noise level so determined is entered in the noise level register for the premises. Again, there are rights of appeal to the Secretary of State against the council's decision.

The council may also serve a noise reduction notice in respect of premises to which a noise abatement zone order applies, if it considers that the level of noise emanating from those premises is unacceptable, provided that the proposed reduction of noise is achievable at reasonable expense and would result in benefit to the public. A noise reduction notice may include conditions as to times of the day and days of the week during which the noise level is to be reduced. The details of the notice are also entered in the noise level register. There is a right of appeal against the notice to the magistrates' court, but it is an offence punishable by a fine not to comply with a noise reduction notice if no appeal is made, or if an appeal has failed.

Summary

Optional enquiry 11.2 concerns whether there are any entries in the noise level register relating to the premises. A buyer will prefer a negative reply, meaning that there is no restriction on the level of noise caused by operations on the premises. If the reply is affirmative, the buyer will want to know details, such as the level of noise registered for the premises; measurements taken by the council; whether any appeals have been made to the Secretary of State, and if so the outcome; and whether or not a noise reduction notice has been served in respect of the premises.

Optional enquiry 11.3 is about the place where the register can be inspected and how copies of entries can be obtained. A buyer will want to know this, if the reply to optional enquiry 11.2 is in the affirmative, so that details of all registrations can be ascertained. The register must be kept at the principal office of the council and is administered by environmental health officers. The council must provide facilities for copies of entries to be taken, but is entitled to levy a reasonable charge for this service.

Optional Enquiry 12: Urban Development Areas

"12.1. Is the area an urban development area designated under Part XVI of the Local Government, Planning and Land Act 1980?
12.2. If so, please state the name of the urban development corporation and the address of its principal office."

This optional enquiry concerns areas designated as urban development areas, and urban development corporations. It is normally asked by a buyer of property in an area of derelict or run down land, mainly in the centres of old towns or where it is known that an urban development corporation has been established.

The Local Government, Planning and Land Act of 1980 provided for the designation of urban development areas and the establishment of urban development corporations. These corporations are set up with the purpose of regenerating areas of derelict and run down land, in the national interest.

The areas are designated by the Secretary of State, and the corporations established to provide their regeneration are also established by Parliament.

A corporation consists of a chairman, deputy chairman and up to eleven other members appointed by the Secretary of State (they are not elected). They are people who have a special knowledge of the relevant locality.

The objects of an urban development corporation are principally to secure regeneration of its area. It must do this by bringing derelict land and buildings into effective use; by encouraging the development of new industry and commerce; by measures designed to enhance the environment; and by ensuring that housing and social facilities are available within the area to encourage people to live and work there.

Wide powers are conferred on urban development corporations by the Local Government, Planning and Land Act. In particular they have power to purchase, manage, reclaim and sell land and buildings; carry out building operations; make arrangements for the provision of water, electricity, gas and sewerage services; carry on businesses for these purposes; and do anything else necessary to achieve the primary object of regenerating the area. In addition, the corporations may make financial contributions toward the costs of councils and statutory undertakers in the discharge of these functions, and may contribute towards the costs of providing certain amenities.

Powers of Urban Development Corporations

The particular powers and functions of an urban development corporation are contained in the order of the Secretary of State establishing the corporation. Specific powers vested in the corporations are as follows.

Power to Acquire Land

The Secretary of State may confiscate land vested in a council or other public body such as a statutory undertaker and vest it in the corporation by order, subject to the payment of compensation. The corporation may also buy land by agreement or by the use of compulsory powers. Land acquired by an urban development corporation must be in the urban development area; adjacent to that area and required for the discharge of the corporation's functions in the area; or, whether or not adjacent to the area, required for the provision of services within the area.

Disposal of Land

The urban development corporation has a relatively free hand in disposing of its land for securing the overall object of regeneration of the area which it administers. The corporation must, so far as is possible, provide for the reaccommodation of people who were living or carrying on business or other activities on the land when it was acquired, and who wish to return to the area. Land offered to these people by the corporation must be suitable for their reasonable requirements, although, curiously, the corporation is not obliged to offer to such a person who was previously carrying on the business of a public house or off-licence, alternative accommodation suitable for this purpose.

The corporation, in both disposing of land and developing it, must have regard to the need for preserving features of special architectural and historic interest, and in particular listed buildings.

Planning Functions

The urban development corporation may submit to the Secretary of State proposals for the development of any land in its area. The Secretary of State consults the council as the local planning authority for the area and may then approve the proposals. When the proposals are approved, the Secretary of State may make a special development order granting automatic planning permission for any development within the urban development area which is in accordance with the proposals. In this way, the council, which is normally the local planning authority, may have its responsibilities for considering planning applications taken away. The urban development corporation virtually becomes, in these circumstances, the local planning authority. Indeed, the Secretary of State may actually make the urban development corporation the local planning authority for part or all of its area, giving it the power and duty to receive and consider all applications for planning permission for development within the area or that part of the area defined in the order.

Orders of the Secretary of State vesting planning control duties and powers in urban development corporations may also make the corporation responsible for the exercise of a wide variety of powers otherwise exercised by the council as local planning authority, and the council is not able to exercise the powers in its own area if the order so specifies.

Powers of local planning authorities under the Town and Country Planning Act and the Planning (Listed Buildings and Conservation Areas) Act, which may be vested in an urban development corporation, include the following:

- control of listed buildings;
- building preservation notices;
- tree preservation orders;
- control of advertisements;
- enforcement notices;
- stop notices;
- listed building enforcement notices;
- urgent works for preservation of unoccupied listed buildings;
- compulsory purchase of listed buildings in need of repair;
- listed buildings repairs notices;
- conservation area designation.

Other Powers

Further powers which may be vested in an urban development corporation may include building control functions; housing authority functions; the granting of rent rebates; the declaration of streets as highways maintainable at the public expense; sewerage functions; public health functions; and the granting of loans.

The first urban development corporations to be established were the Merseyside Development Corporation (covering approximately 865 acres of land in Liverpool and the Wirral) and the London Docklands Development Corporation (approximately 5,120 acres in Greater London). Further corporations were established in 1987 at Trafford, the Black Country, Teesside, Tyne and Wear and Cardiff Bay.

The intention always was that urban development corporations would be dissolved when their work is done and the area has been regenerated. At this time the assets of the corporation are transferred to the relevant councils or statutory undertakers. All the corporations in England have been, or are in the final processes of being, wound up. No future corporations have been created.

Summary

Optional enquiry 12.1 concerns whether the property is situated in an urban development area. If so, the buyer is well advised to make enquiries as to the powers of the urban development corporation and its functions, since it may well be that it was the corporation, and not the council, which was the effective local planning authority for the area. If the corporation has not been fully wound up, further enquiries could be made as to when this process is expected to be complete, and as to whom any enquiries relating to the property should be addressed.

Optional enquiry 12.2 should reveal the name and principal office address of the urban development corporation, to facilitate the buyer's enquiries into the corporation's powers and responsibilities. If the winding-up of the corporation is complete, the enquirer will normally be referred back to the council for advice.

Optional Enquiry 13: Enterprise Zones

"Is the area an enterprise zone designated under Part XVIII of the Local Government, Planning and Land Act 1980?"

This optional enquiry concerns enterprise zones established in the area where the property is situated, and is normally asked by a buyer of industrial or commercial premises, or a buyer of land who wishes to construct or adapt premises for these purposes.

Under the Local Government, Planning and Land Act 1980 (section 179 and schedule 32), provision was made for selected district councils (or London borough councils) to be invited by the Secretary of State to prepare schemes for areas with a view to their being designated as enterprise zones. Once a scheme is adopted and the zone designated, development for purposes specified in the scheme is granted automatic planning permission, and certain premises in the zone were originally exempted from the liability to pay business rates. There are therefore, in designated enterprise zones, considerable planning control and other advantages for industrial and commercial premises. The idea is to encourage industrial and commercial activity by the removal of some tax burdens and by speeding up planning and other administrative controls.

The Procedure for Designation

The first step in designating an enterprise zone is for the Secretary of State to invite the council to prepare a scheme. The Secretary of State specifies the proposed area and may make directions as to what provisions the scheme shall contain.

The council then prepares the scheme, if it wishes (it is not obliged to do so, but if it does, it must contain the provisions as directed by the Secretary of State). The council must publicise the scheme it has prepared, and give an opportunity for representations about it to be made to the council within a specified period of time. The council must then consider any representations made.

Once any representations have been considered, the council may formally adopt the scheme, with or without modifications, and give public notification of its adoption in the *London Gazette* and local newspapers, placing a copy of it on deposit at the offices of the council for public inspection. The public may request copies of the scheme, which must be provided at reasonable cost. The importance of the opportunity to inspect the scheme lies in the fact that it will reveal the forms of development that will automatically be granted planning permission in the event that the area is designated as an enterprise zone.

Any person who is aggrieved by the provisions of the scheme adopted by the council may question the validity of the scheme within six weeks of its publication in the press, by making application to the High Court.

The final step is designation of the enterprise zone. This is done by the Secretary of State, if he thinks it expedient to do so, once the six-week period referred to above has passed or, if an application to question the scheme's validity has been made to the High Court, once those proceedings have been dealt with.

The Secretary of State designates the enterprise zone by order which specifies:

(i)   the date the designation takes effect;
(ii)   the period it is to remain in force (normally ten years);
(iii) the boundaries of the zone (by reference to a map); and
(iv) the enterprise zone authority (the council which was invited to prepare the scheme).

Further publicity must then be given about the designation, and an advertisement must be placed in the *London Gazette* and local newspaper containing a statement that the enterprise zone has been created and that a copy of the scheme pursuant to which it was created can be inspected at the council's offices.

The Secretary of State may modify enterprise zones but not so as to alter boundaries, change the enterprise zone authority or reduce the period during which the zone is to be an enterprise zone.

Over one hundred enterprise zones have to date been designated in areas such as Swansea, Salford, Trafford, Gateshead, Newcastle, Hartlepool, Liverpool, the Isle of Dogs, Wellingborough, North West Kent, North East Lancashire and Telford.

Certain consequences of designation as an enterprise zone may be of advantage to a buyer of commercial or industrial property, or a buyer who wishes to establish commercial or industrial undertakings in the zone. These are outlined below.

Planning and Development Control

One of the main reasons for designating an area as an enterprise zone is to encourage and attract the growth of industrial and commercial undertakings in the area, and for this reason it is desirable that planning permission for such development should be easier to obtain. The order designating the zone has the effect of granting automatic planning permission for any class of development specified in the scheme. These automatic planning permissions are subject only to the conditions specified in the enterprise zone scheme, and if none is specified, the permission for that class of development is unconditional. The scheme therefore provides a form of permitted development rights, although the enterprise zone authority may, with the approval of the Secretary of State, withdraw these rights by direction.

Development authorised under an automatic planning permission provided by the order designating an enterprise zone is no longer permitted once the zone terminates (normally ten years from its designation). Thereafter, application for formal permission to implement development must be made to the council as local planning authority, unless the development had commenced before the enterprise zone terminated.

Rates and Other Advantages

Exemption from the liability to pay business rates (but not water rates or charges) was originally granted in respect of any premises exempted under an enterprise zone scheme for so long as the zone remains so designated. All premises in an enterprise zone used to qualify for this exemption, except private dwellinghouses, garages and storage premises, and certain premises owned by public utility companies. The exemption, and other financial advantages associated with enterprise zones, have, however, since been removed.

Apart from the streamlining of the planning process in enterprise zones, there are further advantages to owners of such premises in such zones. These include exemption from the requirement to pay industrial training levies under the Industrial Training Act 1982. The last enterprise zone, however, was designated in 1996, and further designations are unlikely.

Summary

Optional enquiry 13 concerns whether the property lies within an enterprise zone. A buyer of commercial or industrial property, or one who wishes to establish such an undertaking, would be pleased with an affirmative reply in view of the substantial planning advantages available. Such a buyer would, however, be wise to request a copy of the scheme on which the designation was based for full details of permitted development and the conditions that may be imposed on such development by the automatic planning permission provisions of the scheme.

Optional Enquiry 14: Inner Urban Improvement Areas

"Have the Council resolved to define the area as an improvement area under s. 4 of the Inner Urban Areas Act 1978?"

This optional enquiry is concerned with improvement areas declared in inner urban areas under provisions contained in the Inner Urban Areas Act 1978. It is normally asked by the buyer of industrial or commercial property or a buyer who wishes to establish such a concern within an inner urban area.

The Inner Urban Areas Act introduced measures intended to deal with inner city decay. The measures are intended to attract new development to these areas by the offer of grants and loans to facilitate such development.

Districts may be designated under the Act by the Secretary of State if it is considered that "special social need" exists in an "inner urban area" within that district, and that conditions could be alleviated by invoking the powers in the Act. The Secretary of State may designate by order the whole or any part of the district concerned, and the council for the district or county becomes the "designated district authority".

Once designated, the council, as designated district authority, may make loans to persons to enable them to acquire land or carry out works if such acquisition or works would benefit the designated district. Loans of up to ninety per cent of the value of the property to be purchased, or of the value of that property after the works have been carried out, may be made; these loans are secured by mortgages at rates of interest fixed by the Treasury, repayable over a maximum of thirty years.

A number of districts have been designated under this Act. They include Barnsley, Burnley, Doncaster, Dudley, Greenwich, Hartlepool, Lewisham, Rotherham, Walsall and Wigan.

The district authority for each of the areas designated by the Secretary of State (generally, the district or county council for the area concerned) may declare an improvement area under section 4 of the Act if satisfied that conditions within an area (which is predominantly industrial or commercial in nature) could be improved by the exercise of their powers to make grants and loans.

The council, as designated district authority, must first pass a resolution declaring the area to be an improvement area, specifying a date on which the declaration is to take effect (at least three months after the date of the resolution). The council must then publish in the local newspaper notice of the effect of the resolution, identifying the area to be declared an improvement area, and specifying a place where a copy of the resolution and a map defining the area concerned can be inspected at all reasonable times. A copy of the resolution and the map must also be sent to the Secretary of State.

Termination of an improvement area (whether all of the area or part of it) is dealt with in a similar way, that is, by resolution of the council, publicity of the resolution and a map, and despatch of a copy of the resolution and map to the Secretary of State.

Within areas declared by designated district authorities (that is, councils) as improvement areas under section 4, the council may, if satisfied that the carrying out of certain works on land would benefit the area, make loans and grants for enabling those works to be carried out. The works for which such loans or grants may be made are as follows:

- the construction of fencing and walls;
- landscaping and the planting of trees, shrubs and plants;
- clearance or levelling of land;
- cleansing, painting, repair or demolition of structures or buildings; and
- construction of parking spaces, access roads, turning heads or loading bays.

The council may also make grants to people to enable them to carry out, in improvement areas, the conversion, extension, improvement or modification of industrial or commercial buildings, and the conversion of other buildings into industrial or commercial buildings. These grants may not exceed fifty per cent of the cost of carrying out the works, and the authority must be satisfied that the works would benefit the areas concerned.

Summary

Optional enquiry 14 concerns whether the property is situated in an improvement area which the council has resolved to define under section 4 of the Inner Urban Areas Act. A buyer of commercial or industrial premises, or of land which it is intended to be developed for these purposes, normally prefers an affirmative reply since the loans and grants outlined above may then be available.

Optional Enquiry 15: Simplified Planning Zones

"15.1. Is the area a simplified planning zone adopted or approved pursuant to s. 83 of the Town and Country Planning Act 1990?
15.2. Have the Council approved any proposal for designating the area as a simplified planning zone?"

This optional enquiry relates to simplified planning zone schemes proposed or adopted by the local planning authority or approved by the Secretary of State since their introduction to the regime of planning control in 1987.

The adoption (or approval by the Secretary of State) of a simplified planning zone has the effect of granting, in relation to the zone (or any particular part of it), planning permission for the classes of development specified in the scheme. Thus, simplified planning zone schemes operate to confer a form of permitted development rights in respect of property to which they relate. Development of land, within the limits laid down in the scheme, does not require individual planning permission; this is automatically granted by the scheme, subject to any specified conditions or limitations.

The provisions relating to simplified planning zones were first brought into force on 2 November 1987, and are now contained in sections 82 to 87 of the Town and Country Planning Act 1990. There is generally no obligation upon a local planning authority to promote a simplified planning zone. The duty of the local planning authority was to consider, as soon as practicable after the provisions came into force, whether or not such a scheme was desirable for its area (or part of its area), and to keep this question under review. If such a scheme is considered desirable, the local planning authority is under a duty to prepare one.

However, any person has a right to ask the local planning authority to make or alter a scheme. If the authority refuses such a request, the Secretary of State may be asked to intervene. If the Secretary of State, after consultation, is satisfied that a scheme should be made or altered, he may so direct the local planning authority.

Procedure for Establishing a Simplified Planning Zone

The procedure for the introduction of a simplified planning zone scheme is very similar to the local development plan procedures (see enquiry 1.2 above). In outline, it is as follows:

(i) The local planning authority decides to make a scheme (or is directed by the Secretary of State so to do). The Secretary of State must be notified of the local planning authority's decision and the date upon which preparation will begin.

(ii) The local planning authority must consult the Secretary of State for Transport, the county planning authority, parish and community councils, affected landowners and other prescribed consultees, on the proposals.

(iii) The draft scheme must be placed on deposit for public inspection, and sufficient time for objections to be lodged must be given. A copy of the draft scheme must be forwarded to the Secretary of State. Objections must be made in writing within six weeks of the date upon which the proposals are first available for inspection.

(iv) An inquiry may be held into any objections made within the six weeks' time limit. The inquiry inspector reports to the local planning authority rather than to the Secretary of State.

(v) The local planning authority must consider any objections made and the inspector's report, and make decisions and recommendations for action in the light of the report, giving a statement of its reasons for any action proposed. The proposals, as originally prepared or as modified to take account of objections, may then be formally adopted by the local planning authority. The Secretary of State may direct the local planning authority to consider further modifying the proposals, and there is power for the Secretary of State to call them in for his own approval at any time before they are adopted by the authority.

(vi) Adoption (by the local planning authority) or approval (by the Secretary of State) has the effect of granting planning permission in accordance with the scheme in respect of land covered by it, from the date of adoption or approval and for a period of ten years thereafter, but the permission so granted does not lapse with the scheme if development permitted by it has commenced before the scheme expires.

(vii) A simplified planning zone scheme may be altered at any time (subject to the approval of the Secretary of State if the original scheme was subject to such approval). The procedures for alteration of an existing simplified planning zone scheme are substantially the same.

Nature and Effects of a Simplified Planning Zone

A scheme must consist of:
- a map;
- a written statement;
- diagrams, illustrations and descriptive matter, as appropriate.

It must specify:
- the development or classes of development permitted by the scheme;

- the land in relation to which permission is granted;
- any conditions, limitations or exceptions subject to which permission is granted.

A scheme may specify conditions or limitations in respect of particular descriptions of development, much as an ordinary planning permission granted by the local planning authority on application is, more often than not, conditional. However, a simplified planning zone scheme cannot affect the right of any person to do anything which does not itself amount to development (as defined in the Act); or to carry out development for which planning permission is not required (permitted development) or for which planning permission has been granted. Conditions imposed in a simplified planning zone scheme are enforceable by the local planning authority in the same manner as those imposed on the normal grant of planning permission (that is, by service of enforcement notice or breach of condition notice, etc.; see enquiry 3.9 above).

Simplified planning zones cease to have effect ten years after the date of adoption or approval, and planning permission under such a scheme ceases to have effect at that time, except in so far as development authorised by it has been begun.

Certain classes of land may not be included in a simplified planning zone. These are:

- land in a national park;
- land in a conservation area;
- land within the Broads;
- areas of outstanding natural beauty;
- green belt land;
- areas of special scientific interest.

Summary

Optional enquiry 15.1 concerns whether the area including the property enquired about is a simplified planning zone either adopted (by the local planning authority) or approved (by the Secretary of State). If a negative response is given, the general regime of planning control applies, in the absence of any contrary indication elsewhere in the replies (for instance, a reply to the effect that the property lies in a conservation area or enterprise zone). If the response is in the affirmative, the prudent buyer is well advised to press for full details of what is comprised in the scheme, since it may affect future intended development of the property and facilitate those intentions by means of automatic planning permission. The buyer may also be concerned about the possible uses to which premises in the immediate vicinity may be put, without the requirement for formal application for planning permission. The buyer will wish to know the date of adoption (or approval) and the expiry date of the scheme.

Optional enquiry 15.2 asks whether the council has considered and approved proposals for designating a simplified planning zone. This part of the enquiry is relevant where the council has decided to introduce a scheme but the scheme has not yet gone through all the stages – preparation, publicity, consultation and inquiry – leading to formal adoption or approval. Depending on his future intentions for the property, the prudent buyer who obtains an affirmative response to this part of the enquiry is well advised to press for full details of the approved proposals.

Optional Enquiry 16: Land Maintenance Notices

"Have the Council authorised the service of a maintenance notice under s. 215 of the Town and Country Planning Act 1990?"

This optional enquiry concerns the council's powers to secure the proper maintenance of land in its area by the service of a land maintenance notice under the Town and Country Planning Act 1990. The relevant provisions are contained in sections 215 to 219 of that Act.

The council, as local planning authority, is empowered by these provisions to take action, principally in respect of neglected wasteland which has become derelict or unsightly to such an extent that the amenity of the area (or the amenity of an adjoining area) is adversely affected. The power extends to any land within the authority's area and is not, as previously was the case, limited to vacant sites or open land. This provision is a rare example of planning control directed at acts of omission, rather than commission.

If the local planning authority is satisfied that the amenity of part of the area is "adversely affected" by the condition of a particular piece of land, it may serve a notice under section 215 of the 1990 Act on the owner and the occupier of the land in question. The notice requires steps to be taken to remedy the condition of the land within a time specified in the notice. The notice takes effect, subject to any appeal, on the date specified for this purpose in the notice (which must be at least twenty-eight days after service).

Failure to comply with the requirements of a land maintenance notice within the time specified renders the owner or occupier of the land liable to summary prosecution and, on conviction, a fine. It is a defence to prove that failure to comply was attributable to the default of another person specified in the original notice and that the defendant took all reasonable steps to ensure compliance in the circumstances.

Conviction of the offence of non-compliance with the notice does not itself relieve the defendant from the obligation to comply with its requirements; and if all necessary steps are not taken, the offender may be liable to a daily penalty for so long as the requirements of the notice remain unfulfilled.

There are provisions in section 217 of the Act for appeal against a land maintenance notice. Any person on whom such a notice has been served, or any other person with an interest in the land to which it relates, may appeal to the magistrates' court on any of the following grounds:

(i)   the condition of the land does not adversely affect the amenity of the area;

(ii)   the condition of the land is attributable to and arises out of the carrying out of operations which have the benefit of planning permission;

(iii) the requirements of the notice are excessive;

(iv) the period allowed for compliance with the notice is insufficient.

Any appeal must be lodged before the date specified in the notice as the date on which it is to become effective. If an appeal is lodged, the effectiveness of the notice is suspended pending final determination of the appeal, or its withdrawal. In determining an appeal the magistrates may quash the notice, uphold it, or vary its terms in favour of the appellant (but not in favour of the local planning authority).

Either the appellant or the local planning authority may further appeal to the Crown Court.

In default of compliance with the notice the council, as local planning authority, has further direct powers (under section 219 of the Act) to take the required action itself. The council may enter the land to take remedial action, and may recover from the owner of the land for the time being any expenses reasonably incurred. Any expenses are recoverable from the owner or occupier as a simple contract debt.

Land maintenance notices served under section 215 of the 1990 Act are registrable in the register of local land charges and should be revealed by an official search of the register. Until drafted, prepared and served, however, the notice has no legal effect and is not registered. The decision to serve such a notice is normally taken by the council, or its planning committee, after consideration of a report made by its officers. It is this, as yet unexecuted, decision of the council to serve a land maintenance notice that this enquiry is designed to reveal.

Summary

Optional enquiry 16 is intended to reveal whether the council has authorised the service of a land maintenance notice under section 215 of the Town and Country Planning Act. A buyer will prefer a negative answer. If an affirmative response is given, the buyer ought, at the very least, to require full details of the circumstances giving rise to the decision to serve the notice. A buyer who proceeds with the transaction would be obliged to comply or secure compliance with the notice, or appeal against its provisions, and may have to meet any consequential costs of compliance.

Optional Enquiry 17: Mineral Consultation Areas

"Is the area a mineral consultation area notified by the county planning authority under Schedule 1 para 7 of the Town and Country Planning Act 1990?"

This optional enquiry concerns the processing of planning applications by district planning authorities in those areas notified by county planning authorities as mineral consultation areas. The enquiry is not relevant where the property enquired about is in the area of a metropolitan county, London borough or unitary authority.

The general system of planning policy and control under the Town and Country Planning Acts provided for preparation of structure plans by county councils and of local plans by district councils. Preparation of these plans is considered in the commentary on enquiry 1.2 (see above). The day-to-day functions of the local planning authority – considering and determining applications for planning permission and enforcing the regime of planning control by enforcement notice and prosecution – are generally carried out by district councils, acting as the district planning authorities, in areas where there is still a two-tier structure of local government.

Schedule 1 to the Town and Country Planning Act 1990 defines "county matters". These are specific matters in respect of which the local planning authority's functions of determining applications for planning permission are to be exercised by the county planning authority. Most of these "county matters" relate to the winning and working of minerals or the disposal of mineral waste. Some of the more important county matters are:

(i)   the winning and working of minerals in, on or under land, or the erection of buildings, plant and machinery to be used in connection with such an operation;
(ii) the use of land, adjoining land used for the winning and working of minerals, in connection with the adaptation for sale of the minerals;
(iii) the carrying out of searches for and tests of mineral deposits;
(iv) the depositing of mineral waste;
(v)   the use of land for transport by rail or water of aggregates (i.e., sand and gravel, crushed rock, artificial materials of similar appearance);

(vi) the erection of buildings, plant or machinery to be used for the coating of roadstone or production of concrete, on land adjoining land used for the winning and working of minerals;

(vii) the erection of buildings etc. to be used for the manufacture of cement.

Although all applications for planning permission are still to be made to the district planning authority (generally, the district council), that authority must send a copy of any planning application relating to a county matter to the county planning authority, within seven days of receipt. It is then for the county planning authority (county council) to determine the application.

Paragraph 7 of schedule 1 to the 1990 Act provides that local planning authorities in non-metropolitan counties must, when determining planning applications and carrying out statutory consultation procedures, seek the achievement of the overall objectives of any structure plan which is in force in the area. This provision is aimed at securing consistency of approach between district and county planning authorities where the planning function is split between them.

In the interests of reinforcing this consistency of approach and co-operation where there are two tiers of planning authority (that is, other than in London and the metropolitan counties and where new unitary authorities have come into existence), district planning authorities have a statutory obligation to consult their county planning authority colleagues before determining applications for specified types of development.

Of first importance is the duty of the district planning authority to consult the county planning authority before determining any application for planning permission for development which would, by virtue of its scale, nature or effect, conflict with or prejudice policies or proposals contained in a structure plan.

In view of their status as county matters, the county planning authority may notify the district planning authority of any area in which development is considered to be likely to affect or be affected by the winning and working of minerals other than coal. If such notification has been given in writing, the district planning authority is obliged, by virtue of schedule 1 to the 1990 Act, to consult the county planning authority before determining any application for development of land within that area (unless the county planning authority has issued directions authorising such determination without consultation). It is with these so-called "mineral consultation areas" that this enquiry is concerned.

Summary

Optional enquiry 17 is concerned with whether the area in which the property is situated has been notified to the district planning authority as one in respect of which applications for planning permission require consultation with the county planning authority in view of their implications for mineral extraction operations. A buyer normally requires a response to this enquiry only if the intention is to use the property in connection with such an operation, or if such operations are already being undertaken on or in close proximity to it. Consultation with the county planning authority may give rise to delay in the process of a planning application. Close proximity to mineral workings may affect the outcome of an application for planning permission, and special conditions may be attached to the grant.

Optional Enquiry 18: Hazardous Substance Consents

"18.1. Please list any entries in the register kept pursuant to s. 28 of the Planning (Hazardous Substances) Act 1990.

18.2. If there are any entries:

    (a) how can copies of the entries be obtained

    (b) where can the Register be inspected"

This optional enquiry concerns the public register of applications, consents, revocations, modifications and directions issued or made in accordance with the Planning (Hazardous Substances) Act 1990.

The Act brought into force an outline regime of control in respect of defined "hazardous substances", in excess of the "controlled quantity", kept on, over or under land. It is the presence of a hazardous substance on (or over or under) land which requires the consent of the hazardous substances authority, not the use of the land or any buildings on it *per se*. This is an extension of the duties of traditional local planning authorities. Although the regime of hazardous substance control is similar in many ways to the regime of planning control, the emphasis on the presence and nature of the substance, as opposed to the use of the land on which it is present, is recognised by the fact that provisions originally contained in the Town and Country Planning Acts were extracted and consolidated in the 1990 Act.

The Hazardous Substances Authority

The hazardous substances authority for the area, to which application for consent is made, is, in most cases, the local planning authority. In Greater London the authority is the relevant London borough council. Outside London, the district council (or metropolitan district council in a metropolitan area) has this duty; in urban development areas (see optional enquiry 12) it is generally a function of the urban development corporation. In respect of national parks, the hazardous substances authority is the county council. There are separate arrangements relating to the Norfolk and Suffolk Broads (the Broads Authority).

"Hazardous substances" and their respective "controlled quantities" are defined in the Planning (Hazardous Substances) Regulations 1992. Examples include arsenic pentoxide, bromine, chlorine, acetylene and petroleum spirit. The Secretary of State may also prescribe, by regulation, descriptions of land and other circumstances in respect of which hazardous substances consent is not required.

Hazardous Substances Consent

Consent for hazardous substances (referred to in the Act as "hazardous substances consent") is not required if the aggregate quantity of the substance on the land (including other land or structures within 500 metres and controlled by the same person) is less than the prescribed controlled quantity for that substance. The temporary presence of a hazardous substance in transit is not taken into account unless it is unloaded.

Application for Consent

Hazardous substances consent may either be granted on application to the relevant authority; or, in certain limited circumstances, may be deemed to have been given. An applicant need not have an interest in the land to be the subject of the consent, but the owner of the land is required to be notified of any application. Once granted, the consent runs with the land in question and for the benefit of all persons interested in the land from time to time, subject to revocation (see below).

The 1992 regulations set out detailed provisions relating to the form and manner in which applications for consent are to be made; particulars which such applications must contain; the consultation to be conducted and publicity to be given to applications; and the time within which they must be dealt with. Applications must be recorded in part 1 of the consents register established under section 28 of the Act, within fourteen days of receipt by the council. The details remain in part 1 until the application is finally determined, whereupon the decision is recorded in part 2.

The hazardous substances authority to which application for consent is made may grant consent unconditionally or subject to conditions, or may refuse consent. In reaching its decision on the application, the authority is required to have regard to other land uses in the area and any planning permission granted for other land in the vicinity. Regard must also be had to any advice given by the Health and Safety Executive or the Health and Safety Commission following consultation. Application for hazardous substances consent often goes hand in hand with an application for planning permission in respect of the same land. However, the presence of hazardous substances on land does not always require planning permission (as, for example, where existing storage facilities are used), so that the only controls available to the authority may be those conferred by the Planning (Hazardous Substances) Act.

Conditions

Conditions may be imposed on the grant of hazardous substances consent. Conditions may relate to the site itself; and to each substance it is sought to introduce to the site including, for example, the times between which each substance may be present. There is, perhaps surprisingly, no requirement in the

Act relating to the qualifications or experience of the person having control of a site the subject of a hazardous substances consent.

Application may be made to remove conditions from a hazardous substances consent. On such application, the hazardous substances authority is entitled only to review the conditions attached to the consent. The authority is not entitled to review the question of whether consent should or should not have been granted in the first place.

Deemed Consent

As a transitional measure, deemed consent applied in relation to the established presence of a hazardous substance on land if it had existed for at least twelve months before the date upon which the Act came into force and was claimed within six months after that date. If a claim for such deemed consent was made, and not rejected as invalid within two weeks of the claim, deemed consent would apply.

A government department may direct that hazardous substances consent is deemed to have been granted in respect of a development to be carried out by a local authority or statutory undertaker (railway, water supplier, gas supplier, sewerage undertaker etc.).

Revocation of Consent

Hazardous substances consent may, by order of the authority, be revoked or modified, subject in some cases to confirmation by the Secretary of State. In certain cases the hazardous substances authority is liable to pay compensation to the landowner, or others affected by a revocation order, for depreciation in the value of the interest in the land or for disturbance. The circumstances giving rise to the revocation of consent are, in brief, as follows:

(i) generally, where the authority considers it expedient, having regard to a "material consideration" (compensation payable);

(ii) where there has been a material change of use of the land to which the consent relates (no compensation payable);

(iii) where the substance or substances have not been present in a controlled quantity for at least five years (no compensation payable);

(iv) where there has been a change of person in control of part (as opposed to the whole) of the land – this gives rise to automatic revocation unless an application for continuance of the consent has already been made (no compensation payable except where an application for continuance has been made and the consent is modified or revoked);

(v) where a contravention notice (see below) has been served requiring removal of the substance from the land (no compensation payable if the requirements of the contravention notice are upheld on appeal).

Appeals

An appeal may be made to the Secretary of State against refusal by the authority to grant hazardous substances consent, or against conditions imposed by the authority on such a consent. An appeal may also be brought where an application for continuation of a consent on a change of person in control of the land is refused or granted subject to conditions unacceptable to the person in control.

Offences

The following criminal offences are created by the Planning (Hazardous Substances) Act 1990:

- equalling or exceeding the controlled quantity of a hazardous substance where there is no hazardous substances consent;
- exceeding the maximum quantity permitted by a hazardous substances consent;
- failure to comply with a condition attached to a hazardous substances consent.

Contravention Notices

Hazardous substance contravention notices may be served by the authority as a method of enforcing compliance with the provisions of the Act. These notices may be served independently of, or in addition to, the bringing of criminal proceedings. They have a parallel in the enforcement notice provisions and procedures contained in the Town and Country Planning Act (see enquiry 3.9 above), although there is no procedure equivalent to the service of a stop notice.

A contravention notice must specify the alleged breach of control and the steps to be taken to remedy the contravention. It is served on the owner of the land to which it relates, and any other person in control of the land. A reasonable period of time (not less than twenty-eight days) must be allowed for compliance. Provision has been made for an appeals procedure, with a right of appeal to the Secretary of State; the effectiveness of the contravention notice is suspended pending final determination or withdrawal of any appeal.

The Hazardous Substances Register

A hazardous substances authority must, by virtue of section 28 of the Act, maintain a register available for inspection by the public at all reasonable hours. The register must record details of all applications, consents, revocations, modifications and directions issued. Each consent granted by the authority must contain:

- a description of the land to which the consent relates;
- a description of the hazardous substance(s) to which it relates;
- a statement of the maximum quantity of each substance permitted by the consent to be present at any one time.

Summary

Optional enquiry 18.1 is designed to produce a list of entries in the register of hazardous substances. The buyer of residential property is not normally concerned with this enquiry, but a buyer of industrial or warehouse premises or land will want to know of the existence of any entries, particularly if it is proposed to carry on an operation dependent upon the storage of hazardous substances (as defined). A buyer of part, as opposed to the whole, of premises or land in respect of which a hazardous substance consent has been given should consider applying, under section 17 of the Act, for continuation of the consent before completion of the purchase; failure to do so would result in automatic revocation of the consent.

Optional enquiry 18.2.(a) concerns how copies of the entries may be obtained. Since the register is open to public inspection the authority should be prepared to supply copies on request, but a charge may be made.

Optional enquiry 18.2.(b) concerns where the register may be inspected. Since the administration under this Act is an extension of provisions originally contained in the Town and Country Planning Act, and in view of the similarity of the two regimes, the register is likely to be maintained in the planning department of the council (if, as is usually the case, the council is the hazardous substances authority).

Optional Enquiry 19: Environmental and Pollution Notices

> "What outstanding statutory or informal notices have been issued by the Council under the Environmental Protection Act 1990 or the Control of Pollution Act 1974? (This enquiry does not cover notices under Part IIA or Part III of the EPA, to which enquiries 3.12 or 3.7 apply)."

This optional enquiry concerns statutory or informal notices issued under powers contained in the Environmental Protection Act 1990 and the Control of Pollution Act 1974. Notices under part IIA and part III of the Environmental Protection Act (which relate, respectively, to contaminated land, and statutory nuisances and clean air) are specifically excluded from the ambit of this enquiry and are dealt with by enquiries 3.12 and 3.7 respectively (see above).

The Environmental Protection Act is extremely wide-ranging and introduced new and modified powers and duties for local authorities to deal with a large number of issues. Together with the Control of Pollution Act, which it largely supersedes, it is perhaps the most important piece of legislation in its field. The Act includes provisions on the following:

- control of industrial and air pollution;
- the collection, disposal and treatment of controlled waste;
- statutory nuisances and clean air;
- litter control;
- abandoned shopping trolleys;
- the control of genetically modified organisms;
- the use of injurious substances;
- oil pollution from ships;
- the identification and control of dogs;
- burning of crop residues (straw and stubble).

Numerous powers to serve and enforce notices are conferred upon councils by the Act's provisions. Some of the more important of these notices are:

(i) Section 13 – enforcement notice served on a person carrying on a "prescribed process" (which is capable of causing environmental pollution and requires authorisation) in contravention of the conditions of an authorisation, requiring steps to be taken to remedy the breach within a time specified in the notice.

(ii)   Section 14 – prohibition notice served in respect of the carrying out of a "prescribed process" where it is considered that the process, or the manner in which it is being carried on, involves an imminent risk of serious pollution.

(iii) Section 10 – variation notice served on the holder of an authorisation to carry out a "prescribed process", varying the terms of the authorisation.

(iv) Section 46 – notice requiring the occupier of property to place household waste in the receptacle provided for the purpose.

(v)   Section 47 – notice requiring occupier to provide receptacles for storage of commercial or industrial waste where nuisance would otherwise result.

(vi) Section 59 – notice requiring the occupier of land on which controlled waste has been deposited unlawfully to remove it in not less than twenty-one days.

(vii) Section 80 – nuisance abatement notices (see the commentary on enquiry 3.7 above).

(viii) Section 92A – litter clearing notice requiring litter to be cleared from land which is open to the air and prohibiting it from becoming defaced by litter in the future.

(ix) Section 93 – street litter control notice served on the occupiers of premises in and around any street or open land, requiring steps to be taken to alleviate the problem of litter accumulating in the vicinity.

(x)   Section 110 – prohibition notice served on a person proposing to import, acquire, market or release genetically modified organisms where there is a risk of damage to the environment.

(xi) Section 149 – notice served on the owner of a dog that it has been seized and will be disposed of within seven days if not claimed.

Most of these notices may be appealed against, either in the magistrates' court or to the Secretary of State, and their requirements may be modified or quashed. In most cases breach of the notice gives rise to an offence punishable by a fine.

The Control of Pollution Act was perhaps the earliest attempt to address the problem of pollution of the environment in a comprehensive enactment. It originally covered such matters as:

• waste on land, including the licensing of disposal of controlled waste;
• pollution of water, including control of discharges of trade effluent into the public sewer;
• noise nuisance;
• pollution of the atmosphere.

Many of the Act's provisions have now been superseded and replaced by provisions in the Environmental Protection Act. However, the following powers to issue and serve notices under the 1974 Act remain:

(i)   Section 23 – notice by the council as highway authority prohibiting the parking of vehicles during certain hours of the day to facilitate street cleaning.

(ii)   Section 60 – notice in connection with a building site imposing requirements as to the way in which works are to be carried out in the interests of reducing noise.

(iii) Section 66 – noise abatement notice; see the commentary on optional enquiry 11 (on noise abatement; see above).

Again, most of these notices may be appealed against, and their requirements may be modified, quashed or upheld on appeal. In most cases breach of a notice gives rise to an offence punishable by fine.

Summary

Optional enquiry 19 is intended to reveal details of notices, whether statutory or informal, issued by the council under powers contained either in the Environmental Protection Act or the earlier Control of Pollution Act. Clearly, a buyer will prefer a negative response. If, however, any outstanding notices are revealed in response to this enquiry, the buyer should seek full details of them and the extent to which they may have been complied with. Further enquiries of the council should be made in any such case.

Optional Enquiry 20: Food Safety Notices

"What outstanding statutory notices or informal notices have been issued by the Council under the Food Safety Act 1990 or the Food Hygiene Regulations 2006?"

This optional enquiry deals with improvement notices issued in respect of the premises under the provisions of the Food Safety Act 1990, and hygiene improvement notices issued under the Food Hygiene Regulations 2006. It is appropriate to raise this enquiry only if the premises which are the subject of the search are used for the purposes of a food business, or are intended to be so used.

"Food" includes drink, articles of no nutritional value used for human consumption, chewing gum and substances used as ingredients in food preparation. The definition does not include live animals or fish, animal fodder or feeding stuffs, controlled drugs or medicines.

"Business" includes canteens, clubs, schools, hospitals or institutions and activities carried out by local authorities and the like.

The Food Safety Act 1990 is the basis of a system of food law designed to control food manufacture, composition, labelling and advertising. The regime, which consists of this Act and many detailed sets of regulations, also regulates food distribution practice. It is enforced variously by the county, district and London borough councils as food authorities for their areas.

A variety of offences is created by the Act, including the rendering of food injurious to health (by adulteration, for example) and selling food not complying with food safety requirements (for example, where it is unfit for human consumption). Authorised officers of food authorities may inspect food intended for human consumption at all reasonable times if it is being, or has been, offered for sale.

Improvement Notices
An authorised officer of an enforcement authority may, if he has reasonable grounds for believing that the proprietor of a food business is failing to comply with certain regulations (for instance, for prohibiting the use of any process in the preparation of food, or for securing hygienic conditions and practices), serve on the proprietor an improvement notice under section 10 of the 1990 Act.

149

The notice must state the grounds for the officer's belief in failure to comply with the regulations; specify the failure to comply and the measures which should be taken to secure compliance; and give at least fourteen days for the proprietor to comply.

The proprietor may appeal against the requirements of an improvement notice to the magistrates' court. The court may either cancel or affirm the notice, with or without modification. An appeal against a notice suspends its effectiveness until the appeal has been finally dealt with.

Failure to comply with the provisions of an improvement notice renders the offender liable to a fine or imprisonment.

Emergency Prohibition Notices

Where there is an imminent risk of injury to health in connection with a food business, an emergency prohibition notice may be issued by an authorised officer of an enforcement authority. To issue such a notice (under section 12 of the 1990 Act), the officer must be satisfied that one of the following involves a risk of injury to health, which is imminent:

(i)   the use for the purposes of the business of any process or treatment;
(ii) the construction of the premises or the use of any equipment;
(iii) the state or condition of any premises or equipment used for the business.

This notice, which must be affixed in a conspicuous position on the premises to which it relates, effectively prohibits the use of the process or treatment, the premises or the equipment complained of.

Application must be made, by the enforcing authority, for an emergency prohibition order within the three days following service of the notice, failing which it ceases to have effect. Application for the order is made to a magistrates' court. Before making an order, the court must be satisfied on the evidence that the circumstances give rise to an imminent risk of injury to health.

Emergency prohibition notices and orders cease to have effect on the issue by the enforcement authority of a certificate to the effect that the proprietor has taken sufficient measures to secure that the health risk condition has been remedied.

It is an offence, punishable by a fine or imprisonment, knowingly to contravene an emergency prohibition notice or order.

Prohibition Orders

There are provisions in the 1990 Act for the issue of a prohibition order (that is, an order other than an emergency prohibition order) by a magistrates' court at the suit of the enforcing authority. These orders are not preceded by notice served by the enforcing authority but clearly have a serious impact. They may prevent the effective use of the premises for the purposes of a food business, or the use of specified processes or equipment for such a business. If a proprietor of a food business has been convicted of an offence under hygiene regulations, he may be prohibited from participating in the management of any food business.

Hygiene Improvement Notices, Prohibition Orders and Remedial Action Notices

The Food Hygiene Regulations 2006 provide a regime for environmental health officers to deal with the condition of food business premises specifically from the point of view of hygiene. While the provisions of the Food Safety Act referred to above continue to be operated by trading standards officers, who are largely concerned with the constituents of food and its proper packaging, labelling, and so on, hygienic conditions at food *premises* are largely within the purview of environmental health officers and the Food Hygiene Regulations.

The regime, and indeed the provisions, are very similar to those described above. Hygiene improvement notices may be served on a food business operator specifying those matters within hygiene regulations which have not been complied with, and the measures which should be taken to secure compliance. At least fourteen days must be given to the operator to comply, and failure to comply renders the operator guilty of an offence. Hygiene prohibition orders may be applied for in cases where a food business operator has been convicted of an offence under the regulations and the court is satisfied that a health risk arises in connection with the use of any particular process or treatment, the construction of the premises themselves or the use of equipment in them, or the state of the premises or equipment concerned. The court may prohibit, as appropriate, the use of the premises, the process or the equipment. Hygiene emergency prohibition notices and orders apply in much the same way as the emergency prohibition notices and orders described above, and, like them, must be served on the food business operator and affixed to the premises.

Remedial action notices may be served on a food business operator prohibiting the use of equipment or premises where proper inspection under the hygiene regulations is being hampered.

There are rights of appeal against these notices and prohibition orders, and a breach is an offence.

Summary
Optional enquiry 20 concerns whether there are any outstanding statutory or informal Food Safety Act or Food Hygiene Regulation notices in respect of the property. The enquiry is relevant only to a person purchasing a food business as a going concern, or purchasing premises intended for such use. Any such buyer will clearly prefer a negative response. If any statutory notices are revealed, the prudent buyer would require dates and full details of all of them, to ascertain what attention is required to the premises before they can be used for a food business. Any indication of informal (that is, non-statutory) notices issued by the council as enforcing authority should be treated with the same caution.

Optional Enquiry 21: Hedgerow Notices

"21.1. Please list any entries in the record maintained under regulation 10 of the Hedgerows Regulations 1997.
21.2. If there are any entries:
    (a) how can copies of the matters entered be obtained
    (b) where can the record be inspected"

This optional enquiry relates to hedgerow removal and retention notices, consent notices and determinations of appeals under the Hedgerow Regulations 1997. It is normally asked only by a buyer of agricultural land on which significant hedgerows are in evidence.

Section 97 of the Environment Act 1995 first conferred power on the Secretary of State to make regulations for the protection of "important hedgerows in England and Wales". This enabling measure permitted the Secretary of State to make, by regulation, provisions prohibiting the removal of hedgerows, except in prescribed cases; for appeals against notices issued under the regulations; and for the prosecution of persons contravening them.

"Hedgerow", for the purposes of the Act and Regulations, includes any stretch of hedgerow.

Protection of Hedgerows

The Hedgerow Regulations 1997 were promulgated following increasing concern about the wholesale destruction of hedgerows which had taken place over the preceding fifty years, with the mechanisation of British agriculture and the introduction of intensive farming methods. Unprotected by the general planning control regime, and the special control afforded to trees by virtue of tree preservation orders, certain hedgerows now enjoy their own protection under these regulations.

Protected hedgerows are those growing in, or adjacent to:
- common land (including town or village greens);
- protected land (managed as a nature reserve by a local authority under the National Parks and Access to the Countryside Act 1949, or areas notified as of special scientific interest);

- land used for agriculture, forestry or the breeding or keeping of horses, ponies or donkeys.

To be protected, a hedgerow must be of a continuous length of twenty metres or more, or meet by intersection or junction another hedgerow at each end.

"Important" hedgerows are those which have existed for over thirty years and satisfy one of the archaeological or wildlife criteria listed in part II of schedule I to the regulations (for example, the hedgerow marks the boundary of a historic parish; is situated within an archaeological site; marks the boundary of a pre-1600 AD estate or manor; or contains protected animal or plant species).

Removal of a Protected Hedgerow

Removal of a protected hedgerow in compliance with the regulations may be lawfully achieved only following service on the council, as local planning authority, of a "hedgerow removal notice" in the form prescribed and with a plan attached. The notice must specify the reasons for the removal of the hedgerow and give evidence of the date of planting, showing, marked "X", those stretches that are less than thirty years old.

If the council approves the proposal, or fails to notify approval within forty-two days of receipt of the notice, the landowner may carry out the removal as specified in the hedgerow removal notice, but must do so within two years of the date of service of the original notice.

The council, as local planning authority, may, in response to the hedgerow removal notice, serve a "hedgerow retention notice", prohibiting the carrying out of removal works, but it may do this only if the hedgerow is an "important" one, as defined in the regulations and outlined above. Indeed, if the hedgerow is considered "important" in light of the criteria contained in schedule I, the council is bound to reply with a hedgerow retention notice.

Regulation 6 permits the removal of any hedgerow if removal is required:

- for making a new opening for access (subject to a requirement to replant the old opening);
- for temporary emergency access;
- for access where another means of access is prohibitively expensive;
- for purposes of national defence;
- for carrying out a development permitted by a planning permission;
- for flood defence or land drainage;
- for preventing or eradicating pests;
- for certain highway functions;
- to prevent interference with electric lines;
- for proper management of the hedgerow.

Enforcement

Intentional (or reckless) removal of a hedgerow in contravention of the requirement to serve a hedgerow removal notice or the requirements of a hedgerow retention notice can give rise to prosecution and, on conviction, an unlimited fine. In imposing a fine, the court is bound to have regard to any financial benefit which may accrue to the guilty party.

The council's enforcement powers in defence of hedgerows are quite draconian. Whether or not a prosecution is brought for an offence, the owner may be required, again by notice, to plant another hedgerow. Such a notice specifies the species and position of trees or shrubs to be planted, and the period within which the planting is to be carried out. A hedgerow forcibly planted in accordance with these provisions is accorded the same protection as "important" hedgerows for the period of thirty years beginning with the date of completion of the planting.

Appeals

The regulations specify an appeals mechanism. Hedgerow retention notices and hedgerow replacement notices may be appealed against to the Secretary of State within twenty-eight days of their service. The Secretary of State may allow or dismiss an appeal, either as to the whole or as to part, and may quash or modify a notice. An opportunity of being heard by a person appointed by the Secretary of State must be afforded to the appellant and to the council as local planning authority. This may be done by means of a formal local inquiry, or by written representations.

Records

Regulation 10 of the Hedgerow Regulations provides that each local planning authority must compile and keep available for public inspection, free of charge and at all reasonable hours at a convenient place, a record containing a copy of:

(i)   every hedgerow removal notice received by it;
(ii)   every hedgerow retention notice issued by it;
(iii) every hedgerow removal consent issued by it;
(iv) every determination of an appeal by the Secretary of State notified to it.

Summary

Optional enquiry 21.1 is intended to produce a list of any entries in the record maintained under regulation 10 of the Hedgerow Regulations. The buyer will be interested in the details of any hedgerow removal notice revealed, but should be aware that if removal is to take place in accordance with its terms, it must take place within two years of the date of original service of the notice. A buyer would also be wise to check whether consent for removal has been issued, which should be apparent from the same list; or whether forty-two days have elapsed since service of the original removal notice, in which case it may be possible to claim "deemed" consent to removal.

A buyer does not normally wish to find a hedgerow retention notice, since this indicates that an "important" hedgerow is included in the property. Of course, if there are no plans to remove any of the hedgerows, a buyer would not be deterred by the existence of an "important" hedgerow.

The determination of any appeal to the Secretary of State, which should also be listed in reply to this part of the enquiry, will be of interest to the buyer in that it would give a full picture of the hedgerow protection situation of the property. Responsibility for replacing, and maintaining for at least thirty years, a hedgerow prescribed in a hedgerow replacement notice could be a considerable financial and troublesome burden, however ecologically minded the buyer happens to be.

Optional enquiry 21.2.(a) concerns how copies of the matters entered in the record can be obtained. Details are normally held in the planning department of the relevant council, and the buyer can expect to be provided with copies at a modest charge.

Optional enquiry 21.2.(b) concerns where the record can be inspected. The regulations specify that it must be available for public inspection, free of charge, at all reasonable hours, "at a convenient place". The record should be readily available in the planning department of the council.

Optional Enquiry 22: Common Land, Town and Village Greens

"22.1 Is the property, or any land which abuts the property, registered common land or town or village green under the Commons Registration Act 1965 or the Commons Act 2006?

22.2 If there are any entries, how can copies of the matters registered be obtained and where can the register be inspected?"

This enquiry relates to property, or land abutting it, which is registered common land or town or village green, and the registers of such land which are kept by local authorities (notably county councils). The enquiry would normally be raised only by buyers of significant tracts of land, or of properties adjoining land which is or has in the past been used in common with the public. It is particularly relevant since the Countryside and Rights of Way Act 2000 introduced new provision for public access to the countryside, including rights of access over registered common land. This optional enquiry replaces the former statutory arrangements for searches of the commons registers, with effect from 1 October 2007.

Common Land

The Commons Registration Act 1965, which made provision for the registration of common land, defines "common land" as:

    (i)   land subject to rights of common, whether those rights are exercisable at all times or only during limited periods; and

    (ii)   waste land of a manor not subject to rights of common,

but as not including a town or village green, or any land which forms part of a highway.

The rights of common, enjoyed over common land by "commoners" or the public at large include:

- commons of pasture (the right to feed cattle, horses, sheep or other animals);
- commons of turbary (the right to dig turves or peat from another's soil);
- commons of estovers (the right to take wood to sustain a house or agriculture);

- commons of piscary (the right to fish in another's waters); and
- commons in soil (the right to take sand, gravel and stone).

Town and Village Greens

Town and village greens were required to be registered under the Commons Registration Act 1965. They are defined as land which has either been allotted under an Act for the exercise or recreation of the inhabitants of a locality, or on which such inhabitants have a customary right to indulge in lawful sports and pastimes, or on which for at least twenty years a significant number of such inhabitants have indulged in such sports and pastimes as of right.

The Requirement of Registration

Provision was made by the 1965 Act for the registration of all common land and town or village greens in England and Wales, together with the rights of common claimed over them and their ownership. If they are not registered, no land capable of being registered (apart from new common land) is deemed common land or a town or village green, and no rights of common are exercisable over them unless they are subsequently registered.

The registration of land as common land affects the use which can be made of it. Registered common land is subject to restrictions on works, such as fencing, which may be carried out, and it is an offence to build on, or otherwise interfere with the public enjoyment of, greens.

Powers of the Local Authorities

A local authority has the power to assist persons in maintaining the ancient rights of common if, in its opinion, extinction of the rights would be prejudicial to the inhabitants of the area. In addition, the council may make schemes for the regulation and management of commons, and spend money on drainage, levelling and improvement; and may make by-laws and regulations for preventing nuisance and preserving order. The stationing of caravans on a common may be prohibited. On the other hand, the authorities have certain powers to improve and provide facilities such as refreshment places, parking places, shelters and lavatories, for the convenience of the public.

Public Rights of Access

A number of statutory provisions protect the public right of access over open spaces including common land. The Countryside and Rights of Way Act 2000 makes general provision for public access over registered common land which is shown on a map issued by the Countryside Agency (or the Countryside Council for Wales); such land is referred to as "access land". The public is entitled, subject to certain specific restrictions, to enter this land for the purposes of open-air recreation on foot. Certain types of land cannot constitute "access land", notably land within twenty metres of a dwelling (for people or livestock); land used as a garden, golf course or railway; land used for training racehorses at specified times of the day; and land being used for the planting or sowing of crops or trees. Subject to that, any person may enter and remain on any registered common land which has been designated as access land or dedicated as such by its owner, for the purpose of open-air recreation, provided that person does not break or damage any wall, fence, hedge, stile, or gate and observes the general and specific restrictions in relation to the land.

The Registers

Registration of any land as common land or as a town or village green, or of any rights of common over such land, is conclusive evidence of the matters registered. The registration authorities are the county council for land situated in a county (or county borough, in Wales); and in any metropolitan county, the metropolitan district council. In Greater London the registration authority is the relevant London borough council, and unitary authorities, where they exist, are also registration authorities.

Every registration authority must maintain a register of common land and a register of town or village greens, and the registers must be open to inspection by the public at all reasonable times. The register consists of:

(i) a register map;
(ii) as many register units as there are registrations of land in the register;
(iii) supplemental maps, if necessary.

In addition to the particulars registered in respect of the land, the registration authority may note in the land section of the register any schemes made under the Commons Acts for regulation of the common; local Acts regulating the land; and any limitations and conditions imposed in respect of the common land to which the public has access. If required to do so by the owner of the right, the authority must also register rights such as easements, profits à prendre, franchises and any rights and interests of the lord of the manor.

Until June 2007, any person who required a search to be made in the registers could, on payment of a prescribed fee, lodge a requisition for search (in form 21). The authority would then make the search required and issue a certificate of the result. It has been held that failure by a solicitor to make a search in the case of vacant land may amount to negligence.

On payment of the prescribed fee certified copies of, or extracts from, the general part of the register or any map may be required.

The Commons Act 2006 repeals the provision in the Commons Registration Act relating to statutory searches, and there is no replacement provision for statutory searches of the register. Optional enquiry 22 must now be used to elicit information relating to commons and town and village greens.

DEFRA (The Department for Environment Food and Rural Affairs) has issued a guidance note on the new arrangements for searches of the commons registers. This is reproduced in the Appendix to this book.

Summary

Optional enquiry 22.1 asks about the status of the property, or any land abutting the property in terms of common land, town or village green. Clearly the enquiry would normally be raised only in respect of a large vacant site, in the country, or in the neighbourhood of an apparent town or village green. An intending buyer may well prefer the property not to be registered common land, in view of the access to the public granted by the Countryside and Rights of Way Act 2000. On the other hand, there may be advantages in owning common land if it is well maintained and has the benefit of a regulation scheme operated by a suitable local authority. Again, buying land abutting a sleepy town or village green might have its attraction for the cricket enthusiast, but the average buyer might be dismayed at the prospects of frequent and noisy gatherings on or near his estate.

Optional enquiry 22.2 asks for copies of any entries in the register. These should be supplied, on payment of the requisite fee, by the appropriate registration authority, at whose offices one might expect to inspect them. The reply to this enquiry may not disclose details of any rights exercisable over the land. If these details are of interest to a prospective buyer, supplementary enquiries should be raised.

Part III: Drainage and Water Enquiries

The Water Act 1989 provided for the privatisation of the water industry in England and Wales. From 1 September 1989, water and sewerage functions formerly performed by the water authorities were transferred to the new public limited companies by virtue of section 4 of the Act. It is now the duty of the sewerage undertakers to provide, improve and extend the system of public sewers and to cleanse and maintain them. By virtue of section 97 of the Water Industry Act 1991, local authorities may enter into agency arrangements with the undertakers to carry out sewerage functions on their behalf, and this they may do individually or by way of consortium arrangements with other local authorities.

Drainage and water enquiries relating to property became the subject of a separate form – Con 29DW. The form was agreed between representatives of the sewerage undertakers and the undertakers charged their own separate fee for replying to them. Most searches are conducted electronically. Thus sewerage undertakers usually reply in report form, without specific reference to the enquiries as they appear on the form.

The enquiries on Con 29DW have been given statutory recognition by virtue of the Home Information Pack (No. 2) Regulations 2007, with effect from 1 August 2007. The search report required by the regulations must contain the enquiries and the appropriate responses as set out in schedule 8. The commentary which follows is based upon the requirements of the Home Information Pack Regulations. A new paper Form Con 29DW is available, in full compliance with the regulations. Alternatively, a written or electronic request for a drainage and water search in respect of a particular property, accompanied by the appropriate fee, will suffice to elicit a search which complies with the Home Information Pack (No. 2) Regulations. The sewerage undertakers pledged to the government that they would, by 1 June 2007, supply drainage and water searches in compliance with the regulations in respect of properties which are situated within their areas, and that where there are separate water companies, responsible only for water supply, they, the undertakers, will take responsibility for supplying comprehensive search reports, covering water as well as sewerage issues.

Drainage and Water Enquiries (Con 29DW)

These enquiries are concerned with the manner in which effluent and surface water are removed from buildings or land, and responsibility for the maintenance of the public sewer system. They also concern arrangements for premises that are not connected to a drainage system, and the supply of water from the public main.

Public Sewer Map

"Where relevant, please include a copy of an extract from the public sewer map."

Water and effluent (or sewage) is generally removed from premises through an enclosed line of pipes. In so far as those pipes form a drain within the premises, responsibility for their upkeep rests with the owner of the premises. In so far as they form a sewer, that is, a public sewer vested in a sewerage undertaker, rather than being owned privately, they are the undertaker's responsibility. In general, a drain is intended for the passage of fluids from a single building, while a sewer is a system of drainage designed to deal with liquids from a number of buildings or yards.

The principal sewerage undertaker for a locality is the company appointed by the Secretary of State under the Water Industry Act 1991. The sewerage undertaker has a duty to provide, improve and extend the public sewer system, and to cleanse and maintain it, so that the area is effectively drained. By virtue of section 97 of the Act, a sewerage undertaker may enter into agency arrangements with the relevant local authority (district or London borough council) whereby the sewerage undertaker's functions, other than sewage disposal and discharge of trade effluent, are delegated to the council for the area. In these areas, the enquirer may still find the council able and willing to reply to the drainage and water enquiries.

Section 32 of the Public Health Act 1936, now repealed, required local authorities to keep maps showing the existing public sewers and to make them available for public inspection. Section 199 of the Water Industry Act now imposes the duty on the sewerage undertaker to keep records of every public sewer and disposal main vested in it. But the undertaker is not obliged to keep records of sewers laid before 1 September 1989 if it does not know of, and has no reasonable grounds for suspecting, their existence. In addition, it must transfer to its own records details of sewers, drains and mains laid before that date only if they were shown on the old section 32 map, and the undertaker was permitted ten years to transfer these details, if they existed. Copies of the old maps must be sent to the undertakers by the local authorities previously maintaining them.

The information recorded on a public sewer map includes the location of the pipe, and whether it is a drain, sewer or disposal main, and the effluent it carries. The record also shows whether the pipe is vested in the undertaker, or is likely to become so vested by virtue of an agreement under section 104 of the Water Industry Act 1991 (see below). Undertakers must keep separate records for each local authority area in which they operate, and, for the purposes of providing the information to the public, should keep them in the form of a map. Once drawn up, free copies must be sent to the local authority (ies) to whose area(s) they relate, and any modifications should be similarly treated, so that a council is at all times informed of the records relevant to its area. The council should keep the copy of the map at one of its offices, available for public inspection at all reasonable times. The undertakers must themselves keep copies available for public inspection.

The responses to this enquiry, set out in the Home Information Pack (No. 2) Regulations, are as follows:

(a)   a copy of an extract from the public sewer map is included in which the location of the property is identified; or

(b)   a copy of an extract of the public sewer map is included, showing the public sewers, disposal mains and lateral drains in the vicinity of the property; or

(c)   no map is included, as there are no public sewers in the vicinity of the property.

Summary

This drainage and water enquiry is a request for a copy extract from the public sewer map relevant to the area and, in particular, relevant to the property. A buyer would hope to be provided with a copy extract showing a public sewer in the close vicinity of the property, so that if inspection or search reveals that connection has not already been made, it can be. The buyer should, however, be aware that no such map may yet have been drawn, and sewers constructed before 1 September 1989 may not be shown in any case. A buyer of new or recently built property should make further enquiries of the developer or seller before assuming that a negative response to this part of the enquiry implies that there are no adopted, or public, sewers serving the property.

Foul Water

"Does foul water from the property drain to a public sewer?"

The second enquiry relates to the drainage and sewerage of the property and responsibility for maintenance of drains and sewers.

A drain generally conveys effluent from one building or a group of buildings within one curtilage and deposits it in a sewer, cesspool or septic tank.

Responsibility for maintenance of a drain is that of the property owner and the drain remains in private ownership.

A sewer conveys the effluent to a sewage treatment works. It generally runs under a road, but may be in public or private ownership. It serves more than one property.

Foul drainage is effluent produced from within the premises. Surface water consists of rainwater.

The responses to this enquiry, set out in the Home Information Pack (No. 2) Regulations, are as follows:

(a) records indicate that foul water from the property drains to a public sewer; or

(b) records indicate that foul water from the property does not drain to a public sewer; or

(c) this enquiry appears to relate to a plot of land or a recently built property. It is recommended that drainage proposals are checked with the developer.

Summary

This drainage and water enquiry concerns whether foul drainage from the premises drains into a public sewer, that is, a sewer owned and maintained by the sewerage undertaker, rather than into a cesspool or septic tank. A buyer will prefer a positive reply, since drainage into a cesspool or septic tank means that the owner has to bear the costs of maintenance and emptying the cesspool or septic tank, whereas drainage into a public sewer ensures the effluent is eventually treated at a treatment works.

Surface Water

"Does surface water from the property drain to a public sewer?"

Surface water, that is, rainwater, lands on the roof of the premises and generally runs down the roof and into a series of gutters. From there it passes along the gutters and into downpipes and eventually underground. Surface water may drain straight into the ground into what is known as a "soakaway", but more commonly it flows into a drain and thence into a sewer – often the same sewer as that which takes the foul drainage.

A highway drain is constructed in or under a road for the purpose of carrying away surface water from the road surface. Highway drains are not sewers since they are not used primarily for the drainage of buildings and yards. They belong to, and are maintained by and at the expense of, the county council (or London borough or metropolitan council) in its capacity as highway authority.

The responses to this enquiry, set out in the Home Information Pack (No. 2) Regulations, are as follows:

(a) records indicate that surface water from the property does drain to a public sewer;

(b) records indicate that surface water from the property does not drain to a public sewer; or

(c)   this enquiry appears to relate to a plot of land or a recently built property. It is recommended that drainage proposals are checked with the developer.

Summary

This drainage and water enquiry concerns whether the surface water drainage is to a public sewer, that is, a sewer maintainable by the sewerage undertaker, or to a highway drain maintainable by the highway authority. A buyer will prefer an affirmative response. If the property is not connected for surface water drainage, the buyer may be eligible for a rebate of the surface water drainage charge.

Public Adoption of Sewers and Lateral Drains

"Are any sewers or lateral drains serving or which are proposed to serve the property the subject of an existing adoption agreement or an application for such an agreement?"

Developers constructing new buildings may enter into agreements with the sewerage undertaker whereby the developer agrees to construct the sewer or sewage disposal works necessary to serve the development and, subject to satisfactory completion of the works, the sewerage undertaker declares the sewer vested in itself and assumes responsibility for future maintenance. Such agreements are entered into under section 104 of the Water Industry Act 1991 and are commonly referred to as section 104 agreements. They are very often associated with agreements under section 38 of the Highways Act 1980 in respect of new roads (see required enquiry 2, above).

If such an agreement is in force, it should be supported by a bond, much as a section 38 (Highways Act) agreement should be. The bond is a financial commitment on the part of a financial institution such as a bank, insurance company or pension fund, guaranteeing due performance of the agreement. A buyer will wish to be satisfied that the bond is of a sufficient value to ensure completion of the works on the sewer so that it will be adopted by the undertaker.

The responses to this enquiry, set out in the Home Information Pack (No. 2) Regulations, are as follows:

(a)   records indicate that in relation to sewers and lateral drains serving the development of which the property forms part–
  (i)   an adoption agreement is currently in preparation;
  (ii)   an adoption agreement exists and the sewers and lateral drains are not yet vested in the sewerage undertaker, although the maintenance period has commenced;
  (iii) an adoption agreement exists and the sewers and lateral drains are not yet vested in the sewerage undertaker and the maintenance period has not yet commenced;
  (iv)   an adoption agreement exists and is supported by a bond;
  (v)   an adoption agreement exists and is the subject of a bond waiver; or

(vi) an adoption agreement exists and is not supported by a bond or by a bond waiver; or

(b) records confirm that sewers serving the development, of which the property forms part are not the subject of an existing adoption agreement or an application for such an agreement; or

(c) the property is part of an established development and is not subject to an adoption agreement.

Summary

This enquiry concerns whether any sewer, existing or proposed to serve the premises, is subject to a section 104 agreement. Normally a buyer of a newly constructed house expects such an agreement to be in force, or at least in preparation. An affirmative response to the enquiry, or information about the stage the adoption process has reached, is therefore to be expected. A prudent buyer may wish to be satisfied of the developer's compliance with the conditions of any such agreement, and further enquiries in this direction could be addressed to the sewerage undertaker.

This enquiry further concerns whether there is a bond to support any agreement entered into under section 104 of the Water Industry Act. The buyer will expect an affirmative response if a subsisting section 104 agreement is shown to exist. If there is no such bond, the buyer would have concerns about the prospects of the property being drained into a public sewer, or the expense of ensuring a connection if the developer becomes insolvent.

Public Sewers Within the Boundaries of the Property

"Does the public sewer map indicate any public sewer, disposal main or lateral drain within the boundaries of the property?"

This enquiry concerns sewers within the boundaries of the property enquired about, and their status with regard to the statutory sewer map.

Sewer Maps

As mentioned above, the statutory sewer map is maintained by the sewerage undertaker for the area in accordance with the duty, under section 199 of the Water Industry Act, to keep certain records. The map must show every public sewer and disposal main vested in the sewerage undertaker; all drains and sewers which are the subject of section 104 agreements; and those sewers in respect of which a vesting declaration has been made under section 102 of the Act but has not taken effect. Records of sewers laid before 1 September 1989 may not appear on the map if the sewerage undertaker is not aware of them, and it may be worth making an approach to the council which was responsible for this function before 1991 for further details.

The information recorded should show the location of the pipe; whether it is a drain, sewer or disposal main; the effluent it carries; and details of any section 102 declaration or section 104 agreement (see below). Records should be modified and kept up to date with developments.

Once prepared by the sewerage undertaker, free copies of the statutory sewer map must be provided to any council to whose area it relates, as should details of any modifications made, so that the council should at all times be informed of the detailed records in respect of its area. The map must be kept at the council's offices and be made available for inspection by the public, without charge, at all reasonable times. Copies of the maps must also be kept available for public inspection at the offices of the sewerage undertaker.

Vesting Declarations

A sewerage undertaker has power, subject to the provisions of section 102 of the Water Industry Act, to declare sewers (or parts of sewers) in its area and constructed after 1 October 1937 to be vested in the undertaker with effect from a date specified in a vesting declaration. Owners of sewers may apply to the sewerage undertaker for a vesting declaration to be made, effectively divesting the owner of future maintenance responsibilities and liabilities.

Sewerage undertakers may also make vesting declarations on their own initiative.

Before making a vesting declaration the sewerage undertaker must give two months' notice of its intention to do so, to all owners of the sewer. An appeal may be made in this time to the Director General of Water Services against the proposal of the sewerage undertaker to vest the sewer in itself. If this is done the vesting declaration may not proceed until the appeal has been determined. In considering any appeal, regard must be had to all the circumstances of the case, and in particular to whether the making of the vesting declaration would be seriously detrimental to the appellant owner. In most cases, adoption is likely to be considered beneficial to an owner, who will be divested of future maintenance responsibilities. Compensation may be payable to owners in respect of a vesting declaration on the part of the undertaker, but in view of the benefits which vesting brings, the power to award compensation is likely to be used sparingly.

A person who has applied to have a sewer vested in the undertaker, and is refused, may appeal to the Director General against refusal. In determining an appeal, the Director General must have regard to:

(i)   whether the sewer is adapted to the general sewerage system for the area;

(ii)   whether the sewer is under a highway or land reserved for a street;

(iii)   the present number of buildings served by the sewer and possible future numbers;

(iv)   the method of construction of the sewer and its state of repair.

On hearing the appeal the Director General may allow or reject the statutory undertaker's proposal, and specify conditions for the adoption with a proviso that the vesting declaration shall not take effect unless such conditions are accepted.

Section 104 Agreements

Sewerage undertakers may enter into agreements under section 104 of the Water Industry Act with developers of land to the effect that if a sewer is constructed in accordance with the terms of the agreement the undertaker will, on its completion, declare the sewer to be a public sewer vested in it. Agreements may also be made in respect of drains, but only when they have become sewers.

To an extent, developers may seek to compel sewerage undertakers to enter into section 104 agreements. If the sewerage undertaker refuses to enter into such an agreement when the developer has made a request supported by adequate information for the purpose, the developer may appeal to the Director General, who will adjudicate on the matter.

Agreements made under section 104 are enforceable against the sewerage undertaker by the owner or occupier for the time being of any premises served by the sewer to which it relates.

The responses to this enquiry, set out in the Home Information Pack (No. 2) Regulations, are as follows:

(a) the public sewer map included indicates that there is a public sewer, disposal main or lateral drain within the boundaries of the property; or

(b) the public sewer map indicates that there are private sewers or lateral drains subject to an existing adoption agreement within the boundaries of the property; or

(c) the public sewer map indicates that there are no public sewers, disposal mains or lateral drains within the boundaries of the property. However, it has not always been a requirement for such public sewers, disposal mains or lateral drains to be recorded on the public sewer map. It is therefore possible for unidentified sewers, disposal mains or lateral drains to exist within the boundaries of the property.

Summary

This drainage and water enquiry concerns whether the statutory sewer map, prepared and maintained by the sewerage undertaker and held by the council, shows any public sewers within the boundaries of the property. The enquiry effectively extends to any sewers in respect of which a vesting declaration has been made but is not yet in force, but which, when in force, will make those sewers public sewers; it also extends to any drains and sewers subject to agreements under section 104 of the Water Industry Act. If the property enquired about is not already connected to the public sewer, a buyer raising this enquiry normally prefers an affirmative response, rather than one or other of the alternatives. This will ensure the likelihood of early connection at reasonable cost to an existing public sewer, or adoption in the near future of an existing private sewer.

This enquiry is normally of concern only in respect of an undeveloped site or premises which are not already connected to the public sewerage system (such as those served by a cesspool or septic tank).

A buyer receiving an affirmative response to this enquiry should, however, be aware that the presence of a public sewer running within the boundary of the property may restrict further development. Sewerage undertakers have a statutory right of access to carry out work on their assets, subject to due notice.

This may result in the sewerage undertakers' employees or its contractors needing to enter the property to carry out work.

Public Sewers Near To The Property

"Does the public sewer map indicate any public sewer within 30.48 metres (100 feet) of any buildings within the property?"

This enquiry is intended to reveal information about the public foul and surface water sewers nearest to the property which is the subject of the enquiries. It is normally raised only in respect of an undeveloped site, or premises which do not drain to a public sewer but rely on more primitive methods of sewerage disposal (such as a cesspool or septic tank).

Private sewers and drains are usually constructed by the developer of a housing or industrial estate. Local authorities have no specific statutory powers to require developers to lay private sewers, but the provisions of the Building Act 1984 and the Building Regulations, and the council's power to deal with statutory nuisances, are usually sufficient to ensure that sewers are constructed. New premises constructed with drainage to a cesspool or septic tank are a rarity, perhaps confined to remote and outlying districts, upland regions or the islands.

Connection to a Public Sewer

Developers, and private individuals constructing their own dwellinghouses, normally prefer to arrange for drainage to the public sewer, thus divesting themselves of future maintenance liabilities and costs. It is for this reason that developers commonly enter into agreements with sewerage undertakers under section 104 of the Water Industry Act 1991, making provision for the construction of sewers by the developer and the subsequent adoption of them by the sewerage undertaker. Section 104 agreements have been considered above.

Under sections 106 to 109 of the Water Industry Act the owner of premises or the owner of a private sewer has a limited right to connect a drain or sewer to a public sewer belonging to a sewerage undertaker. Before making a connection the owner must give notice of the proposed works, whereupon the undertaker may, within twenty-one days, refuse to allow the connection if it is considered that the mode of construction or the condition of the private sewer is such that it would be prejudicial to the sewerage system. If connection is allowed, the works may be carried out either by the owner, under supervision of the sewerage undertaker, or by the sewerage undertaker by agreement, and on an undertaking or security to meet the undertaker's costs.

An outline of the contents of the statutory sewer map, maintained by the sewerage undertaker and copied to the council, has been given above. It should show, among other details, the location of all public foul and surface water sewers for which the sewerage undertaker is responsible.

The responses to this enquiry, set out in the Home Information Pack (No. 2) Regulations, are as follows:

(a) the public sewer map included indicates that there is a public sewer within 30.48 metres (100 feet) of a building within the property; or

(b) the public sewer map indicates that there is a public sewer or lateral drain subject to an existing adoption agreement within 30.48 metres (100 feet) of a building within the property; or

(c) the public sewer map indicates that there are no public sewers within 30.48 metres (100 feet) of a building within the property. However, it has not always been a requirement for such public sewers to be recorded on the public sewer map. It is therefore possible for unidentified sewers or public sewers to exist within the boundaries of the property.

Summary

This enquiry concerns whether the statutory sewer map shows public foul and surface water sewers within 100 feet (30.48 metres) of the property. The buyer of premises or a site not already connected to the public sewer will prefer an affirmative response. This would facilitate an assessment of the problems and likely costs of connection to the public sewerage system.

Any reply will be based on the statutory sewer map which the sewerage undertaker has provided to the council, and other records the undertaker may hold. These records may be incomplete, and a prudent buyer in any doubt may wish to commission a physical inspection.

If the sewerage undertaker replies enclosing an extract of the statutory sewer map, the enquirer should check the notation carefully, and clarify any queries with the sewerage undertaker direct.

Building Over a Public Sewer, Disposal Main or Drain

"Has a sewerage undertaker approved or been consulted about any plans to erect a building or extension on the property over or in the vicinity of a public sewer, disposal main or drain?"

The general position relating to the drainage of property is dealt with above. This enquiry is concerned with the Building Act 1984 and the building or extension of a building over, or in the vicinity of, drains and sewers.

Sewerage undertakers have special statutory powers to protect the structure and integrity of public sewers. By section 18 of the Building Act 1984, where building plans were deposited with the local authority for approval, and they disclosed that a new structure was to be erected over a drain, sewer or disposal main (or would interfere with use of such pipes), the local authority was required to reject the plans, unless in the particular circumstances it was considered that consent could be granted.

The provisions of section 18 have been repealed and effectively replaced by an amendment to the Building Regulations 2000. Part H4 of the regulations now provides that the erection or extension of a building is to be carried out in a way that is not detrimental to the building or building extension, or to the continued maintenance of the drain, sewer or disposal main. The sewerage undertaker must be consulted by the local authority as soon as practicable after plans have been deposited with it and before issuing any completion certificate in relation to the building work where any proposal to build over sewers is made. The undertaker may require the local authority to refuse consent or make consent subject to conditions based upon the type of development involved.

A "disposal main" for these purposes is any outfall pipe or other pipe which is a pipe for the conveyance of effluent to or from any sewerage disposal works, whether of a sewerage undertaker or of any other person; and is not a public sewer.

Buildings or extensions erected over a sewer in contravention of building controls may have to be removed or altered as required by a notice served under section 36 of the Building Act 1984. If such a notice is not complied with the authority may carry out any necessary works in default.

The responses to this enquiry, set out in the Home Information Pack (No. 2) Regulations, are as follows:

(a) records indicate that a sewerage undertaker has approved or has been consulted about plans to erect a building or extension on the property over or in the vicinity of a public sewer, disposal main or drain; or

(b) records indicate that a sewerage undertaker has rejected plans to erect a building or extension on the property over or in the vicinity of a public sewer, disposal main or drain; or

(c) there are no records in relation to any approval or consultation about plans to erect a building or extension on the property over or in the vicinity of a public sewer, disposal main or drain. However, the sewerage undertaker might not be aware of a building or extension on the property over or in the vicinity of a public sewer, disposal main or drain.

Summary

This enquiry concerns whether there is in force an agreement or consent under section 18 of the Building Act 1984 or, now, the Building Regulations 2000, for a building or extension over or near a public sewer or disposal main. A buyer will ideally prefer a negative response; if the reply is affirmative, the buyer should request full details of the agreement or consent, and confirmation that the conditions of any such agreement or consent have been complied with to date. This matter is, effectively, raised with the council as building control authority by required enquiry 3.3 (Part I, above), but if the council is unable to supply the information, an approach may have to be made to the sewerage undertaker direct.

Map of Waterworks

"Where relevant, please include a copy of an extract from the map of waterworks."

Originally, domestic water was supplied to premises by statutory water companies or local authorities under the provisions of a local Act of

Parliament. The Water Act of 1973 transferred the powers of local authorities to supply water to the new water authorities established under that Act, and the powers of local authorities to supply water in their areas ceased. By virtue of section 37 of the Water Industry Act 1991, it is now the duty of water undertakers to develop and maintain efficient and economical systems of water supply to premises in their areas, and to make supplies available to persons who require them.

Water undertakers have powers of entry under the 1991 Act for the purposes of exercising their water supply functions. These powers include power to enter premises to disconnect or cut off a supply; in normal circumstances seven days' prior notice must be given to the occupier of the premises concerned.

Owners and lawful occupiers of premises and local authorities may, by written notice, require a water undertaker to provide a water main to supply water for the "domestic purposes" of those premises. "Domestic purposes" comprise drinking, washing, cooking, central heating, and sanitary purposes. The owner must first enter into a binding undertaking to pay the water undertaker its loan charges for the period of twelve years following installation of the main, in so far as those loan charges exceed the income received by the water undertaker over that period arising from the supply of water to the premises or development in question. Once the financial undertaking has been entered into, the water undertaker has three months to comply with the demand for a new main. The undertaker must lay the water main in such a way that the service pipes of the relevant premises can be reasonably conveniently connected.

An owner, occupier or developer of any premises may serve a "connection notice" on a water undertaker, requiring it to connect a supply pipe in the premises to one of its mains, so that water for domestic purposes can be supplied to the premises.

By virtue of section 195 of the Water Resources Act 1991, water undertakers must keep an up-to-date record of where their resource mains, water mains, discharge pipes and other underground works (except service pipes) are located. The records kept by virtue of this provision must be available for public inspection free of charge at all reasonable hours at the office of the relevant water undertaker. The information must be shown in the form of a map.

The responses to this enquiry, set out in the Home Information Pack (No. 2) Regulations, are as follows:

(a) a copy of an extract from the map of waterworks is included in which the location of the property is identified;

(b) a copy of an extract of the map of waterworks is included, showing water mains, resource mains or discharge pipes in the vicinity of the property; or

(c) no map is included, as there are no water mains, resource mains or discharge pipes in the vicinity of the property.

Summary

This enquiry is a request for a copy extract from the public water main map. The sewerage undertaking company of which this enquiry is raised should be able to supply such an extract, and may well be carrying out the water supply functions itself in the locality. A buyer will be concerned to ensure that a public water main is situated in the immediate vicinity so that, if mains water is not already connected to the premises, it may conveniently be obtained. If there are no vested water mains in the vicinity of the property, connection will be expensive, and the buyer without water may have to consider obtaining a private water supply (from a spring, well or bore hole) to the property to be purchased.

Adoption of Water Mains and Service Pipes

"Is any water main or service pipe serving or which is proposed to serve the property the subject of an existing adoption agreement or an application for such an agreement?"

Water undertakers may enter into agreements with developers who are constructing, or proposing to construct, water mains or service pipes, by virtue of which, if the main or pipe is constructed in accordance with the terms of the agreement, the undertaker will, on completion of the work, declare the main or pipe vested in itself. These agreements are normally triggered on an application by the developer. In considering the application, the water undertaker must have regard to any effect the new main or pipe may have on the quality of water supplies and any increased danger to life or health which is considered may result.

The agreement itself may also provide for associated infrastructure works downstream of the point of connection with the undertaker's supply system as may be necessary, and to ensure that the proposed main will be of a sufficient size to cater for later development works, the water undertaker generally agreeing to pay for any additional cost involved. The agreement provides for connection of the new water main to the existing supply system, and for vesting the new main and service pipes in the water undertaker so that the undertaker becomes responsible for future maintenance. These agreements are enforceable against the water undertaker by the owner or occupier for the time being of premises connected, or to be connected, to the water main or service pipes to which they relate.

These provisions, which are contained in section 51A of the Water Industry Act 1991, are mirrored by sewer adoption agreements entered into under section 104 of the 1991 Act (see page 168 above) and are similar in many respects to highway adoption agreements under section 38 of the Highways Act (see required enquiry 2(b) above). Like those agreements, water main adoption agreements may be supported by a bond ensuring proper performance of the developer's obligations. If a developer's application for an agreement is refused, or the water undertaker does not, within two months, give notice of the terms upon which it will be accepted, the applicant may appeal to the Water Services Regulation Authority, which will adjudicate on the matter. A water undertaker cannot, however, be forced to enter into an agreement for water mains or service pipes that are to be used for non-domestic supplies.

The responses to this enquiry, set out in the Home Information Pack (No. 2) Regulations, are as follows:

  (a) Records confirm that in relation to water mains and service pipes serving the development, of which the property forms part–

      (i) an adoption agreement is currently in preparation;

      (ii) an adoption agreement exists and the water mains or service pipes are not yet vested in the water undertaker;

      (iii) an adoption agreement exists and is supported by a bond; or

      (iv) an adoption agreement exists and is not supported by a bond. *or*

  (b) Records confirm that water mains or service pipes serving the property are not the subject of an existing adoption agreement or an application for such an agreement.

Summary

This enquiry concerns whether the water main or service pipes serving (or proposed to be serving) the property are the subject of a section 51A adoption agreement. An intending buyer of newly developed residential accommodation will certainly hope for, and expect, an affirmative response, indicating that if the water mains are not already vested in a competent water company, they eventually will be.

Sewerage and Water Undertakers

"Who are the sewerage and water undertakers for the area?"

Sewerage and water undertakers are appointed to exercise the functions of public sewerage and water supply in their areas, and their powers and functions are found in their memoranda and articles of association. Companies carrying out these functions may also be empowered to carry out functions outside their own areas. One water company, or undertaker, for instance, may supply water in the area of another.

The responses to this enquiry, set out in the Home Information Pack (No. 2) Regulations, are as follows:

  [*Give company name and address*] is the sewerage undertaker for the area, and [*give company name and address*] is the water undertaker for the area.

Summary

This drainage and water enquiry simply asks for the name of the company or companies carrying out the functions of public sewerage and water supply for the area. The buyer will want to know who is supplying water to the property, or who to approach to organise a supply, and who is responsible for public sewerage, particularly if that function is not yet being carried in respect of the property to be purchased. The water undertaker for the property may well be the same company as that carrying out the sewerage functions.

Connection to Mains Water Supply

"Is the property connected to mains water supply?"

If the property is connected to the mains water supply, maintenance of the supply and all the public infrastructure is the responsibility of the water undertaker. Some properties in remote areas are situated so far from the nearest public main as to render connection to a main either impracticable or prohibitively expensive. These properties often have to rely on a private water supply, either from a culvert or well, or from a bore hole and pump sunk into the land at a location well below the water table, so that water can be obtained all year round regardless of seasonal weather fluctuations. Responsibility for the maintenance, cleansing and filtration of these supplies rests on the shoulders of the property owner.

Planning permission for the laying of pipes, erection of water tanks and so on may be required in connection with the installation of a private water supply, and an abstraction licence may be required under section 24 of the Water Resources Act 1991. If the route of a proposed private water supply is to traverse land in the ownership of another, the owner will have to negotiate private easements with adjoining owners, the owner having no statutory powers of compulsory purchase. On the other hand, once installed, a private water supply is within the control of the property owner; exemption from water rates and charges is available and may prove attractive.

The responses to this enquiry, set out in the Home Information Pack (No. 2) Regulations, are as follows:

(a) records indicate that the property is connected to mains water supply; or

(b) records indicate that the property is not connected to mains water supply and water is therefore likely to be provided by virtue of a private supply; or

(c) this enquiry relates to a plot of land or a recently built property. It is recommended that the water supply proposals are checked with the developer.

Summary

This enquiry simply concerns whether the property is connected to a mains water supply. A buyer will normally expect, receive and prefer an affirmative response, so that the water supply to the property is both secure and safe to use. If the response is in the negative, the prudent buyer should make further enquiries. If the enquiry relates to a plot of land or a recently built property, the buyer should check the water supply proposals with the developer or owner. If the property already has a private supply, not connected to the mains, the water undertaker will not be able to assist much further, and enquiries should be raised with the seller as to the route, condition, maintenance and performance history of the supply, and liabilities in respect of it. Where no supply exists at all, and connection to the public main is either impracticable or prohibitively expensive, the buyer would be well advised to research, before proceeding with the purchase, the practicality and likely cost of sinking a well or bore hole.

Water Mains, Resource Mains or Discharge Pipes

"Are there any water mains, resource mains or discharge pipes within the boundaries of the property?"

A water undertaker is responsible for all the mains vested in it, and has the power to maintain them as provided by sections 158 and 159 of the Water Industry Act. The water undertaker is normally also responsible for its communication pipes. Liability for individual supply pipes (that is, to individual properties) normally rests with the water consumer.

The power of the water undertaker to maintain its pipes includes power to clean them. The power, in section 158 of the Water Industry Act, to alter the size or course of pipes, includes power to move or remove them, and replace them. Water undertakers may inspect, maintain, adjust, repair or alter any of their mains, resource mains, discharge pipes or service pipes, both under streets and situated elsewhere, subject to the duty to pay compensation for loss or damage caused by the exercise of these powers.

Local Acts of Parliament may authorise the council to carry out urgent repairs to water supply pipes or water fittings, to ensure that premises affected by defects in them have an adequate supply for domestic purposes. If works are to be carried out on the premises of an owner occupier, that person's consent is necessary, but otherwise the owner must be notified of works either before they are carried out or, in an emergency, as soon as possible after they have been done. Normally twenty-four hours' notice is given (except in an emergency). Local Acts may allow recovery of the expense of the works from the owner of the premises. These powers are not exercised by the council without the consent of the relevant water undertaker, except in emergency, and the undertaker may elect to carry out the works itself.

The responses to this enquiry, set out in the Home Information Pack (No. 2) Regulations, are as follows:

(a) the map of waterworks indicates that there are water mains, resource mains or discharge pipes within the boundaries of the property;

(b) the map of waterworks does not indicate any water mains, resource mains or discharge pipes within the boundaries of the property; or

(c) the map of waterworks indicates that there is a water main subject to an existing adoption agreement within the boundaries of the property.

Summary

This enquiry concerns whether there are any water mains or other assets vested in a water undertaker within the boundaries of the property. The buyer will prefer a negative response. If the reply is in the affirmative, however, the buyer would be well advised to enquire further about the precise route of any main or the location of other assets; whether work on them is anticipated in the future or has been undertaken in the recent past; and whether any claims for compensation, either by or against the present owner, are outstanding or anticipated. The buyer should also be aware that the presence of a vested water main within the boundary may restrict further development. The water undertaker has a statutory right of access to carry out work on its assets, subject to short notice.

Current Basis for Sewerage and Water Charges

"What is the current basis for charging for sewerage and water services at the property?"

This enquiry is concerned with the charges that water and sewerage undertakers may make for the services they render.

Water Charges

Every water and sewerage undertaker has power to fix its own charges by reference to such criteria as it considers appropriate. Water undertakers must have, in effect, a charges scheme by which they fix charges for domestic water. Normally, water supply charges schemes exist for both domestic and non-domestic supplies. Copies of these schemes must be available for public inspection at the offices of the water undertaker, and the latest edition should be sent free of charge to any person on request.

Unmeasured supplies of water to premises for domestic purposes may be charged for on the basis of the rating system. If so, the charge is expressed as an amount in the pound fixed annually by resolution of the water undertaker, multiplied by the net value of the premises, as shown on the local valuation list, to which the supply is made. An alternative to the rate-based system is a flat rate charge, levied on a standard property basis or on a band of properties, or in other ways.

Metered supplies are provided for in the Water Industry Act 1991, supplemented by regulations. Metering of premises is normally optional and is introduced at the request of the property owner. Meters must normally be installed within fifteen working days of a request by the owner, provided the installation charge has been paid.

The charge for a metered water supply is assessed by multiplying the volume of water supplied as measured by the meter, by a rate per thousand gallons or per cubic metre, as fixed by the undertaker. The customer may be charged under the scheme for all water passing through the meter, including water lost by leakage, waste or otherwise, except for water used for fire fighting purposes.

The occupier of premises supplied through a meter is liable to pay the charges for the supply, even after he has given up occupation, unless he informs the undertaker at least two working days in advance.

Sewerage Charges

Sewerage undertakers have power to fix charges for any of the services they provide, including their trade effluent functions. Charges for ordinary sewerage services are fixed in accordance with a scheme made under section 143 of the Water Industry Act 1991.

The occupier of the premises to which sewerage services are provided is liable to pay general sewerage charges. Services are provided to premises if they are drained to a public sewer, vested in the sewerage undertaker, which is used for foul or surface water or both.

A sewerage charges scheme may comprise a rate-based charge according to the net annual value of the premises. This is calculated in the same way as for water supply charges (see above). Alternatively, a volume charge may be made, based on the assessed or metered water supply to the premises, or calculated by reference to returns showing the amount of water abstracted for use on the premises.

Sewerage undertakers may fix a meter to a drain or private sewer connecting premises to a public sewer, and base a volume charge on the actual amount of effluent discharged from the premises. More commonly, sewerage undertakers rely on readings from water meters to establish the volume of water supplied to the premises and base their charges on that.

Trade effluent charges may be imposed either as a standard charge by a scheme made under section 142 as above, or as a term of an agreement made under schedule 8 to the 1991 Act. A charges scheme may, for instance, empower the undertaker to make a charge when a "trade effluent notice" is served on it; when it grants consent; and when a discharge is made under that consent. In each case, the person liable to pay the charge is the person who served the notice, the person to whom consent was granted or the person who makes the discharge in pursuance of the consent.

Charges for trade effluent can be made on a measured or unmeasured basis, and conditions imposed on trade effluent consents may require the occupier of the premises in question to provide and maintain meters to measure volume and rate of discharge.

Other charges that may be levied, both by water and sewerage undertakers, include charges for connection to a water supply or to a public sewer. Generally, such charges can be imposed only in respect of premises that have never before been connected to a domestic water supply or, as appropriate, for domestic drainage purposes.

The responses to this enquiry, set out in the Home Information Pack (No. 2) Regulations, are as follows:

(a) the charges are based on actual volumes of water measured through a water meter ("metered supply");

(b) the charges are based on the rateable value of the property of £ *give rateable value* and the charge for the current financial year is £ *give amount of charge*;

(c) the charges are made on a basis other than rateable value or metered supply. They are based on *give basis for charges* and are £ *give amount of charge* for each financial year;

(d) records indicate that this enquiry relates to a plot of land or a recently built property.

Summary

This enquiry is intended to reveal the basis for charging for sewerage and water supply at the property. Because charging schemes for both services are company-specific, the replies vary considerably depending on the area in which the property is situated. The buyer should, however, expect to receive details of those services for which a charge is made, and to be told whether charges are measured or unmeasured.

Whether the buyer prefers charges to be on a measured or unmeasured basis depends largely on the size of the family unit and its normal living habits. Single people and couples with relatively low use of domestic water normally benefit from a metered supply, particularly if the rateable value of the property is high. On the other hand, large families living in modest accommodation where the rateable value is low often benefit from charges based on an unmeasured supply.

In any case, it is helpful for a buyer to obtain a copy of the water and sewerage undertakers' charges schemes, which are available on request and free of charge.

The buyer of trade premises, who intends to discharge significant quantities of trade effluent into the system, should certainly be prepared to enquire after the sewerage undertaker's charging mechanisms for this service.

Charges following Change of Occupation

"Will the basis for charging for sewerage and water services at the property change as a consequence of a change of occupation?"

This enquiry relates to the power sewerage and water undertakers have to change the basis for charging for their services following a change in occupation of the premises.

Undertakers have a wide discretion in setting their own charges schemes. The schemes have to be approved by the Director General, but the power of approval may not be exercised so as to limit the total resources available from the scheme in question. Although sections 142 and 143 of the Water Industry Act 1991 allow this wide discretion, undertakers are not entitled to charge for services that have not been provided. Charges schemes may prescribe items with respect to which a consumer is to be liable to pay a charge, or not. Regulations may require alternative bases of charging to be made available, and special provision may be made exempting from certain charges vulnerable sections of the community.

In general, the liability of an occupier of premises for charges is dealt with by section 144 of the Act. Liability is, by that section, treated as being that of the occupier for the time being of the premises concerned. Charges fixed and imposed by reference to volume supplied or treated may be so imposed that a person is made liable in relation to premises even after he has ceased to be the occupier, unless he informs the relevant undertaker of the cessation of his occupation at least two working days before ceasing to occupy them.

A water consumer is entitled, by virtue of section 144A of the Act, to elect to be charged for water by reference to volume consumed. To do this, the consumer simply serves a "measured charges notice", requiring the undertaker to fix charges by reference to volume supplied. The water undertaker is not obliged to comply with the notice if it is not reasonably practicable to fix charges in this way in respect of the premises, or if to do so would require the undertaker to incur unreasonable expense. In the case of dispute, the Director General adjudicates.

There are circumstances in which a consumer is permitted to remain on an unmeasured (unmetered) charge. A water company may not charge domestic consumers on a measured basis unless any consumer has requested or agreed to be charged on that basis by means of a "measured charge notice", or by agreement, or a consumer has recently moved into the premises and has not yet received a bill referable to an unmeasured charge. To take advantage of this regime, a consumer may be obliged to satisfy certain conditions, for example, the consumer may be denied the use of a garden sprinkler on the premises.

The responses to this enquiry, set out in the Home Information Pack (No. 2) Regulations, are as follows:

(a) The basis for the charges will change and will be based on an unmeasured supply.

(b) The basis for the charges will change and will be based on a metered supply.

(c) The basis for the charges will change and will be based on *give basis for charges*.

(d) The basis for the charges will change and will be based on rateable value.

(e) There will be no change in the current charging arrangements as a consequence of a change of occupation. *or*

(f) Records indicate that this enquiry relates to a plot of land or a recently built property. It is recommended that the charging proposals are checked with the developer.

Summary

This enquiry concerns the future basis of charging for sewerage and water services after a change of occupation. The reply preferred by a prospective buyer will depend largely upon his intended use of the property, the size of his family and other factors. Perusal of the scheme of charging should reveal a suitable reply, but a prudent buyer will want to know where he stands regarding the future basis of charging.

Surface Water Drainage Charges

"Is a surface water drainage charge payable?"

The subject of this inquiry is the obligation to pay surface water drainage charges.

"Surface water" is defined, by the Home Information Pack Regulations (No. 2) 2007 which specify these enquiries, to include water from roofs and other impermeable surfaces within the curtilage of the property. It derives, mainly, from aquatic precipitation in the form of rain, snow and hail, most of which soaks harmlessly into the ground where it falls. When surface water falls upon impermeable surfaces such as the roofs of houses, it usually finds its way through the system of gutters, downpipes and lateral pipes into a public sewer.

From that point on, surface water receives much the same treatment as foul water and is dealt with by the sewerage undertakers.

The sewerage undertaker is entitled to make charges for its services, and charges schemes are made under section 143 of the Water Industry Act 1991. The charges scheme, which is normally in force for a period of twelve months, has to be approved by the Director General. However, undertakers have a wide discretion in connection with their schemes of charges, and may fix sums to be paid for any services provided in the course of their functions. Liability for the charges falls, by virtue of section 144, on the occupier for the time being of premises drained by a sewer or drain connecting with such a sewer of the undertaker as is provided for foul or surface water or both.

The sewerage undertaker may elect not to levy a charge for surface water, but usually does so. Because it is virtually impossible to measure the quantity of surface water attributable to a particular property, the charge for this service is normally dealt with on the same basis as foul water sewerage.

Sewerage undertakers may not charge for services which have not been provided. If it can be shown, to the satisfaction of the undertaker, that surface water from a particular property does not drain to a public drain or sewer, then no surface water charge may be made. For example, in some rural locations foul sewerage is to a septic tank or cesspool, and surface water drains to a soakaway in the ground.

The responses to this enquiry, set out in the Home Information Pack (No. 2) Regulations, are as follows:

(a) Records confirm that a surface water drainage charge is payable for the property at £ *give level of charge* for each financial year. *or*

(b) Records confirm that a surface water drainage charge is not payable for the property.

Summary

This enquiry concerns liability for surface water drainage charges. Clearly, a prospective buyer would prefer a negative response, but is likely to receive an affirmative one. If the reply to this enquiry does not reveal the actual charge, the prospective buyer might ask the sewerage undertaker for a copy of its charges scheme, which should be readily available at no cost. If a surface water drainage charge is levied, and it is apparent that the property's surface water does in fact drain to a soakaway and not to a public sewer, the buyer may at some time wish to challenge liability for this aspect of the sewerage undertaker's charges.

Water Meters

"Please include details of the location of any water meter serving the property"

This enquiry simply relates to the physical location of any water meter serving the property. A water meter is defined as "any apparatus for measuring or showing the volume of water supplied to, or of effluent discharged from any premises".

Section 144A of the Water Industry Act 1991 confers a right on consumers paying water and sewerage charges on an unmeasured basis by virtue of a charging scheme to require a water company to levy charges by reference to volume, by means of a "measured charges notice". A water company is not obliged to install a meter where it is not practical, or where it would be unreasonably expensive to do so, and disputes on this issue are referred to the Director General. The water undertaker's charges scheme prescribes the time within which a meter will be fitted by a water company and the date from which the consumer will be charged by volume.

A tenant, other than a tenant under a fixed term tenancy of less than six months, may exercise this right without the consent of his landlord.

The responses to this enquiry, set out in the Home Information Pack (No. 2) Regulations, are as follows:

(a)   Records indicate that the property is not served by a water meter. *or*

(b)   Records indicate that the property is served by a water meter, which is located–

    (i)   within the dwelling-house which is or forms part of the property, and in particular is located at *give details of location*; or

    (ii)   is not within the dwelling-house which is or forms part of the property, and in particular is located at *give details of location.*

Summary

This drainage and water enquiry simply asks where the water meter, if any, is located. If there is no water meter, after completion of the purchase, the buyer may, depending on his personal circumstances, consider serving a "measured charges notice" and being billed on the basis of a measured supply.

Sewerage Bills

"Who bills the property for sewerage services?"

The sewerage bills enquiry simply asks for the name and address, telephone number and website address of the billing company in respect of sewerage services. If no details are available or forthcoming, it is likely that the property is not connected to the public sewer. If the buyer wishes to dispute a bill for sewerage services, he should in the first instance take up the matter with the billing company. Section 150A of the Water Industry Act 1991 makes provision for the resolution of billing disputes by referral to the Director General. Proceedings may not be commenced in respect of any charge for the provision of sewerage services, other than the carrying out of trade effluent functions, without at least twenty-eight days' prior notice to the consumer of intention to commence proceedings and of the customer's rights to have billing disputes adjudicated by the Director General.

The responses to this enquiry, set out in the Home Information Pack (No. 2) Regulations, are as follows:

(a) The property is billed for sewerage services by *give company name, billing address, enquiry telephone number and website address. or*

(b) The property is not billed for sewerage services.

Summary

This enquiry simply asks for the details of the billing company in respect of sewerage services.

Water Bills

"Who bills the property for water services?"

This enquiry simply asks for the name and address, telephone number and website address of the billing company in respect of water services. If no details are available or forthcoming, it is likely that the property is not connected to the public main, and either has its own water supply or has not yet been completed. A person wishing to dispute a bill for water services should take the matter up in the first instance with the billing company. Section 150A of the Water Industry Act 1991 makes provision for the resolution of billing disputes by referral to the Director General. Proceedings may not be commenced in respect of any charge for the supply of water for domestic purposes without at least twenty-eight days' prior notice to the customer of intention to commence proceedings and of the customer's rights to have billing disputes adjudicated by the Director General.

The responses to this enquiry, set out in the Home Information Pack (No. 2) Regulations, are as follows:

(a) The property is billed for water services by *give company name, billing address, enquiry telephone number and website address. or*

(b) The property is not billed for water services.

Summary

This drainage and water enquiry simply asks for the details of the billing company in respect of water services.

Risk of Flooding due to Overloaded Public Sewers

"Is the dwelling-house which is or forms part of the property at risk of internal flooding due to overloaded public sewers?"

This question relates to dwelling-houses only, and to the risk of internal flooding (not, for example, the flooding of streets or gardens external to the house) due to overloaded public sewers. It does not concern, for example, flooding caused solely by abnormal weather conditions, as where a river bursts its banks, or the occurrence of an abnormally high tide.

The sewerage undertakers have wide powers and duties, under the provisions of the Water Industry Act 1991, to carry out works for sewerage purposes. These include the power to carry out works for the construction, laying, alteration and repair of sewers and drains, and to ensure that water in main waterworks is not contaminated or polluted. They have powers to carry out incidental works, such as the breaking open of streets, tunnelling or boring under them and moving earth and materials, and their powers apply equally to land not in, under or over a street. They have powers to enter premises and land to carry out surveys or tests to determine whether it is appropriate or practicable to execute any relevant works, and to carry out these works if necessary.

Where a sewerage undertaker exercises its powers to do works on private land, any complaints arising may be made to the Water Services Regulation Authority. The authority must investigate any such complaint, unless it appears to it to be vexatious or frivolous; or it has already been brought to the undertaker's attention and a reasonable opportunity of dealing with it has not been given; or if the complaint is more than twelve weeks old. If satisfied that the undertaker has failed adequately to consult the complainant in the exercise of the powers, and that the complainant has suffered loss, damage or inconvenience, the Authority may award compensation.

The responses to this enquiry, set out in the Home Information Pack (No. 2) Regulations, are as follows:

   (a)   Records confirm that the property is at risk of internal flooding due to overloaded public sewers (following an actual flooding event or otherwise) and a report is included describing–

        (i)   this and the action proposed by the sewerage undertaker to remove the risk;

        (ii) who will undertake this action and when; and

        (iii) whether mitigation measures have been installed to reduce the risk of flooding to the property. *or*

   (b)   An investigation is currently being carried out by the sewerage undertaker to determine if the property should be recorded on a register as being at risk of internal flooding due to overloaded public sewers, and a report is included describing–

        (i)   the action proposed by the water undertaker to remove the risk; and

        (ii) who will undertake the action and when. *or*

   (c)   The property is not recorded as being at risk of internal flooding due to overloaded public sewers.

Summary

This enquiry may be relevant where there is a history of internal flooding to dwelling-houses in the area. Obviously, an intending buyer will prefer a negative response, and if records reveal that the house is at risk of internal flooding, the intending buyer will want to be advised of all and any steps that have been taken or are proposed to alleviate the risk. These should be detailed in any report accompanying the reply to this enquiry. Many buyers of residential properties may be dissuaded from proceeding with the purchase of a property if it has a history of risk of internal flooding, and the intending buyer should also check the insurance and mortgage finance situation before proceeding any further.

It is repeated that the reply to this enquiry, as worded, does not necessarily reveal any history of properties which are not "dwelling-houses", nor any history of internal flooding caused by factors other than "overloaded public sewers".

Risk of Low Water Pressure or Flow

"Is the property at risk of receiving low water pressure or flow?"

This enquiry concerns the duty of a water undertaker to ensure constancy and sufficiency of water pressure or flow to its consumers.

Section 65 of the Water Industry Act 1991 imposes a duty on the water undertaker to ensure that the water in those of its mains and other pipes that are used for domestic water supplies or have fire hydrants fixed in them is constant and kept at such a pressure as will cause the water to reach the top of the top-most storey of every building within its area. The water undertaker may comply with this duty by supplying water by gravitational flow through its mains from a service reservoir or from a tank, so long as the reservoir or tank is at such a height that the water naturally flows, by gravitational forces, to the top of the top-most storey. The level of the pressure to be maintained is nowhere specifically or scientifically prescribed.

Temporary reductions in constancy, pressure or flow are permissible to enable waterworks to be carried out.

Enforcement of this water undertaker's basic duty is by the Secretary of State using his powers under section 18 of the Act, and water undertakers may be prosecuted for criminal offences (the defence of due diligence and of having taken all reasonable steps to avoid breach of the duty applies).

To maintain the constancy of supply, the water undertaker has the power to require certain buildings to be provided with a cistern with a float-operated valve. This applies to buildings (or parts of buildings) where a constant supply under pressure is not necessary, and certain houses where water is required to be delivered at a height greater than a point 10.5 meters below the draw-off level of the service reservoir or tank from which the water undertaker is providing the supply.

As stated, there appears as yet, no statutory definition of low water pressure or flow.

The responses to this enquiry, set out in the Home Information Pack (No. 2) Regulations, are as follows:

    (a)   Records confirm that the property is recorded on a register kept by the water undertaker as being at risk of receiving low water pressure or flow, and a report is included describing–

        (i)   the action proposed by the water undertaker to remove the risk; and

        (ii) who will undertake the action and when.

    (b)   An investigation is currently being carried out by the water undertaker to determine if the property should be recorded on a register as being at risk of receiving low water pressure or flow, and a report is included describing–

(i) the action proposed by the water undertaker to remove the risk; and

(ii) who will undertake the action and when. *or*

(c) Records confirm that the property is not recorded on a register kept by the water undertaker as being at risk of receiving low water pressure or flow.

Summary
This drainage and water enquiry concerns water pressure and flow, and whether the property is at risk of receiving low pressure or flow, neither of which is defined in the Act. The prospective buyer will prefer a negative response, but the extent to which an affirmative response will discourage an intending buyer would depend largely upon his intentions for the property. Keen gardeners, and those who prefer to hose wash their cars, will prefer a reasonable level of pressure and flow. Others may not be so concerned. Electric pumps may be installed in line with the water supply, which will significantly enhance water pressure if no alternative is proposed.

Water Quality Analysis

"Please include details of a water quality analysis made by the water undertaker for the water supply zone in respect of the most recent calendar year".

This enquiry concerns the water undertaker's duty to provide a supply of wholesome water to domestic and food production premises, and the standards of "wholesomeness" prescribed by the Water Supply (Water Quality) Regulations.

The basic duty of a water undertaker in relation to quality of water supply is contained in section 68 of the Water Industry Act 1991. When supplying water to any premises for domestic or food production purposes, the undertaker must supply water which is "wholesome" at the time of supply; and this duty applies up to the point where the supply reaches the consumer's own pipes. It is a most serious offence to supply water that is unfit for human consumption and a water undertaker may be fined up to £20,000 for such a breach of the law.

Standards of "wholesomeness" are set by the Secretary of State by regulations which prescribe specific requirements as to the substances which should be present in, and absent from, the water (and their relevant concentrations); other specific characteristics of the water, such as its taste; and sampling and monitoring arrangements. The Secretary of State may authorise relaxation of, and departures from, the prescribed requirements, and authorise local authorities to exercise similar powers in relation to private water supplies. These standards, and their application, are enforced by the Secretary of State under section 18 of the Water Industry Act. Water which is not so bad as to be unfit for human consumption, justifying a prosecution, may nevertheless be unwholesome in the terms of the regulations, justifying enforcement by the Secretary of State.

To ensure compliance with the section 68 duty to supply and preserve the supply of wholesome water, regulations may require undertakers to monitor and record whether water for domestic or food production purposes is wholesome, to monitor it at source, and to ensure that records are kept of the localities within which all the premises are normally supplied from the same source. Regulations may also deal with the analysis of water samples.

The Water Supply (Water Quality) Regulations 2000, as amended by the 2001 Regulations, make detailed arrangements for the monitoring and sampling of water quality, for the maintenance of records and provision of information.

Before the beginning of each year, a water undertaker must designate the names and areas within its area of supply that are to be its water supply zones for that year. Such a zone may not comprise an area with a population over 100,000. Within each of these zones, the water undertaker must take and analyse a number of samples of water, at regular intervals. The samples must be representative of the quality of the water at the time of sampling; not contaminated during the process of being taken; kept at controlled temperatures; and analysed as soon as may be after being taken.

Analysis is carried out against an extremely technical backdrop, but, basically, water samples which contain certain micro organisms, parasites, or substances at a concentration which would constitute a danger to human health will not be deemed "wholesome".

Water undertakers must keep records in respect of each of their water supply zones containing:

- the name of the zone;
- the name of all water treatment works or service reservoirs from which water is supplied to the zone;
- an estimate of the population;
- particulars of any departures authorised under part 6 of the regulations (see below);
- particulars of action taken or required to be taken by the water undertaker;
- particulars of the result of any analysis of samples; and
- other particulars as the undertaker may determine.

These records must be available for inspection by the public at all reasonable hours, free of charge, at one of the offices of the water undertaker. Copies must be provided free of charge to people receiving a supply of water in the relevant water zone, and, at a reasonable charge, to others.

The responses to this enquiry, set out in the Home Information Pack (No. 2) Regulations, are as follows:

(a) The analysis confirmed that all tests met the standards prescribed by the 2000 Regulations or the 2001 Regulations.

(b) The analysis confirmed that tests met the standards prescribed by the 2000 Regulations or the 2001 Regulations, except that *give number* tests of *give total number* tests failed to meet the standard for nitrate.

(c) The analysis confirmed that tests met the standards prescribed by the 2000 Regulations or the 2001 Regulations, except that *give number* tests of *give total number* tests failed to meet the standard for lead.

(d)   The analysis confirmed that tests failed to meet the standards of the 2000 Regulations or the 2001 Regulations, in relation to both nitrate and lead, and these are *give further details of such tests. or*

(e)   The analysis records confirmed that tests failed to meet the standards of the 2000 Regulations or the 2001 Regulations in relation to another substance or substances, and these are *include further details.*

Summary

This enquiry elicits details of any water quality analysis made by the water undertaker for the previous or most recent calendar year.

The buyer of domestic premises, or premises which are to be used for food production, will be particularly concerned to be receiving a supply of good, potable "wholesome" water, and will be interested in the results of any analyses. Most buyers would hope that the response reveals that all standards prescribed by the regulations have been met. Any failure to meet a standard may not, of itself, be fatal to the purchase (or, indeed to the buyer), but a prospective buyer will be concerned to know what remedial action is being taken, and when a supply of water to the required standards is to be expected.

Authorised Departures from Water Quality Standards

"Please include details of any departures–

(a)   authorised by the Secretary of State under Part 6 of the 2000 Regulations from the provisions of Part 3 of those Regulations; or

(b)   authorised by the National Assembly for Wales under Part 6 of the 2001 Regulations from the provisions of Part 3 of those Regulations."

This enquiry is intended to elicit details of any relaxations of the requirements of the Water Supply (Water Quality) Regulations which have been authorised by the Secretary of State in England (2000 Regulations) or the National Assembly for Wales (2001 Regulations). It would normally be particularly relevant to prospective buyers of domestic residential accommodation or premises used or intended to be used for food production purposes.

The basic duties of water undertakers in relation to the supply of water of wholesome quality, monitoring, sampling, analysis and recording are contained in sections 68 and 69 of the Water Industry Act 1991 and the Water Supply (Water Quality) Regulations made thereunder. These were dealt with above.

Part 6 of the regulations makes provision for the water undertaker to investigate any suspected failure to reach the standards of wholesomeness prescribed by the regulations. If such failure is suspected, the water undertaker must investigate the cause and extent of the failure, or apprehended failure, and whether it is due to the domestic distribution system itself, maintenance of the system, or neither of these. The water undertaker must then report, as soon as may be, to the Secretary of State, or the National Assembly, as appropriate, on the failure and on any action taken to remedy it.

The Secretary of State (or National Assembly) may authorise departures from the part 3 standards of "wholesomeness" if satisfied that:

(i)   such an authorised departure is necessary in order to maintain, in the water zone, a supply of water for domestic purposes (cooking, drinking, food preparation or washing) or to premises in which food is produced;

(ii)   the supply cannot be maintained in the zone by any other reasonable means; and

(iii) the supply of water in accordance with the authorisation does not constitute a potential danger to human health.

Application for such an authorisation must be accompanied by a statement of the grounds on which it is sought; the name of the water zone in respect of which it is sought; details of analyses over the proceeding twelve months; the average daily quantity of water supplied to the zone; the estimated population of the zone; whether food production undertakings would be affected; the period of the requested authorisation; and the reasons why supply cannot be maintained by other reasonable means. A scheme for monitoring water quality in the zone, and a summary of the steps to be taken, with a timetable and costings, must also be provided. The water undertaker must notify the local authority and health authorities of the application, and these bodies may make representation to the Secretary of State (or National Assembly) within a period of thirty days from the date of application.

The Secretary of State (or National Assembly) may authorise departures for such periods of time as are reasonably necessary for securing a supply of wholesome water as required by the regulations. The authorisation will specify:

- the grounds on which it is granted;
- the water zones in respect of which it is granted;
- the extent of the departure from the standards that is granted;
- results of analysis of samples for the preceding twelve months;
- the average daily quantity of water supplied to each of the zones affected;
- the estimated population of the zones affected;
- whether or not any food production undertaking would be affected;
- the "departure period" – that is, the period of time for which the departure from water quality standards is authorised.

The authorisation must also require the implementation of monitoring schemes and the carrying out of steps to secure that the supply returns to proper standards of "wholesomeness"; and it must set out timetabling arrangements and costings. The water undertaker would also be required to give advice as to the measures people in the water supply zones should take in the interests of their health, during the "departure period".

Publicity must be given to all authorised departures from the standards, in newspapers circulating in the areas to which the departure applies.

Water undertakers must maintain records containing particulars of any departures authorised under part 6 of the regulations which apply to water supplied in the zone. These records must be available for inspection by the public at all reasonable hours free of charge in at least one of the water undertaker's offices.

The responses to this enquiry, set out in the Home Information Pack (No. 2) Regulations, are as follows:

(a)   There are no such authorised departures for the water supply zone.

or

(b)   The Secretary of State or the National Assembly for Wales has authorised a departure from the standards prescribed by the 2000 Regulations or the 2001 Regulations, in the water supply zone, and–

   (i)   the departure permits the water undertaker or water supplier to supply water that does not meet the standard for *give substance* whilst remedial action to restore normal water quality is taken;

   (ii)   the maximum permitted departure is up to *give number* micrograms per litre; and

   (iii)   the measures taken to restore normal water quality are due to be completed by *give approximate month and year*.

Summary

This drainage and water enquiry is designed to produce details of any departures from the requirements of the Water Supply (Water Quality) Regulations which have been authorised by the Secretary of State (England) or the National Assembly (Wales). The availability of wholesome water from the public main is usually of great importance to a buyer of residential accommodation, and vital to a buyer of a food production undertaking. Both would clearly prefer a negative response. But if the response reveals any departures from the statutory standards of wholesomeness, the prospective buyer would normally be most interested in the replies to this enquiry and may wish to study the detailed terms of the departure authorisation; a copy should be readily available on request, normally at no fee if the buyer is already a customer for water services in the area.

Sewage Treatment Works

"Please state the distance from the property to the nearest boundary of the nearest sewage treatment works".

The final enquiry simply asks for the location of the nearest sewage treatment works. It is normally of concern only to a developer wishing to construct a new housing development of significant size, which is to be connected to the public sewerage system.

The duty of sewerage undertakers to provide a public sewer for the drainage of domestic premises is the subject of sections 98 and 99 of the Water Industry Act 1991, which deal with sewer requisitions and the financial conditions for complying with them.

The location of the nearest public sewer and the practicability of connecting to it, together with the financial implications of so doing, are of concern to a developer of a new site which is not connected to the public sewerage system. Such a developer would also be concerned to be reassured that the treatment works are of sufficient capacity to handle the estimated outflow of sewage from the proposed development. Planning permission for such new development has in the past been hampered by the fact that the available sewage treatment works have been inadequate to cater for significant new demands.

The response to this enquiry, set out in the Home Information Pack (No. 2) Regulations, is as follows:

> The nearest sewage treatment works is *give distance in kilometres or miles* to the *give direction* of the property. The name of the nearest sewage treatment works is *give name.*

Summary

This enquiry asks for confirmation of the distance between the property and the nearest sewage treatment works. It is suggested that this enquiry is of interest only in the context of proposals for new development. An intending buyer, or developer, would require an accurate and factual response. If a developer is concerned about the impact his proposal may have on the operation of the sewage treatment works, or of the effect of that on his application for planning permission, he should make further enquiries in this respect of both the sewerage undertaker and the local planning authority.

Appendix

The Commons Act 2006: New Arrangements for Searches of the Commons Registers. July 2007

The following guidance note was issued by the Department for Environment, Food and Rural Affairs in July 2007. It is Crown copyright and may be downloaded from the DEFRA website, www.defra.gov.uk.

New Arrangements for Searches of the Commons Registers

Summary

1. New arrangements for searches of the commons registers will begin on 1 August 2007. They will comprise a modification of the existing non-statutory form used for supplementary searches of local authorities on a purchase of land or property, formerly known as the CON29 part II, so as to include an optional question 22 about the commons registers. The existing statutory form 21 for searches of the commons registers will be abolished on 1 October. The new arrangements apply to England and Wales, and will particularly affect local authorities and solicitors and conveyancers, at whom this guidance note is targeted.

2. Details of the new search question on the commons registers may be found at annexe A and frequently asked questions may be found at annexe B.

3. This guidance note replaces the first version, which was published in March 2007 in anticipation of the changes described in this guidance note taking place on 1 June 2007. In the event, owing to the postponement of the timetable for the introduction of Home Information Packs, announced on 22 May, the introduction of new arrangements for commons searches was put back to 1 August 2007.

The commons registers

4. Registered common land and town or village greens are defined by their inclusion in the relevant registers held by commons registration authorities (referred to collectively below as the 'commons registers'). Commons registration authorities were appointed under the Commons Registration Act 1965 (the 1965 Act), and are county councils, metropolitan district councils and London Borough councils (including any unitary authorities). The registers show the extent of common land and greens, and any rights of common which are exercisable over the land (such as rights to graze cattle). The registers are open to public inspection.

5. The registration of land affects the use which can be made of the land. For example, registered common land is subject to restrictions on 'works' (such as fencing)[1], and it is an offence to build on, or otherwise interfere with the enjoyment of, greens[2]. Nearly all registered common land and greens are likely to be subject to rights of access for recreation[3]. People wishing to buy land may therefore wish to enquire (ahead of their purchase) whether the land is included in either of the two registers — particularly where the land is in a rural area, or known to be close to a recognised area of common land or a green.

6. Searches are most commonly undertaken by conveyancers (on behalf of their clients) on a purchase of a house or land, to check whether the local authority holds any information which would have a bearing on the purchase (such as whether a new house has planning permission). The

CON29 forms parts I and II are non-statutory forms by which representatives of local authorities and conveyancers have agreed to the supply of information held by local authorities in England and Wales in return for a fee.

7. To undertake a search, conveyancers send a CON29 part I form to the local authority (the district council in two tier local authority areas), together with a fee (set by each authority). They may also send a CON29 part II form with additional optional questions (such as whether the property is crossed by a public right of way). The CON29 forms are negotiated between (principally) the Local Government Association and the Law Society, are non-statutory, and (until now) central Government has had no direct role in their management.

8. Forms CON29 part I and II are routinely used for local authority searches on nearly every purchase of land or residential property. Neither of the existing forms included any question about the commons registers.

9. From 1 August 2007, forms CON29 parts I and II will be amended and known as forms CON29R and CON29O, respectively.

Statutory searches of the commons registers and form 21

10. Purchasers of land or residential property may undertake a statutory search of the commons registers using a procedure prescribed under the 1965 Act[4]. They must complete a form 21[5], which must be submitted to the commons registration authority (the county council in two tier local authority areas) in writing with the prescribed fee (which is £14[6]). A duplicate of the form is returned by the authority, duly completed, again in writing.

Home Information Packs

11. Home Information Packs (HIP) will ensure that the vendors of residential properties make available essential information about the property to potential purchasers. HIPs will become compulsory in England and Wales (on homes with four bedrooms or more brought to the market) after 1 August 2007[7]. Regulations[8] will require HIPs to include the results of a local authority search similar to the form CON29R, and will enable (but not require) HIPs to include the results of a search using the form CON29O[9].

12. Because every HIP must include the results of a form CON29R search, but may often not include the results of a CON29O search, local authorities will, from 1 August, often receive requests from purchasers of residential property for a CON29O search without any requirement for a repeat CON29R search (which will already be available in the HIP): this is a significant departure from present practice, where the part II search is often available only as an optional addition to a part I search.

The Commons Act 2006

13. The Commons Act 2006 updates the legislation relating to common land, and repeals the 1965 Act. It continues to require commons registration authorities to maintain registers of common land and greens, open to public inspection. There is no provision in the 2006 Act for statutory searches of the register, and in due course, the existing search form 21 must cease to exist. Instead, Defra has reached agreement for an additional question relating to the commons registers to be included in the new form CON29O.

Modifications to the CON29 part II

14. The launch of HIPs (in relation to homes with four or more bedrooms) on 1 August 2007 required consequential amendments to the form CON29 part I so that it conforms to the requirements of the HIP regulations[10]. The revised form, which will be known as the CON29R, will be available from 1 August 2007. The modified form CON29 part II will instead be known as the CON29O, and will be made available from the same date.

15. The existing versions of forms CON29 parts I and II will be withdrawn from 1 August; however, the new forms will be appropriate for use whether or not the replies to the searches are intended for use in a HIP.

Abolition of form 21

16. Defra intends to make regulations which will revoke form 21[11] in England from 1 October 2007[12]. In Wales, the National Assembly is expected to make regulations for the same purpose to a similar timetable.

17. Consequently, for a short period of time, it will be possible to conduct a search using either form 21 or form CON29O. We accept that a period of 'dual-running' in England and Wales may cause some difficulties for commons registration authorities. However, this approach enabled us to

delay making further regulations until there was clarity about the changes taking place on 1 August, and to ensure that stakeholders have sufficient notice of the abolition of form 21.

18. During the transitional period, local authorities responding to statutory searches submitted using form 21 may wish to include a note about the new arrangements for searches, and the withdrawal of form 21 from 1 October.

The new question on the commons registers

19. Form CON29O will include a new two-part question 22 about the commons registers. The questions, and illustrative answers to the questions, are at annexe A to this guidance note. Local authorities are not obliged to adopt these illustrative answers, but it will help to achieve national consistency if they are used where appropriate. For each question, annexe A also explains the implications of the answer for the end user of the search — please note that these explanations (sidelined in the annexe) are not intended to form part of the authority's formal answer to the search question, but, where appropriate, it may be helpful to include a similar note by way of explanation of how the answer should be interpreted by the potential purchaser or client of the conveyancer.

20. Some searches of the commons registers are at present carried out using form 21 in isolation (without any requirement for other local authority searches). This will remain possible under the new arrangements by using form CON29O, as it is an integral element of the changes wrought by the HIPs that searches using CON29O may be carried out independently of those using form CON29R. Any or all of the questions on the CON29O form may be selected, and a separate fee is payable for each question. Therefore, if required, it will be possible to select only question 22.

Changes from form 21

21. Information is included in form 21 which will not routinely be available from a search using form CON29O:

- register unit number: this may be disclosed voluntarily by the local authority (so as to assist in responding to subsequent enquiries), or if required, may be sought in subsequent enquiries;
- rights of common: the search will identify whether land is registered common or town or village green — if details of any rights exercisable over the land are required, they may be sought in subsequent enquiries;
- ownership and registration in the register of title: this information is no longer needed, as a copy of the proprietorship register (from the Land Registry register of title), or a deduction of title, will be included in the HIP.

22. The fee for a search using form CON29O will be determined by the local authority (in two tier local authority areas, the district council will need to set a fee in consultation with the commons registration authority). At the present time, the fee imposed by a local authority for a search of this kind must be set in accordance with the Local Authorities (Charges for Land Searches) Regulations 1994, i.e. that: "The amount of a charge is to be at the local authority's discretion, and in determining that amount the authority shall have regard to its costs in dealing with enquiries within the description in regulation 2(1)."[13]

23. A search using form CON29O must normally be sent to the district council in two tier local authority areas. In such cases, where question 22 is selected, the district council may be expected to refer the search to the commons registration authority for a response (only the commons registration authority is likely to have a complete and up-to-date register). The response will then be integrated with responses to other questions before an overall reply is sent by the district council. Local authorities may sometimes wish to make alternative arrangements in their particular area.

24. Many searches using forms CON29R and CON29O are conducted using electronic exchange media. It is not legally possible for a search using form 21 to be exchanged electronically[14] (although some commons registration authorities use electronic means on request), but it will be possible for a search using the CON29O form to be exchanged electronically. However, commons registration authorities cannot at present hold their commons registers in an electronic form, and it may not be possible for a response to be given to question 22 without manual intervention. Section 25 of the Commons Act 2006 will enable registration authorities to hold the commons registers in electronic form when the section is brought into force[15].

Regulatory impact assessment

25. A regulatory impact assessment (RIA) of the change in searches of the commons registers was included in the RIA prepared for the Commons Bill[16]. The RIA noted that the change could result in "wide variance in the charges made by commons registration authorities for such searches", with

search fees increasing for some users of the service, but delegation of responsibility for setting fees is in line with Government policy. The RIA also noted that the change would facilitate electronic searches (which under the present stand-alone system, must be conducted manually), and that it would promote greater awareness and use of the search, so reducing the likelihood of purchasers being unaware of the status of the land.

Annexe A : New Questions

Q.22. Registered Common Land and Town or Village Green

Q.22.1 Is the property, or any land which abuts the property, registered common land or town or village green under the Commons Registration Act 1965 or the Commons Act 2006?

Informatives: These standard answers are provided for guidance only. Local authorities may choose to use the bulleted answers (as appropriate) or to formulate their own answers. Final users of the searches may also find it helpful to receive the sidelined explanatory text with answers, where the authority considers it practicable to communicate the explanation.

- Informative 22.1.A: Yes, all or part of the property is registered as common land [, register unit no. CL___]

Explanation of Informative 22.1.A: All or part of the property is registered in the register of common land held by the commons registration authority. Generally, there are restrictions on the use which you may make of the registered land, and the land may be subject to rights held by others. For example, you may need consent from the Secretary of State (in Wales, the National Assembly for Wales) to construct works on the land which interfere with others' access to it. The land may be subject to a public right of access, and subject to rights of common (such as a right to graze animals) held by others. You should consult your conveyancer for further advice if any part of the property is registered.

- Informative 22.1.B: Yes, all or part of the property is registered as town or village green [, register unit no. VG___]

Explanation of Informative 22.1.B: All or part of the property is registered in the register of town or village greens held by the commons registration authority. Generally, there are restrictions on the use which you may make of the registered land, and the land may be subject to rights held by others. For example, the land is likely to be subject to rights of recreation for the local community. The land may be subject to rights of common (such as a right to graze animals) held by others. It is likely to be an offence to do anything on the land which interferes with these rights, or which damages the green. You should consult your conveyancer for further advice if any part of the property is registered.

- Informative 22.1.C: Yes, the property abuts registered common land [, register unit no. CL___]

Explanation of Informative 22.1.C: Land abutting the property is registered in the register of common land held by the commons registration authority. 'Abut' may not mean in practice that the registered land is directly adjacent to the boundary of the property. It would be a good idea to check the exact boundary to the registered land. If vehicular access to the property is obtained over registered land, you may wish to confirm your entitlement to use that means of access. Registered common land is generally subject to public rights of access, and may be subject to rights of common (such as a right to graze animals) held by others: such rights may affect the use you make of the property (e.g. there is likely to be a customary obligation for you to fence the property to exclude grazing animals). You may wish to consult your conveyancer for further advice.

- Informative 22.1.D: Yes, the property abuts registered town or village green [, register unit no. VG___]

Explanation of Informative 22.1.D: Land abutting the property is registered in the register of town or village greens held by the commons registration authority. 'Abut' may not mean that the registered land is directly adjacent to the boundary of the property. It would be a good idea to check the exact boundary to the registered land. If vehicular access to the property is obtained over registered land, you may wish to confirm your entitlement to use that means of access. Registered town or village green is generally subject to rights of recreation for the local community, and may be subject to rights of common (such as a right to graze animals) held by others: such rights may affect the use you make of the property (e.g. local people may be entitled to use land adjacent to the property for sports and pastimes). You may wish to consult your conveyancer for further advice.

- Informative 22.1.E: No, but an application is pending for an amendment of the register affecting the property[17]

Explanation of Informative 22.1.E: An application has been made (but not decided) to register all or part of the property in the register of town or village greens held by the commons registration

196

authority. If the application were successful, registration would place restrictions on the use which you may make of the property. You should consult your conveyancer for further advice.
- Informative 22.1.F: No, but the property [is][abuts] land which was[18] exempt from registration by order under section 11 of the Commons Registration Act 1965

Explanation of Informative 22.1.F: Some land which is common land or a town or village green was exempt from registration under the Commons Registration Act 1965, and so is not formally registered as common land or a green. The New Forest, Epping Forest and the Forest of Dean are exempt from registration, and you should consult your conveyancer for further advice if the property lies within these areas. Other land was exempted from registration by order under the 1965 Act, and the exempt areas are shown on the commons and greens registers. You should consult your conveyancer for further advice if any part of the property was exempt from registration by order.
- Informative 22.1.G: No

Explanation of Informative 22.1.G: The property is not registered in the commons registers. But it is possible that an application may be pending for registration of the property as a town or village green, or that an application may be made at a later date. If you think that either possibility is likely, or you are in doubt, you should consult your conveyancer for further advice.

Q.22.2 If there are any entries, how can copies of the matters registered be obtained and where can the register be inspected?

Informative:
- Informative 22.2: A copy of the register, including a map of the registered land, may be obtained from [insert contact details for commons registration officer]. [Please quote the above-mentioned register unit no. in any request.] [A charge of £[ ] will be made for a copy of the register.]

Explanation of Informative 22.2: If the property, or any land abutting the property, is registered, it would be sensible to obtain a copy of the register map. In some cases, it would also be sensible to obtain a copy of the full register entries relating to the registered land. The commons registration authority's response to this question will explain how these copies may be obtained. If, in response to either question, a register unit number has been quoted, it will help the commons registration authority respond to your re-quest if you quote the number.

Annexe B : Frequently asked questions

Q1. Why abolish form 21 — it works fine?
Form 21 is an anomaly — outside the local land charges régime, it is the only statutory search mechanism. Most local authority held information is searched using the proprietary CON29 forms, and this works well. Retaining stand-alone searches for the commons registers means that these searches are less well known, administratively inconvenient for conveyancers, and therefore sometimes overlooked. And the fees for statutory searches are set by Government, rather than local authorities, so they cannot reflect local circumstances.

Q2. Why change now?
The Commons Act 2006 makes no provision for searches. So the existing search mechanism, which is prescribed under the Commons Registration Act 1965, must cease to exist within the next few years, when the 1965 Act is repealed. The CON29 forms have been revised this year in anticipation of the partial introduction of Home Information Packs on 1 August 2007, so this makes it a good time to replace the commons registers search too.

Q3. Why the abortive start earlier this year?
Defra originally planned to deregulate the present statutory commons search, by replacing it with a modification to the form CON29 part II, following agreement with the Law Society, the Local Government Association and others controlling the use and content of that form. These changes were due to be introduced on 1 June 2007 at the same time as modifications required to the form CON29 part I in consequence of the introduction of Home Information Packs (HIPs). Following the announcement of the Secretary of State for Communities on 22 May to postpone the introduction of HIPs, the controlling parties decided to defer the introduction of the modified forms CON29 pending further discussions, and it was therefore unacceptable to proceed with the abolition of the existing statutory search mechanism on the original timetable.

Q4. What's happening in Wales?
Responsibility for abolition of form 21 in Wales is devolved to the National Assembly for Wales. Arrangements for Home Information Packs are not devolved, and will be partially introduced in both England and Wales on 1 August 2007. The new commons registers search will be available in

both England and Wales from the same date. It will continue to be possible to use the old form 21 search in both England and Wales until 1 October 2007.

Q5. Won't this mean searches cost more?

Not necessarily. The fee for a search using form 21 was set in 2003 at £14, representing slightly less than the fee most frequently proposed in response to a consultation in 2000[19]. Commons registration authorities are obliged to set a fee which has regard to costs[20]. Where the costs of a search are set at a level which exceeds the present prescribed fee, it is only right that the full cost is borne by the person commissioning the search, rather than council tax payers in general.

Q6. I just want to know whether the land is registered!

Searches are designed to deliver reliable evidence to a purchaser of land about information held by a local authority in relation to that land. In relation to the commons registers, the new search arrangements will make it easier to establish whether the land is registered at the same time as other information is obtained (such as whether the property is crossed by a public right of way). If someone wants to find out only whether the land is registered, it may be quicker, more informative and possibly cheaper to ask the commons registration authority to supply a copy of the register. It is best to ask how much this would cost in advance.

Q7. What will happen to form 21 searches submitted before 1 October?

Regulations revoking form 21 are not expected to contain a saving for any form 21 submitted, but not answered, before 1 October, because the Commons Registration Act 1965 does not confer any powers for that purpose. But section 16 of the Interpretation Act 1978 provides that revocation of an enactment does not affect any 'right, privilege, obligation or liability' acquired under it. In Defra's view, an authority may therefore respond to a form 21 submitted before 1 October, after that date.

Q8. What will happen to form 21 searches submitted after 1 October?

Form 21 will cease to exist, in both England and Wales, from 1 October. Any form 21 submitted after that date will therefore have no statutory authority. If a local authority chooses to reply to a form submitted after that date, it should consider whether it has powers to charge and receive a fee for so doing.

Q9. What happens if there is more than one parcel of land to check?

It is up to local authorities to decide whether an additional fee must be paid for additional parcels of land. Local authorities may wish to apply the same 'rules' for the purposes of multiple land parcels in relation to question 22, as they currently apply in relation to other questions on the CON29O.

Q10. Why isn't a commons registers search included in the Home Information Pack?

A search of the commons registers has never been a routine element of the conveyancing process. It is most likely to be sought in relation to undeveloped land, land adjacent to open space, and land to which access is obtained over open space[21]. Requiring a commons registers search to be included in the HIP would significantly add to the cost, but in the vast majority of cases, the information would be redundant. A commons registers search may be included in the HIP at the vendor's discretion[22], or the purchaser may commission a search himself: this would be particularly appropriate where there is a risk that the land might be registered.

Q11. [In question 22.1] What does 'abut' mean?

'Abut' should be given the same meaning as in existing question 5.1: "Is any footpath, bridleway, restricted byway or byway open to all traffic which abuts on, or cross the property, shown in a definitive map…"? The Oxford English Dictionary suggests: "To end at, march with, border on, as contiguous lands or estates do".

1   Section 194 of the Law of Property Act 1925 (expected to be re-enacted with amendments in Part 3 of the Commons Act 2006 with effect in England from 1 October 2007).

2   Section 12 of the Inclosure Act 1857 and section 29 of the Commons Act 1876.

3   In relation to common land, under part I of the Countryside and Rights of Way Act 2000, or earlier legislation, and in relation to town or village greens, at common law.

4   Regulation 32 of the Commons Registration (General) Regulations 1966 (SI 1966/1471).

5   Form 21 is prescribed in Schedule 1 to the General Regulations (see footnote 4), as substituted by the Commons Registration (General) (Amendment) Regulations 1989 (SI 1989/2167).

6   The Commons Registration (General) (Amendment) (England) Regulations 2003 (SI 2003/2260), and The Commons Registration (General) (Amendment) (Wales) Regulations 2003 (SI 2003/994).
7   The Housing Act 2004 (Commencement No 8) (England and Wales) Order 2007 (SI 2007/1668). For the statutory authority for HIPs, see part 5 of the Housing Act 2004. HIPs are expected to be required for properties with fewer than four bedrooms at a later date.
8   The Home Information Pack (No. 2) Regulations 2007 (SI 2007/1667).
9   Regulation 9(m)(ii).
10   The questions required in form CON29R can be found in Part 2 of Schedule 7 to the Home Information Pack (No. 2) Regulations 2007 (SI 2007/1667).
11   The regulations will also revoke General Regulation 32 (see footnote 4).
12   The Commons Registration (General) (Amendment) (England) Regulations 2007 (SI 2007/1032) were made on 26 March 2007 to identical effect, but were revoked by the Commons Registration (General) (Amendment) (England) (Revocation) Regulations 2007 (SI 2007/1553) before they came into force — see paragraph 3.
13   SI 1994/1885. See regulation 3.
14   Section 19(1)(d) of the 1965 Act enables the Secretary of State to make regulations: "for requiring registration authorities to supply by post ... such information relating to the entries in the registers kept by them as may be prescribed."
15   In England, expected to be between 2008 and 2012, depending on the location.
16   The RIA may be seen via: www.defra.gov.uk/wildlife-countryside/issues/common/commonbill/index.htm.
17   An authority may be dealing with an application for registration of a new town or village green. There is no register of such applications, and in our view, an authority cannot be obliged to give such an answer, but may wish to do so.
18   Some land exempted under the Commons Registration Act 1965 will not be exempted under the Commons Act 2006. However, such land will continue to be identified in the registers as exempted, and should be referred to as exempted under the 1965 Act.
19   See Increase in Search Fees, at www.defra.gov.uk/wildlife-countryside/issues/common/registration/index.htm.
20   Local Authorities (Charges for Land Searches) Regulations 1994 (SI 1994/1885).
21   Every purchase of undeveloped land should include a search of the register, and a solicitor might be negligent if a search is not undertaken: *G & K Ladenbau (UK) Ltd. v. Crawley & de Reya* [1978] 1 WLR 266.
22   A search report relating to common land and town or village greens may (but is not required to) be included in a HIP — see regulation 9(m)(ii) of The Home Information Pack (No. 2) Regulations 2007 (SI 2007/1667).

Forms Con 29R and Con 29O

Forms Con 29R: Enquiries of local authority (2007) and Con 29O: Optional Enquiries of local authority (2007) are reproduced below by arrangement with the Law Society.

CON 29R Enquiries of local authority (2007)

The Law Society

A duplicate plan is required for all searches submitted directly to a local authority.
If submitted manually, this form must be submitted in duplicate. Please type or use BLOCK LETTERS

A.

Local authority name and address	■
	Search No:..
	Signed:...
	On behalf of: .... Local authority/private search company/ member of the public (indicate as applicable)
	Dated: ....

B.

Address of the land/property

UPRN(s):

Secondary name/number:

Primary name/number:

Street:

Locality/village:

Town:

Postcode:

C.

Other roadways, footways and footpaths in respect of which a reply to enquiry 2 is required

D.

Fees

£_____ is enclosed/is paid by NLIS transfer (delete as applicable)

Signed:

Dated:

Reference:

Telephone No:

Fax No:

E-mail:

E. (For HIPs regulations compliance only)

Names of those involved in the sale (this box is only completed when the replies to these enquiries are to be included in a Home Information Pack)

Name of vendor:

Name of estate agents:

Name of HIP provider:

Name of solicitor/conveyancer:

Your personal data – name and address – will be handled strictly in accordance with the requirements of the Data Protection Act. It is required to pass on to the relevant authority(ies) in order to carry out the necessary searches.

Notes

A. Enter name and address of appropriate Council. If the property is near a local authority boundary, consider raising certain enquiries (e.g. road schemes) with the adjoining Council.
B. Enter address and description of the property. Please give the UPRN(s) (Unique Property Reference Number) where known. **A duplicate plan is required for all searches submitted directly to a local authority.** The search may be returned if land/property cannot easily be identified.
C. Enter name and/or mark on plan any other roadways, footways and footpaths abutting the property (in addition to those entered in Box B) to which a reply to enquiry 2 is required.
D. Details of fees can be obtained from the Council, your chosen NLIS channel or search provider.
E. Box E is only to be completed when the replies to these enquiries are to be included in a Home Information Pack. Enter the name of the individual(s) and firms involved in the sale of the property.
F. Enter the name and address/DX address of the person or company lodging or conducting this enquiry.

F.

Reply to

DX address:

Oyez 7 Spa Road, London SE16 3QQ

© Law Society 2007

4.2007 F7618

5033382

Conveyancing 29R (Enquiries)

201

CON 29R Enquiries of local authority (2007)

PLANNING AND BUILDING REGULATIONS

1.1. Planning and building decisions and pending applications

Which of the following relating to the property have been granted, issued or refused or (where applicable) are the subject of pending applications?
(a) a planning permission
(b) a listed building consent
(c) a conservation area consent
(d) a certificate of lawfulness of existing use or development
(e) a certificate of lawfulness of proposed use or development
(f) building regulations approval
(g) a building regulation completion certificate and
(h) any building regulations certificate or notice issued in respect of work carried out under a competent person self-certification scheme

1.2. Planning designations and proposals

What designations of land use for the property or the area, and what specific proposals for the property, are contained in any existing or proposed development plan?

ROADS

2. Roadways, footways and footpaths

Which of the roads, footways and footpaths named in the application for this search (via boxes B and C) are:
(a) highways maintainable at public expense
(b) subject to adoption and, supported by a bond or bond waiver
(c) to be made up by a local authority who will reclaim the cost from the frontagers
(d) to be adopted by a local authority without reclaiming the cost from the frontagers

OTHER MATTERS

3.1. Land required for public purposes
Is the property included in land required for public purposes?

3.2. Land to be acquired for road works
Is the property included in land to be acquired for road works?

3.3. Drainage agreements and consents
Do either of the following exist in relation to the property?
(a) an agreement to drain buildings in combination into an existing sewer by means of a private sewer
(b) an agreement or consent for (i) a building, or (ii) extension to a building on the property, to be built over, or in the vicinity of a drain, sewer or disposal main

3.4. Nearby road schemes
Is the property (or will it be) within 200 metres of any of the following?
(a) the centre line of a new trunk road or special road specified in any order, draft order or scheme
(b) the centre line of a proposed alteration or improvement to an existing road involving construction of a subway, underpass, flyover, footbridge, elevated road or dual carriageway
(c) the outer limits of construction works for a proposed alteration or improvement to an existing road involving (i) construction of a roundabout (other than a mini roundabout), or (ii) widening by construction of one or more additional traffic lanes;
(d) the outer limits of (i) construction of a new road to be built by a local authority, (ii) an approved alteration or improvement to an existing road involving construction of a subway, underpass, flyover, footbridge, elevated road or dual carriageway, (iii) construction of a roundabout (other than a mini roundabout) or widening by construction of one or more additional traffic lanes
(e) the centre line of the proposed route of a new road under proposals published for public consultation
(f) the outer limits of (i) construction of a proposed alteration or improvement to an existing road involving construction of a subway, underpass, flyover, footbridge, elevated road or dual carriageway, (ii) construction of a roundabout (other than a mini roundabout), (iii) widening by construction of one or more additional traffic lanes, under proposals published for public consultation

3.5. Nearby railway schemes
Is the property (or will it be) within 200 metres of the centre line of a proposed railway, tramway, light railway or monorail?

3.6. Traffic schemes
Has a local authority approved but not yet implemented any of the following for the roads, footways and footpaths (named in Box B) which abut the boundaries of the property?
(a) permanent stopping up or diversion
(b) waiting or loading restrictions
(c) one way driving
(d) prohibition of driving
(e) pedestrianisation
(f) vehicle width or weight restriction
(g) traffic calming works including road humps
(h) residents parking controls
(i) minor road widening or improvement
(j) pedestrian crossings
(k) cycle tracks
(l) bridge building

3.7. Outstanding notices
Do any statutory notices which relate to the following matters subsist in relation to the property other than those revealed in a response to any other enquiry in this form?
(a) building works
(b) environment
(c) health and safety
(d) housing
(e) highways
(f) public health

3.8. Contravention of building regulations
Has a local authority authorised in relation to the property any proceedings for the contravention of any provision contained in Building Regulations?

3.9. Notices, orders, directions and proceedings under Planning Acts
Do any of the following subsist in relation to the property, or has a local authority decided to issue, serve, make or commence any of the following?
(a) an enforcement notice
(b) a stop notice
(c) a listed building enforcement notice
(d) a breach of condition notice
(e) a planning contravention notice
(f) another notice relating to breach of planning control
(g) a listed building repairs notice
(h) in the case of a listed building deliberately allowed to fall into disrepair, a compulsory purchase order with a direction for minimum compensation
(i) a building preservation notice
(j) a direction restricting permitted development
(k) an order revoking or modifying planning permission
(l) an order requiring discontinuance of use or alteration or removal of building or works
(m) a tree preservation order
(n) proceedings to enforce a planning agreement or planning contribution

3.10. Conservation area
Do the following apply in relation to the property?
(a) the making of the area a conservation area before 31st August 1974
(b) an unimplemented resolution to designate the area a conservation area

3.11. Compulsory purchase
Has any enforceable order or decision been made to compulsorily purchase or acquire the property?

3.12. Contaminated land
Do any of the following apply (including any relating to the land adjacent to or adjoining the property which has been identified as contaminated land because it is in such a condition that harm or pollution of controlled waters might be caused on the property)?
(a) a contaminated land notice
(b) in relation to a register maintained under section 78R of the Environmental Protection Act 1990
    (i) a decision to make an entry
    (ii) an entry
(c) consultation with the owner or occupier of the property conducted under section 78G(3) of the Environmental Protection Act 1990 before the service of a remediation notice

3.13. Radon gas
Do records indicate that the property is in a 'Radon Affected Area' as identified by the Health Protection Agency?

NOTES:
(1) References to the provisions of particular Acts of Parliament or Regulations include any provisions which they have replaced and also include existing or future amendments or re-enactments.
(2) The replies will be given in the belief that they are in accordance with information presently available to the officers of the replying Council, but none of the Councils or their officers accept legal responsibility for an incorrect reply, except for negligence. Any liability for negligence will extend to the person who raised the enquiries and the person on whose behalf they were raised. It will also extend to any other person who has knowledge (personally or through an agent) of the replies before the time when he purchases, takes a tenancy of, or lends money on the security of the property or (if earlier) the time when he becomes contractually bound to do so.
(3) This Form should be read in conjunction with the guidance notes available separately.
(4) Area means any area in which the property is located.
(5) References to the Council include any predecessor Council and also any council committee, sub-committee or other body or person exercising powers delegated by the Council and their approval includes their decision to proceed. The replies given to certain enquiries cover knowledge and actions of both the District Council and County Council.
(6) Where relevant, the source department for copy documents should be provided.

CON 29O Optional enquiries of local authority (2007)

The Law Society

A duplicate plan is required for all searches submitted directly to a local authority.
If submitted manually, this form must be submitted in duplicate. Please type or use BLOCK LETTERS

A.

<table>
<tr><td>

Local authority name and address

</td><td>

Search No:..

Signed:...

On behalf of: ....
Local authority/private search company/ member of the public
(indicate as applicable)

Dated: ....

</td></tr>
</table>

B.

Address of the land/property

UPRN(s):

Secondary name/number:

Primary name/number:

Street:

Locality/village:

Town:

Postcode:

D.

Fees

£_____ is enclosed/is paid by NLIS transfer (delete as applicable)

Signed:

Dated:

Reference:

Telephone No:

Fax No:

E-mail:

E.

Reply to

DX address:

C.

Optional enquiries (please tick as required)

☐ 4. Road proposals by private bodies

☐ 5. Public paths or byways

☐ 6. Advertisements

☐ 7. Completion notices

☐ 8. Parks and countryside

☐ 9. Pipelines

☐ 10. Houses in multiple occupation

☐ 11. Noise abatement

☐ 12. Urban development areas

☐ 13. Enterprise zones

☐ 14. Inner urban improvement areas

☐ 15. Simplified planning zones

☐ 16. Land maintenance notices

☐ 17. Mineral consultation areas

☐ 18. Hazardous substance consents

☐ 19. Environmental and pollution notices

☐ 20. Food safety notices

☐ 21. Hedgerow notices

☐ 22. Common land, town and village greens

Notes

A. Enter name and address of appropriate Council. If the property is near a local authority boundary, consider raising certain enquiries (e.g. road schemes) with the adjoining Council.

B. Enter address and description of the property. Please give the UPRN(s) (Unique Property Reference Number) where known. **A duplicate plan is required for all searches submitted directly to a local authority.** The search may be returned if land/property cannot easily be identified.

C. Questions 1-3 appear on CON 29R Enquiries of local authority (2007).

D. Details of fees can be obtained from the Council, your chosen NLIS channel or search provider.

E. Enter the name and address/DX address of the person or company lodging or conducting this enquiry.

Oyez 7 Spa Road, London SE16 3QQ   © Law Society 2007   4.2007 F7619

5033384

Conveyancing 29O (Optional Enquiries)

CON 29O Optional enquiries of local authority (2007)

ROAD PROPOSALS BY PRIVATE BODIES

4. What proposals by others, still capable of being implemented, have the Council approved for any of the following, the limits of construction of which are within 200 metres of the property?
   (a) the construction of a new road
   (b) the alteration or improvement of an existing road, involving the construction, whether or not within existing highway limits, of a subway, underpass, flyover, footbridge, elevated road, dual carriageway, the construction of a roundabout (other than a mini roundabout) or the widening of an existing road by the construction of one or more additional traffic lanes

   This enquiry refers to proposals by bodies or companies (such as private developers) other than the Council (and where appropriate the County Council) or the Secretary of State. A mini roundabout is a roundabout having a one-way circulatory carriageway around a flush or slightly raised circular marking less than 4 metres in diameter and with or without flared approaches.

PUBLIC PATHS OR BYWAYS

5.1. Is any footpath, bridleway, restricted byway or byway open to all traffic which abuts on, or crosses the property, shown in a definitive map or revised definitive map prepared under Part IV of the National Parks and Access to the Countryside Act 1949 or Part III of the Wildlife and Countryside Act 1981?

5.2. If so, please mark its approximate route on the attached plan.

ADVERTISEMENTS

Entries in the register

6.1. Please list any entries in the register of applications, directions and decisions relating to consent for the display of advertisements.

6.2. If there are any entries, where can that register be inspected?

Notices, proceedings and orders

6.3. Except as shown in the official certificate of search:
   (a) has any notice been given by the Secretary of State or served in respect of a direction or proposed direction restricting deemed consent for any class of advertisement
   (b) have the Council resolved to serve a notice requiring the display of any advertisement to be discontinued
   (c) if a discontinuance notice has been served, has it been complied with to the satisfaction of the Council
   (d) have the Council resolved to serve any other notice or proceedings relating to a contravention of the control of advertisements
   (e) have the Council resolved to make an order for the special control of advertisements for the area

COMPLETION NOTICES

7. Which of the planning permissions in force have the Council resolved to terminate by means of a completion notice under s.94 of the Town and Country Planning Act 1990?

PARKS AND COUNTRYSIDE

Areas of outstanding natural beauty

8.1. Has any order under s.82 of the Countryside and Rights of Way Act 2000 been made?

National Parks

8.2. Is the property within a National Park designated under s.7. of the National Parks and Access to the Countryside Act 1949?

PIPELINES

9. Has a map been deposited under s.35 of the Pipelines Act 1962, or Schedule 7 of the Gas Act 1986, showing a pipeline laid through, or within 100 feet (30.48 metres) of the property?

HOUSES IN MULTIPLE OCCUPATION

10. Is the property a house in multiple occupation,or is it designated or proposed to be designated for selective licensing of residential accommodation in accordance with the Housing Act 2004?

NOISE ABATEMENT

Noise abatement zone

11.1. Have the Council made, or resolved to make, any noise abatement zone order under s.63 of the Control of Pollution Act 1974 for the area?

Entries in register

11.2. Has any entry been recorded in the noise level register kept pursuant to s.64 of the Control of Pollution Act 1974?

11.3. If there is any entry, how can copies be obtained and where can that register be inspected?

URBAN DEVELOPMENT AREAS

12.1. Is the area an urban development area designated under Part XVI of the Local Government, Planning and Land Act 1980?

12.2. If so, please state the name of the urban development corporation and the address of its principal office.

ENTERPRISE ZONES

13. Is the area an enterprise zone designated under Part XVIII of the Local Government, Planning and Land Act 1980?

INNER URBAN IMPROVEMENT AREAS

14. Have the Council resolved to define the area as an improvement area under s.4 of the Inner Urban Areas Act 1978?

SIMPLIFIED PLANNING ZONES

15.1. Is the area a simplified planning zone adopted or approved pursuant to s.83 of the Town and Country Planning Act 1990?

15.2. Have the Council approved any proposal for designating the area as a simplified planning zone?

LAND MAINTENANCE NOTICES

16. Have the Council authorised the service of a maintenance notice under s.215 of the Town and Country Planning Act 1990?

MINERAL CONSULTATION AREAS

17. Is the area a mineral consultation area notified by the county planning authority under Schedule 1 para 7 of the Town and Country Planning Act 1990?

HAZARDOUS SUBSTANCE CONSENTS

18.1. Please list any entries in the register kept pursuant to s.28 of the Planning (Hazardous Substances) Act 1990.

18.2. If there are any entries:
   (a) how can copies of the entries be obtained
   (b) where can the register be inspected

ENVIRONMENTAL AND POLLUTION NOTICES

19. What outstanding statutory or informal notices have been issued by the Council under the Environmental Protection Act 1990 or the Control of Pollution Act 1974? (This enquiry does not cover notices under Part IIA or Part III of the EPA, to which enquiries 3.12 or 3.7 apply).

FOOD SAFETY NOTICES

20. What outstanding statutory notices or informal notices have been issued by the Council under the Food Safety Act 1990 or the Food Hygiene Regulations 2006?

HEDGEROW NOTICES

21.1. Please list any entries in the record maintained under regulation 10 of the Hedgerows Regulations 1997.

21.2. If there are any entries:
   (a) how can copies of the matters entered be obtained
   (b) where can the record be inspected

COMMON LAND, TOWN AND VILLAGE GREENS

22.1. Is the property, or any land which abuts the property, registered common land or town or village green under the Commons Registration Act 1965 or the Commons Act 2006?

22.2. If there are any entries, how can copies of the matters registered be obtained and where can the register be inspected?

NOTES:

(1) References to the provisions of particular Acts of Parliament or Regulations include any provisions which they have replaced and also include existing or future amendments or re-enactments.

(2) The replies will be given in the belief that they are in accordance with information presently available to the officers of the replying Council, but none of the Councils or their officers accept legal responsibility for an incorrect reply, except for negligence. Any liability for negligence will extend to the person who raised the enquiries and the person on whose behalf they were raised. It will also extend to any other person who has knowledge (personally or through an agent) of the replies before the time when he purchases, takes a tenancy of, or lends money on the security of the property or (if earlier) the time when he becomes contractually bound to do so.

(3) This form should be read in conjunction with the guidance notes available separately.

(4) Area means any area in which the property is located.

(5) References to the Council include any predecessor Council and also any council committee, sub-committee or other body or person exercising powers delegated by the Council and their approval includes their decision to proceed. The replies given to certain enquiries cover knowledge and actions of both the District Council and County Council.

(6) Where relevant, the source department for copy documents should be provided.

Index